# DR ANASTASIA ALCOCK

# Your Baby's First Year

## Everything you need to know for the first 12 months

with Beth Graham and Lulu Becker

Quadrille
PUBLISHING

# Contents

# Introduction

What an exciting time! Babies are the most fantastic and fulfilling little beings you could ever wish for. They are totally absorbing and the most wonderful time-wasters: you can sit with them for hours, simply watching their tiny moves and array of expressions. Nevertheless, their arrival gives you a whole lot of new responsibilities and a fresh set of skills to acquire – ones you often have to learn as you go along.

Being a parent can be daunting and sometimes even frightening, but it does not need to be. You will be amazed at how your and your partner's personalities, as well as your beliefs and values, all come together to help you decide how you want to bring up your baby. Of course, there will be things you have never had to think about before, but trust your instincts: it is surprising how much of parenthood is natural and obvious.

However, there may be times when you need a little bit more information. I am sure that, throughout your pregnancy, friends and family have been telling you stories and imparting their wisdom. You may have found this helpful, but the truth is that, until you are in the crazy haze that is new parenthood, you will not really know which bits of guidance work for you. In this book I have tried to give you the facts and the best evidence-based advice that I can so that you can make your own decisions in an informed way. Although I have experience both as a paediatrician and as a mother of two young children, I have also tapped into the knowledge of specialists who have devoted their careers to making sure that they are up to date and relevant with the help that they are giving. In addition to this, always remember that there are teams of healthcare professionals out in the community to help you, such as GPs, health visitors, midwives and paediatricians. My hope is that, together, we will help you to get the most out of this first, incredible year with your baby.

**Dr Anastasia Alcock**

# The early days

Meeting your baby for the first time is an amazing event and one that you will remember for the rest of your life. If this is your first baby, you are now a parent and part of a new family. Knowing what happens next will allow you to relax a little more in those incredible first few days and to focus on getting to know – and enjoying – your wonderful new baby.

# What your new baby looks like

Each baby is unique, but shares some similar characteristics with other newborns. Your baby has just been through an enormous event, whether it was a vaginal delivery or a Caesarean section. Either way, they will have been pushed and shoved and squashed and squeezed, and the results of this can often be seen – temporarily – in their appearance.

## Head

A newborn baby's head can be very different in shape from your own and it is much larger in proportion to their body size. The skull bones are not fixed together, but float between the skin and the brain tissue. This is to allow the head to squeeze through the birth canal and to accommodate the rapid growth of the brain after birth. As a result, babies have a soft spot, the anterior fontanelle, between the two bones on the top of their heads. This can be very disconcerting for first-time parents – particularly as you can often see and/or feel your baby's pulse in the soft spot – but it is entirely normal. The skull bones eventually take up the correct position and fuse together (usually by the age of eighteen months).

Babies who had been engaged for a while tend to have conical-shaped heads for the first few days after birth because the different bones that make up the skull have been pushed together as a result of being confined. After a few days the bones will realign and take a more rounded shape. If you have had a ventouse delivery your baby may have a swollen, raised area of skin where the suction cap was applied, known as a 'chignon'. It rarely causes any problems and usually settles down within ten days. Occasionally, there may be some bruising, but again this settles within ten to fourteen days. However, this bruising can increase your baby's risk of jaundice (see Chapter 8, p.178) and so healthcare professionals will be watching out for this. Rarely, the bruising can calcify (harden), leaving a permanent raised area. This is harmless and can either be left alone or removed surgically.

## Hair

Some babies are born with a full head of hair, while others have hardly any and look almost bald. Any initial hair tends to fall out in the first month and the new hair that follows can be a totally different colour. Some babies, especially premature ones, are born with a fine layer of downy hair (lanugo) covering their entire body. This will be shed naturally within the first few weeks.

## Face

Your baby may initially have swollen eyelids and a reddened face, caused by the pressure endured during the journey down the birth canal. This resolves within the first few days. If you had an assisted delivery using forceps, your baby may have some bruising on their face following the lines of the instrument. This bruising is not permanent and, although it can look distressing, settles very quickly (normally within seven to ten days). Very rarely, the nerve to the facial muscles may be bruised, which can cause muscles on one side of your baby's face to not work properly. This usually improves quickly on its own and requires no treatment.

You are unlikely to see any immediate family resemblance; in any case, a baby's faces changes so much in the first few months that one minute you think it is Dad's nose, the next, Uncle George's!

## Eyes

Your baby's eyes can open at birth or may do so a few hours later. They will initially be blue/grey or brown (it can take between six and eighteen months for them to acquire their final colour).

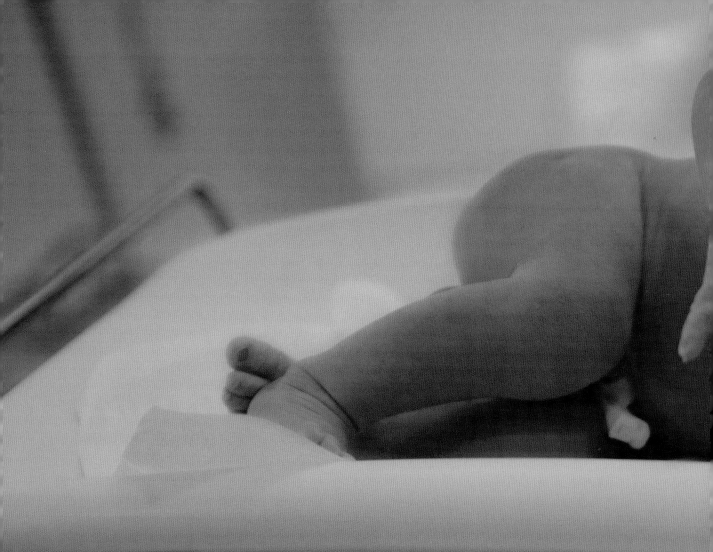

### Skin

Your baby's skin is very delicate – it is not until infants are two years old that they have more adult-like skin. Babies may still be covered with a layer of white, sticky vernix, which prevented the skin from absorbing too much amniotic fluid in the womb. You can either leave it to absorb naturally or wash it off. Overdue babies may have dry, flaky skin.

### Colouring

In the first moments after birth, your baby's colouring is dark red to purple, turning to a brighter red as they take their first breaths. Initially, the fingers and toes are blue. This is normal and, as their circulation improves in the first few hours, they will 'pink up', provided they are warm enough. (It is never normal for a baby's lips to be blue – seek medical advice if you notice this.) If your baby's skin has a yellow tinge, they may be suffering from mild jaundice, common in newborns.

### Umbilicus

The umbilicus (belly button) looks extremely peculiar in a newborn! The jelly-like umbilical cord, which houses the three vessels that provided your baby with blood from the placenta while in the womb, is redundant following birth. It is clamped with a coloured plastic clip and cut in the first moments after delivery, leaving a stump of two or three centimetres. The clip can be removed after 24 hours. The stump is wet and slimy to begin with, but after a week or two it will dry up and drop off. Contrary to popular belief, the shape of your baby's belly button has nothing to do with the way that

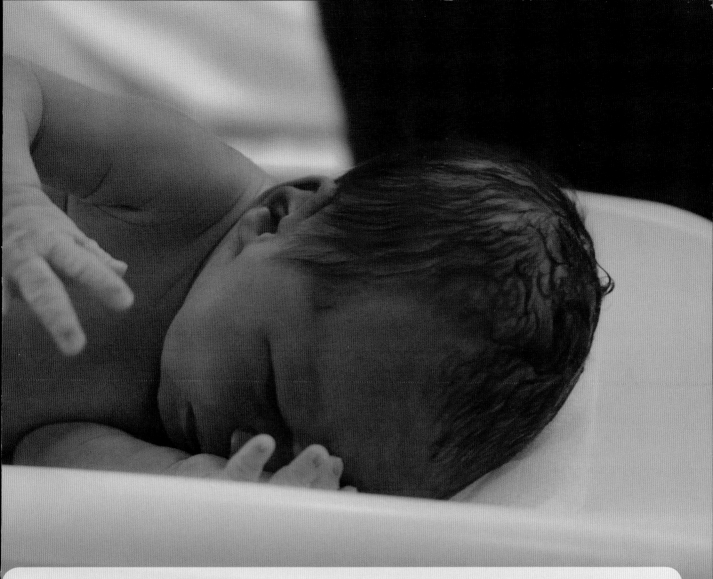

the cord was cut and clamped at birth. This is a genetic phenomenon. See Box in Chapter 2, p.35 for information about cord care.

### Enlarged breasts and genitals

Around 60–95 per cent of babies – both boys and girls – are born with enlarged breast tissue, a condition called gynaecomastia. It usually occurs on both sides, although sometimes it can affect only one. It is caused by oestrogen passing across the placenta at the end of pregnancy, leading to hormone stimulation in your baby. This swollen tissue can sometimes secrete milk. When they are born, babies may also have enlarged genitalia and girls can have discharge or a small bleed. Swelling normally settles during the first few weeks.

### Limbs, hands and feet

Your baby can straighten their arms and legs as soon as they are born, but seem to prefer being curled up when they are calm and quiet. As they grow they adopt this 'fetal position' less and less. Fingers and toes are very flexible. You will also notice that your baby has a grasp reflex: if you put your finger in their palm, they will automatically grab it (see p.16).

### Nails

Many babies – especially ones that are overdue – are born with long finger- and toenails. These can be very sharp and will cause scratch marks, so you will need to trim them with a pair of baby scissors or by carefully tearing or nibbling them off (see Chapter 2, p.40).

# Your baby's first assessments

The healthcare professionals who delivered your baby will be closely monitoring them in the first few days after the birth.

Your baby is assessed within the first, fifth and tenth minutes of delivery in order to gauge their health. Skin colour, breathing, heart rate, muscle tone and responsiveness are all noted and given what is termed an 'Apgar score'. Your baby's score could initially be less than the full score of ten. They may, for example, be stunned at birth and need some help to start breathing. This is very common and babies usually pick up extremely quickly and are breathing on their own within a very short time.

One of the first questions you will be asked is whether you want your baby to have a vitamin K injection. Vitamin K is important for blood-clotting and helps to prevent abnormal bleeding. Babies are born with low levels compared to adults and their blood vessels are delicate and susceptible to rupture, particularly if they are premature or of low birthweight. This puts them at risk of bleeding around the brain, which can lead to serious illness, permanent brain damage and even death. While brain bleeds are extremely rare, I would highly recommend this injection for all newborns, because we have no way of knowing which ones are at risk.

Previous concerns about administering vitamin K as an injection because of a link with childhood cancer have not been borne out by further research. However, if you prefer, you can ask for the medicine to be given orally. The disadvantage of this is that your baby would need three doses, the first two in the first week and the third dose at one month old, the subsequent doses can be easily forgotten. In addition, your baby is not fully protected until all three doses have been given.

Your baby will be weighed as part of the post-birth assessment. This is not always done immediately, so you may need to have a little patience with the medical team. All parents are understandably keen to know what their baby weighs for those all-important phone calls to family and friends, but it is vital to remember that the midwives and doctors first need to make sure that you and your new baby are safe.

## The routine neonatal examination

Within 72 hours of birth your baby will have a head-to-toe examination, commonly termed 'the baby check'. This is often performed by a paediatrician or a specially trained nurse or midwife just before you leave hospital, but it can also be done later by your GP. As well as a thorough look at your baby's overall appearance, the baby check includes a specific examination of your baby's head, heart, lungs, abdomen (including genitalia), hips, limbs, hands and feet (including counting fingers and toes), back, including the spine, eyes, ears, mouth and palate (including the sucking reflex) and movements and posture (if a cause for concern, reflexes will be tested).

The examination will be fully explained and you may be asked about relevant family and antenatal history. You should be able to watch and help if you wish, and can discuss anything that is concerning you. There are some common abnormalities that can be detected during the newborn examination. Most are no cause for alarm, although some may require treatment in order to be rectified.

## Newborn blood spot screening

A blood test is performed when your baby is over five days old to screen for several genetic (inherited) conditions (some of which are very rare), including sickle cell disease and cystic fibrosis. The blood is usually obtained by making a tiny cut on your baby's heel with a small needle. You may hear nothing further if the tests results are normal. However, if the tests show that your baby does have one of the conditions, you will be referred to a specialist and offered counselling.

# Birthmarks

Coloured areas on the skin that appear at birth or soon afterwards are known as 'birthmarks'. There are two main types of birthmark – vascular and pigmented – and your baby could have one or more of each. Vascular birthmarks are caused by abnormal blood vessels under the skin and the pigmented type are made up of melanin (the compound that causes your skin to look tanned or dark) and are therefore usually brown. Birthmarks can occur on any part of the body and are often temporary. They rarely require any treatment.

## Vascular birthmarks

There are three main types of vascular birthmark: stork bites/salmon patches, strawberry marks and port wine stains.

Nearly 50 per cent of babies are born with small pink or red patches, known as 'stork bites' or 'salmon patches', on the eyelids, between the eyes, on the upper lip and on the back of the neck. These are caused by a concentration of tiny immature blood vessels (capillaries) and may be more visible when the baby is crying. Most fade and disappear completely by the end of the first year.

Strawberry marks earn their name because of the bright or dark red, raised or swollen, bumpy area (haemangioma), again formed by a concentration of immature blood vessels. They may not be present at birth, often developing in the first two months, and can appear anywhere on the body. Strawberry marks can increase in size for several months before gradually fading, and nearly all completely disappear by nine years of age. Only a few require treatment, either by surgical removal or with a laser.

Port wine stains are flat pink, red or purple areas on the skin and they are caused by a concentration of dilated blood vessels. These birthmarks usually occur on the head or neck and can vary in size, even covering large areas of the body. Those on the face may be associated with more serious problems. Port wine stains do not change colour when gently pressed and are permanent. They may become darker over time and may bleed when your baby is older or is an adult. The most effective way of treating them is with a special type of laser when your baby is older; smaller ones can be disguised by cosmetics if you wish.

## Pigmented birthmarks

There are three main types of pigmented birthmark: Mongolian blue spots, café-au-lait spots and congenital moles.

Blue or purple patches on the lower back and/or buttocks, known as 'Mongolian blue spots', occur in most dark-skinned babies of all races and are caused by a concentration of pigmented cells. They do not need any treatment and disappear by about four years of age.

Many children are born with one or two coffee-coloured skin patches, called 'café-au-lait spots'. These need no treatment, but if your child has more than six, you should see you GP, as it could be a sign of neurofibromatosis (an extremely rare condition that often runs in families).

Congenital moles, technically known as congenital melanocytic naevi (CMN), are the result of an overgrowth of pigmented skin cells. They are relatively common and range in size. Moles can be left alone, but if they are disfiguring or large, you can seek the advice of a plastic surgeon when your baby is older to discuss removal.

# What your newborn can do

Your new baby may seem tiny, helpless and very fragile, but they can do so much more than you might expect. To help them, they are born with a range of behaviours, instincts and reflexes, which are related to their survival and ability to learn and develop.

## Sleep

The main activity of a newborn is sleep (for as many as sixteen to twenty out of every twenty-four hours). To call it an activity may seem like a contradiction in terms, but sleep is a crucial part of a baby's development. When babies rest they grow and sleep is vital for their ability to process the masses of information they are receiving. Many newborns wake for a feed and then fall straight back to sleep once they are full. You do not need to worry about this, as long as they are feeding well and producing both wet and dirty nappies. For more on sleep, see Chapter 4.

## Crying

Crying is a baby's way of letting you know that they need something. Some newborns cry a lot; others may rarely cry. While older babies have different types of cry that mean different things, newborns have only one type of cry – just different volumes!

*Remember that your baby will be fairly tired at first, especially if they have been through a vaginal delivery. They will need to rest, just like you.*

## Your baby's reflexes

Nature has given all newborn babies some reflexes, automatic responses that their body gives to a stimulus. Here are some of the most visible ones:

- **Moro/startle reflex:** in response to a sudden movement or noise (including their own crying) your baby will fling out their arms and legs, arch their back, throw back their head, then draw their arms back to their chest with the fists clenched; disappears at between four and six months.
- **Grasp reflex:** your baby will automatically grasp at anything in their palm; disappears at three to six months.
- **Stepping reflex:** when your baby's feet touch a flat surface they automatically lift up again, appearing to take a step (although this is not related to real walking); normally disappears at around two months.
- **Rooting reflex:** when their cheek or nose is stroked, your baby will turn their head towards the stimulus and 'root' with their mouth open in order to find the breast or bottle; continues until three to four months and may persist beyond this time when they are sleeping
- **Sucking reflex:** when the roof of the mouth is touched, your baby will start sucking; disappears at about two to four months.

Most will cry because they are hungry, tired, need a cuddle, or have a dirty nappy and are uncomfortable. Within a few weeks you will be able to tell which of these it is. See also Chapter 2, p.42.

## Strength and movement

Your baby will have enough muscle tone to move their arms and legs in an uncontrolled way. However, they do not have the strength in their neck to support their head, so you must be careful to do this when you pick them up and carry them (see p.20). Although babies are born with a grasp reflex that can actually support their bodyweight if necessary (see Box opposite), it will be some months before they can actually hold an object and, in fact, their hands are often tightly closed at first (they will relax over the next few weeks). For more information on how babies gain movement, see Chapter 6, p.133.

## Sight

Newborns can differentiate between light and dark and make out the shapes and silhouettes of objects within 20–30 cm. This means they can probably see the person who is carrying them. In fact, they are programed to search out faces, although this may just be because the two dark spots that are your eyes are the easiest things for them to focus on. Your baby's eyes may seem crossed at times, and may move at slightly different speeds and directions. See also Chapter 6, p.130.

## Hearing

Hearing develops in the womb. From sixteen weeks of pregnancy, the tiny bones in the ear are developed; from nineteen weeks, babies respond to noises of 500 Hz (middle range sound); they next develop the ability to hear the lower ranges and, finally, the higher pitches. It is not until 35 weeks that they are able to hear the full range of sounds.

The intonation and timbre of your voice and that of your partner are already very familiar to your newborn. In a short time, they will turn their heads in response to the direction of a noise. Babies are very responsive to loud and sudden noises (and lights), and so they may need comforting in order to settle once they have been disturbed.

## Top Tips

1 New babies are extremely demanding of your time and energy. Be prepared and ready to adjust!

2 It is normal for babies to cry for as much as three to four hours per day. Your own baby's cry is instantly recognisable and will bother you more than it bothers anyone else – that's nature!

3 Newborns initially sleep a lot, but their sleeping will not have a pattern and they will not yet understand the difference between day and night. They will wake frequently to feed, sometimes as often as every 30 minutes, but more normally every two to three hours.

4 You should expect to feed every two hours if breastfeeding, although it may be more frequent in the first few days before your milk comes in. This continues during the night, too. Formula-fed babies typically feed every two to three hours.

5 Get used to nappy-changing, as babies need a fresh one about eight to twelve times in a 24-hour period.

6 Babies vomit and poo on their clothes frequently! You need to have plenty of vests and sleepsuits, so that you are not constantly putting on the washing machine.

## Sense of smell

Newborns are very sensitive to smell and your unique body smell is an important part of how they learn to recognise you. Your baby is also drawn to the smell of breast milk and can tell the difference between your milk and that of another mother. Even if you are not breastfeeding, your baby will still get to know your distinctive smell, particularly when you spend time together in skin-to-skin contact (see overleaf).

# Bonding with your baby

The time that you and your new baby have together is often referred to as 'bonding'. Establishing a relationship with your baby from the outset is important for both parents. It does not really matter what you do, as long as you are together.

If you are breastfeeding your baby, you will already be forming a close emotional tie through the time you spend together. However, feeding from a bottle also allows bonding time: you are still physically close and looking at each other. Bonding is really only about being in each other's company, and there are many ways in which you and your partner can do that.

### Skin-to-skin contact

Placing your baby directly on your skin while they are wearing just a nappy is sometimes called 'kangaroo care'. This skin-to-skin contact is a lovely way to be close to your baby, but it has many other benefits too. For example, it is a fantastic strategy for calming and reassuring your baby when they are unsettled and for helping them adjust to being 'on the outside' (see Chapter 2, p.45). Skin-to-skin contact is particularly encouraged for premature babies, so that they can benefit from your body warmth. Specifically, skin-to-skin contact can have the following positive effects if it is done within the first hour of a baby's life:

- Blood sugar level remains higher than those babies who have not had skin-to-skin contact (but still within the normal range).
- Babies can be calmer and less likely to cry.
- They are more likely to latch on well to the breast and to breastfeed exclusively for longer.

First make sure that your newborn is dry and wearing a dry hat (this will need to be changed if it gets damp – babies' heads are wet when they are born) and that they have a clean nappy and are not hungry. You need to find a comfortable place to sit (you may be seated in the same position for 15–30 minutes) and wear a loose top with a low neck or a button-through shirt. Pop your baby through the opening directly onto your skin, making sure that their head is peeping out of your top so that they can breathe easily. Keep as much of the baby's body as possible in contact with yours and ensure that their ear is directly against your chest – hearing your heartbeat is very soothing. You should cover your baby with a sheet or blanket to keep warm – however, your body heat will pass through to your baby, so be careful that they do not overheat.

### Baby massage

Massaging your baby is a really wonderful skill and is a good opportunity for parents and babies to enjoy each other's company and relax. There are often free classes at children's centres – ask your midwife or health visitor. See also Chapter 2, p.52.

### Talking, singing and reading

Simply talking to your baby will be soothing and comforting to them. It will also begin the process of language development (see Chapter 6, p.144) – make sure that your face is no more 20–25 cm away, so that your baby can focus on your mouth and expression.

Even if you rarely sing out loud, humming a favourite tune or singing a nursery rhyme can give your baby lots of pleasure – at this stage they will be no judge of quality! In a few weeks, you will also be able to start reading to them. For more information on stimulating your baby, see Chapter 6, pp.137–141.

## When bonding takes time

While many parents instantly feel a rush of love for their newborn, for others it can take a little longer for those emotions to emerge. This is a very normal occurrence, for which there may be many reasons, including:

- Exhaustion from the birth.
- Shock from not having the delivery you were hoping for.
- The hospital environment – bustling, noisy wards are not conducive for resting and getting to know your baby.

You need time to adjust your mind to the events that have just taken place and this may mean actually being a bit selfish for a while. If you are physically and emotionally exhausted, you are not going to have the energy or inclination to bond with your new baby, so need to tell your partner how you are feeling and try to get some sleep and 'me time'.

If, after a few weeks, you are still feeling that you are unable to form a relationship with your baby, you may need some more support. Your midwife or GP should be able to point you in the direction of support groups and others who can help. Do not ignore these feelings; talking to people about it, especially your partner and family and friends, is often all you need. You may find that one of them felt the same and may be able to help you, too.

### When your baby is in the neonatal unit

Some parents do not have the opportunity to form an initial close bond because their baby is very premature or unwell and being cared for in the neonatal unit (see Chapter 8, p.172). There is little evidence to suggest that missing this first 'window' has any long-term effect on the parent-child relationship – after all, bonding is a process, not a one-off event, and bonds have to be constantly worked upon in order to maintain them. In any case, staff in the unit will do all they can to include you in the care of your newborn and, where possible, give you the chance to touch and hold your baby.

To start with, your baby may need the support of an incubator to regulate their body temperature and the environmental humidity in order to protect them while they unstable. This can make it difficult for you to look after them, as you may only be able to touch them through the ports in the sides. As they get better, you will be able to get them out of the incubator for a cuddle, some skin-to-skin contact and to feed them (once they have learnt to suck and swallow).

Your baby may need to stay in hospital for quite a while. It can be very hard on parents to have to go home without their baby, but hospital visits can be very exhausting and you, too, will need time to rest and recover. However, the neonatal unit often has free access times for parents, so you can still be with your baby whenever you want. Bear in mind that they may be too ill for any stimulation other than touch and sound, but reading, singing and talking to them are an extremely important part of the bonding process and their recovery.

### Doing everyday tasks

It sounds obvious, but changing your baby's nappy, feeding and bathing them, placing your baby in a sling or baby carrier while you are out and about, and just simply cuddling them are all ways in which to develop a relationship. Make sure you and your partner share your baby as much as possible between you, so that you both feel equally comfortable with these tasks.

### Making a memory box

Putting together some memorabilia from the birth is a good way to start feeling that your baby is a member of the family. Things to include can be your baby's hospital identity band, the cord clip, a lock of hair, hand and foot prints (in paint), plaster cast hands and feet, antenatal scan photographs, birth congratulations cards and anything else that is meaningful to you.

## How to pick up and hold a newborn

Newborn babies are much more robust than you might at first think. However, they cannot support the weight of their head and so you will need to do this for your baby whenever you move or hold them. You can talk to ten different people and you will get ten different answers as to how this is best done, but the essentials are the same.

The easiest way is to scoop up your baby supporting their head and neck with the palm of your hand and your spread fingers, with the body lying on your forearm. From here you can transfer the baby across your opposite arm, which you should bend at the elbow to allow support for your baby's head and body. You can also hold your baby across your chest, over your shoulder, face down over your forearm or with your baby's back against your abdomen and facing outwards.

When you put your baby down, for example into their Moses basket, once again you need to support their head and neck with your hand, and their back with your forearm or other hand.

# Caring for an adopted baby

This is a topic that is extremely close to my heart, as I myself am adopted. My parents were unable to have their own baby and so decided to pursue adoption. I am not sure I realised the emotional journey they had to go through until I had children of my own.

So how do you start bonding with a baby that has been given to you, one that is not, biologically, your own? Will you have parental instincts when you have not had nine months of pregnancy in which to prepare? Will you love or even like this baby? What if the baby looks odd? (Apparently, when my parents went to collect me, I had a heat rash and a squint, but luckily for me, my mum was able to look beyond my blotchy skin and peculiar gaze!) I do not think that bonding with your newly adopted baby is anything you need to worry about: you obviously wanted a baby, which is why you have gone ahead and adopted. Just get involved from the outset and the bond will develop with time.

A baby is a baby and their needs are exactly the same whether you physically gave birth to them or not. Remember that the first few weeks are just as chaotic for everyone else as they will be for you: your normal routine will be a thing of the past and you will have your share of sleepless nights and restless days. Similarly, you will need the same support and teamwork strategy as any other family.

## Learning the basics

Having a new baby is a full-time job and, from the moment you are given this infant, you are thrown into a world of feeds and nappies. Preparation is key. Make sure that you already know how to do the basics – picking up and holding, changing a nappy, bathing, winding – and that you understand the feeding and sleep patterns that babies have. Through your GP you can find out about local baby care classes. Most women who adopt will formula-feed from the beginning, although it is technically possible to breastfeed an adopted baby with a great deal of help and perseverance. Your baby may already have a feeding routine, so it may be easier, at least initially, to follow that. You can then change it to suit you and the new family unit once you have all had a period of time to settle. If your adopted baby is older, they may be sleeping well already. You will need to find out what their bedtime routine is and try to do something similar, as this will comfort your little one and help them to adapt to their new surroundings and family.

## Telling your child and other people

It is very clear from all the research and accumulated years of experience that children need to be aware that they are adopted at the earliest possible stage. When this is so, it simply becomes normal to them. There are many different ways to tell a child, but the main thing is not to suddenly drop it on them as a huge shock – make it part of life from the beginning. For example, I had a teddy who was called 'Adopted Ted', so as soon as I asked why he was called this, my parents told me and I was able to begin to understand that I was adopted, too. Similarly, if you get used to telling everyone from the start that your baby is adopted, it will become part of your child's 'story' and a natural and comfortable thing to share with other people.

# Your recovery

While much of the focus of the early days will naturally be on your newborn, your healthcare professionals will also be monitoring your recovery. Taking the time to look after yourself as well as your new baby is important for both your physical and mental well-being.

However 'natural' it may be, giving birth is an intense experience from which you need to take some time to recuperate. Hospitals are not always very peaceful places, so do your best to rest whenever it is quiet (you may find an eye mask and earplugs useful) and try to keep visitors to a minimum. If you have had a straightforward vaginal delivery you may be able to leave hospital within six hours of the birth, although this does vary from hospital to hospital. Do remember that although you may be walking around and feeling fine to go home, you will need to take things slowly for a few days. You may prefer to stay in hospital for a bit longer, so that you can take advantage of the midwives' experience and advice in looking after both yourself and your baby. If this is your first baby, having healthcare professionals available to discuss any breastfeeding concerns and babycare techniques, as well as your own health issues, is extremely reassuring. When you decide to leave hospital, a midwife will come and visit you and your new baby at home to assess your ongoing care needs (see p.28).

Your initial elation, excitement and relief may give way to apprehension and even anxiety as you realise that your newborn is totally dependent on you for everything. Although childbirth affects everyone differently, this mix of emotions is normal and will eventually pass as you get to grips with your new role.

Once at home, it is tempting to start getting back to normal as soon as possible – make sure you have plenty of help at hand so that you do not overdo it. Depending on whether you had a vaginal delivery or a Caesarean, there are some specific things you can do to aid your recovery.

## After a vaginal delivery

Until you stop bleeding, rinse your vulva and perineum with clean water each time you go to the toilet. Always wipe from front to back, away from the vagina, and change your sanitary pads often (you must not use tampons as these can cause infection – see also p.24). For the first week at home, gently pat dry using a facial tissue rather than toilet paper, as this is a bit softer. If you feel sore around the perineum, applying creams such as calendula and arnica around your labia/vaginal opening can help reduce any swelling and inflammation. Use once you are clean and dry and reapply throughout the day as necessary. However, do not use creams if you have had an episiotomy or tear (see below).

## Care after an episiotomy or perineal tear

If you have stitches from either an episiotomy or tear to your perineum, you should be especially careful to keep this area clean, following the guidance above – the current advice is to wash just with water rather than using soap (which can irritate sore skin) and to avoid creams. Dabbing on witch hazel with cotton wool can aid healing, as can a soak in a warm bath containing a few drops of tea tree oil. Again, pat rather than rub yourself dry.

Until you have healed, passing urine may sting. Although it makes going to the toilet a little more complicated, a good way of dealing with this is to wash some water over yourself while you are passing urine. This dilutes the urine and so reduces the stinging sensation. Opening your bowels may also be uncomfortable, so follow the measures for dealing with constipation outlined on p.26.

If your perineum is swollen or painful you can apply a cooled gel pack for short periods of time;

some women get relief from sitting on a valley-shaped cushion until the area heals. If you feel you need medication for pain relief, you can take paracetamol.

The perineal area heals very quickly, normally within two weeks. Any stitches you had will dissolve on their own – you do not need to have them removed. Your GP will confirm at your six-week postnatal check (see Box, p.26) that everything has healed well.

## After a Caesarean section

As you have had a major abdominal operation, your stay in hospital will normally be two to three days. You will be kept under close observation by the medical team for the first 24 hours. Try not to expect too much of yourself during this time: the surgery, the effects of an anaesthetic, blood loss and possibly labour beforehand – not to mention dealing with your new baby – are a pretty exhausting combination. If the Caesarean was unexpected, you may also be coming to terms with a birth that was very different from the one you might have imagined you would have.

### Pain management

The pain relief that you will be offered can vary according to your needs and the hospital you are in. In the first 24 hours women are often put on a morphine infusion, which can be topped up by pushing a hand-held button – this is called 'patient-controlled analgesia' (PCA). You may then be given an oral morphine derivative, such as codeine or tramadol, together with paracetamol and either ibuprofen or diclofenac.

My advice is to try to remain as pain-free as possible for the first day or two, as this will help you to move around and become more mobile. If you are breastfeeding, you will be passing some of the medications to your baby through the colostrum/milk, so the quicker you can move onto just paracetamol the better. However, there is a balance to be struck here: if you are in pain and having difficulty moving, you are not going to be able to pick up your new baby for feeds, and regular feeding is essential for stimulating milk production.

*A surgical procedure such as a Caesarean can take six weeks to recover from. Take things easy and ask for help when you need it.*

### Wound care

The incision site will be covered with a sterile dressing for the first 24 hours or so. Once it is removed, you may find it helpful to wear high-waisted underwear so that the elastic does not rub against the wound. You may have been given dissolvable stitches that do not need to be removed; if not, stitches/staples will be removed about five to seven days after surgery. As with any surgery, there is always a small risk of infection. Signs of wound infection are:

- smell
- fluid oozing from the wound
- pain
- redness
- heat from the wound site
- fever and flu-like symptoms.

Seek immediate advice from your midwife, GP or obstetrician if you have one or a combination of these symptoms.

### Other effects of surgery

You should be getting up and about between eight and 24 hours after delivery. This can be difficult, but it is necessary for your recovery. This is because a Caesarean section puts you at higher risk than a vaginal delivery of getting a deep vein thrombosis (DVT). A DVT is a blood clot that occurs in the leg, usually in the calf. If it breaks free and travels into your lungs, it is called a pulmonary embolism (PE) and this can be extremely dangerous (in some cases, fatal). All women are given compression stockings to wear after surgery to help prevent DVT. In addition, as well as generally keeping mobile, you can do some specific exercises, including wiggling your toes, pointing and flexing your feet and gently turning from side to side.

Your abdomen will be sore for quite a few days; twisting and turning will feel very uncomfortable, and others will need to help you with picking up your baby and moving about.

You will still be able to breastfeed your baby if you want to, although you may need to be shown positions that do not press against your abdomen. Your milk tends to take longer to come than it does following a vaginal delivery (about five days). Both these factors can make breastfeeding more challenging, so it is really important that you are not afraid to ask for help. The midwives will offer a wealth of knowledge, and you can also ask to see a specialist lactation consultant. See Chapter 3, pp.60–77 for information about breastfeeding.

You must not do any heavy lifting or driving for at least a month. Your abdominal muscles have been divided and lack the strength to protect your back and pelvis from injury when lifting or to perform an emergency stop. Follow the guidance about back care and do some gentle exercises to help tone the muscles (see Chapter 7, pp.149–153). You can drive again when you are comfortably able to perform an emergency stop, although check with your insurance company. They may need a doctor's letter to confirm that you are well enough to begin driving again.

## Bleeding

Whether you have had a vaginal delivery or a Caesarean section, you will bleed for around two to three weeks, although in some cases bleeding can last for longer. This bleeding is known as lochia and is a combination of blood and sloughed uterine lining. Lochia can vary in flow and consistency: initially, it is heavy and contains clots; as the days pass, the flow gets lighter and eventually it is only a pale pink discharge. You will need to use maternity sanitary pads during this time. Do not use tampons or a vaginal douche before your six-week postnatal

check, as this will increase your risk of getting an infection. You may prefer to sleep on a bath towel in case you leak at night – and be reassured, it does get lighter in time.

While some bleeding after birth is perfectly normal, you should contact your midwife, GP or obstetrician if:

- you have a large, sudden loss of blood
- you are soaking through a large pad every hour
- your vaginal bleeding has increased and does not slow down when you rest
- the amount, colour, smell or duration of your bleeding seems abnormal.

These symptoms may indicate that your placenta was not fully delivered and you may need a procedure to remove it, that you are exhausted and overdoing it or that you have an infection of your uterus (see below).

## Abdominal cramps

You may experience some cramping, often called 'afterpains', as your uterus contracts to return to its pre-pregnancy size. This typically disappears three to four days after birth. If you are breastfeeding, you may experience increased abdominal cramps during and after nursing. This is positive, as it means that the uterus is contracting appropriately, which should reduce how long you bleed for. You can take paracetamol to ease the pain, or discuss with your GP if you need further pain relief.

If you notice increased abdominal tenderness, or are experiencing fever or chills, contact your midwife, GP or obstetrician. If your fever is high and you feel unwell, you should go to the Accident and Emergency department at your local hospital, as this indicates an infection of the uterus and you will need a scan and antibiotics as soon as possible.

## Stress incontinence

Leaking a little urine when you cough, sneeze or laugh, known as 'stress incontinence', is a common postnatal problem. It is due to stretched and weakened pelvic floor muscles, so make sure you start pelvic floor muscle exercises as soon as you can after the birth (see Feature in Chapter 7, p.151).

## Constipation

Hormonal changes in the postnatal period can make you more constipated than usual. Aside from many other unpleasant side effects, long-term constipation and straining also weakens the pelvic floor muscles and can lead to urinary and faecal incontinence (wetting and soiling yourself). Try to keep your stools as soft as possible by drinking lots of water, eating plenty of wholegrains and fruit for fibre and perhaps taking an osmotic laxative (stimulant laxatives can cause abdominal pain).

In addition to adapting your diet, try not to strain, as this will put pressure on your stitches. Adopt more of a squatting position when going to the toilet by placing a large book or footstool under your feet, so that your knees are higher than your hips – hovering over the toilet because you do not feel comfortable is very detrimental to the pelvic floor. Lean forwards, rest your elbows on your knees, relax your abdominal muscles completely and breathe out while opening your bowels. If you are still anxious about going to the toilet, place some folded toilet paper or tissue against your perineum – this pressure will make you feel more supported and may also make it less painful.

## Headaches

If you have had either an epidural for pain relief during labour or a spinal block for a Caesarean section, you may develop a post-dural puncture headache (usually in the front and back of your head). This occurs when the fluid within your spinal cord leaks out through the holes made by the needles used. Up to five per cent of women suffer from headaches following a spinal block. It is much more rare to have a headache following an epidural.

Most headaches do not develop immediately after the epidural/spinal, but occur 24–48 hours afterwards, with 90 per cent of headaches appearing within three days. The headache is worse when you are standing and improves when you are lying down. You may also experience neck stiffness, an inability to look at bright light (photophobia), ringing in your ears (tinnitus) and visual disturbance (e.g. blurred vision, double vision). These symptoms usually resolve spontaneously. Bed rest and extra fluids used to be advised, but recent studies have failed to find any evidence to show that this is beneficial. In more extreme cases, you can be given medication (e.g. caffeine) and there is a procedure to block up the holes that are leaking fluid, called an 'epidural blood patch'.

## Caring for your breasts

You need to support your breasts after birth by wearing a well-fitting bra. If you are breastfeeding, you need special feeding bras (which open at the front to give access) and should be measured when your breasts are at their fullest, as a badly fitting bra creates pressure on the breast tissue, which can lead to blocked milk ducts and mastitis. If you are

### Your postnatal check

Your GP will perform an assessment of your recovery, known as your postnatal check. This is done usually at around six weeks after the birth, although some practices conduct it at eight weeks to coincide with your baby's vaccination schedule (see Feature in Chapter 8, p.173). Your GP will check:

- blood pressure
- urine (to detect infection or diabetes)
- weight.

They will ask about your lochia (see p.24) and whether you have any concerns about your breasts and nipples, your perineum, your Caesarean scar (if applicable) and your bladder control. Your method of contraception will also be discussed. If there are ongoing issues with your own health, such as postnatal urinary incontinence (see p.24), your GP can refer you back to your obstetric consultant or to other specialists for treatment. In addition to your physical well-being, your GP is also interested in your emotional welfare, so if you have any concerns about your mental health (see Chapter 7, pp.156–9), make sure you raise these now.

not breastfeeding, you will still need to be fitted for a new bra, as the breast tissue is enlarged and needs time to settle.

Any bra should be 100 per cent cotton and not underwired. Underwiring can inhibit lymphatic drainage and good flow of the blood, possibly leading to pain and infection. Cotton is breathable and therefore reduces your risk of getting thrush around the nipples. See also Feature in Chapter 3, p.63 regarding breast care while breastfeeding.

## Contraception

It is possible to get pregnant straight after a birth and when you are breastfeeding, so contraception is something that will be discussed with you in hospital, even though sex may be the last thing on your mind. Condoms are highly effective and are probably the simplest method of preventing a surprise pregnancy. The mini pill is the best oral contraceptive if you are breastfeeding. It is extremely effective and when you stop breast-feeding you can convert to your usual pill. A coil is another possibility: they are easier to insert following a vaginal delivery, but you do need to wait for six weeks after the birth before you can have one fitted. A cap is also effective but, if you were using one before your pregnancy, you will need to be measured for a new size after the birth.

## The 'baby blues'

Symptoms of mild depression – commonly known as the 'baby blues' – happen to almost all of us: figures have shown that 60–80 per cent of women will suffer from the baby blues around the third day after the birth, when your hormones are at their most disruptive. Common signs are:

• feeling very unsettled and/or irritable
• feeling like crying for very little or no reason
• being overly anxious about being a good mother.

Remember that this is a temporary phase that normally only lasts a day or two, but you need to warn your partner that this may happen so you can then deal with it together. You may simply need to cry. In this event, you do not need to 'pull yourself together' – you may just benefit from a hug or a bit

of positive encouragement. If you are still having moments like this a couple of weeks after the birth, you should consider talking to your doctor, as you may be suffering from postnatal depression (see Chapter 7, p.158).

## Your ongoing emotional health

The act of giving birth is a very emotional time. Some women have to cope with the added pressure of complications or a birth that was very different from what they wished for, and this can cause disappointment and a feeling of being let down by the whole experience. These emotions can also be accompanied by anger or guilt. In this instance you need to find someone with whom you can discuss your feelings – perhaps your partner or a close friend. Often women who have already been through labour will be a good listening ear and the voice of experience. However, you may feel that you would rather talk to a health professional instead, in which case you should ensure that you meet with someone sooner rather than later.

Being tired is a common feature of new motherhood. Days are long and nights are even longer and this can come as a real shock! Feeling exhausted and sleep-deprived is stressful and may cause you to lose perspective on the new demands and roles that you are trying to fulfil. However, you may be on call 24/7 for your new baby, but you will be no good to anybody if you do not also look after yourself. So, in the early days:

• try to sleep when your baby does
• get help with the household chores
• have some ready meals available or something else that is quick and easy to prepare.

Try to remember that sleep deprivation does not carry on indefinitely and you will gradually learn to adjust to your new lifestyle. You might find it useful to set yourself some simple goals to work towards, based on what is achievable in the early weeks (see also Top Tips, p.17).

# Your support network

Once you have had your baby, you will be cared for by a range of health professionals who can support you both during the first year and beyond.

### Your midwife

A community midwife will visit you at home, normally on the day after you are discharged from hospital (or, if you have had a home delivery, the day after the birth). The midwife will check on your physical recovery, particularly if you have had an episiotomy/perineal tear or a Caesarean section, and will also monitor how your baby is doing. She will discuss with you when a midwife will visit again: for some women, it will be the next day, for others, a few days' time.

The visits are a good opportunity to share any worries or feelings you may have and to seek advice and support with feeding, sleeping, general babycare and so on. If you have any particular medical problems or require medication (e.g. for an infection), your midwife may call your doctor on your behalf. Ideally, community midwives continue to visit you for up to six weeks if you request it, although local demand may mean that this service cannot be delivered to you. However, you may still call the midwives up to 28 days after the birth if you need to. When you are ready, the midwife will transfer your care to your GP and health visitor (see below).

### Your health visitor

At some point between ten and fourteen days after the birth, your health visitor will call on you at home. Based at your local GP surgery, health clinic or Children's Centre, health visitors are trained nurses or midwives who deliver child and family health services up until your child is five years old. They offer parenting support and practical help and advice on general health and minor illnesses and are also a mine of information about babycare (e.g. weaning, dental health), local new mothers' groups (see Chapter 2, p.52) and much more besides.

The home visit will take around an hour, during which time your health visitor will ask you about a number of things, including the birth and your health or that of your partner. She will also check your baby, inform you about the immunisations your baby needs (see Feature in Chapter 8, p.173) and explain how you can arrange your six-week check.

For further contact, your health visitor will suggest that you come to the centre where she is based. She will run at least one weekly clinic, where you can get your baby weighed and seek advice. If necessary, she can assess whether you need further support, referring you to specialists if necessary. If you have a concern that you feel unable to raise at a clinic, you can call her to discuss it or ask her to visit you at home. Some health visitors run courses for new parents, tackling a different aspect of parenting each week, and these classes can be a great way to meet other new mothers in your area in an informal setting. Your health visitor may also perform your baby's routine developmental check at around eight months (see Chapter 6, p.128).

### Your GP

The doctor with whom you are registered, your general practitioner (GP), is there to provide care for any medical problems you or your baby may have. New mothers tend to visit their GP a lot during the first year, so it is worth establishing a relationship with one you like. If you do not feel comfortable with your named doctor, you can ask to see another one in the same practice or even to be transferred to another surgery. Your concerns about your baby's health are normal and natural, so never feel worried about being a nuisance if you need to see your GP. It is far better to seek reassurance that there is no serious problem with your baby than to worry at home alone.

# Officialdom

As soon as your baby is born, their existence is recorded in the 'statutory notification of birth'. Although this marks the beginning of their official profile, in practice there is nothing you need to do other than register your baby's birth at your local register office.

The statutory notification includes your name and address, details of your GP, the date and time of birth and your baby's sex and weight. This is done by the midwife and allows your baby to be issued with an NHS number.

## NHS number

Every baby born in England and Wales is given their own NHS number. This number will last for your baby's lifetime and is subsequently used on all NHS documentation (e.g. labels for blood samples). It also ensures that any healthcare professional can access the correct records. It is useful to keep a note of the number in a safe place and take it with you whenever you have an appointment, but your baby can still receive care if you do not know the number or have mislaid it.

## The Personal Child Health Record

Shortly before or after your baby is born, you will be given a Personal Child Health Record. This has a red cover and so is often called the 'red book'. It is used to keep track of your baby's progress by recording, for example, immunisations and details of developmental checks. You can also add to it yourself, by noting when your baby first rolled over, when teeth appeared, what illnesses they have had, and so on. You should take the red book with you every time you visit the health visitor or GP.

You will notice some charts at the back of the book. These allow healthcare professionals to plot the measurements of babies as a means of assessing their health and progress (see Chapter 6, p.132). They also enable you to find out where your baby is in comparison to the general population. Girls tend to be smaller than boys – hence, there are two versions of the book – one for boys, another for girls – each containing different charts.

## Registering the birth

The birth of all babies must be registered in England, Wales and Northern Ireland within 42 days (21 days in Scotland). You can do this at the register office local to where your baby was born or sometimes at the hospital itself. You do not need to take any documentation with you but you should be prepared to give the following information:

- the place and date of birth
- the name, surname and sex of your baby
- the names and addresses of both parents, along with your places and dates of birth
- the date of your marriage/civil partnership (if applicable)
- your and your partner's jobs
- your maiden name (if applicable).

If you are married, either you or the father can register the birth on your own and can include both parents' details. However, if you are unmarried and want to include both parents' details, you must attend and sign the birth register together unless you, as the mother, have a signed statutory declaration of parentage form (or a court order stating parentage). You can choose not to record details of your child's father if you wish.

Your baby will be issued with a free 'short' certificate detailing the date and place of birth. However, you may choose to pay for a longer version, which includes the information above. Keep the certificate safe: your baby will need to produce it many times throughout their life.

# 2

# Caring for your baby

There are a number of skills that you will need in order to care for your baby. Aside from basic tasks, such as bathing, dressing and changing your baby's nappy, you can master the fine art of soothing your baby. You should also take steps to ensure that your house is safe in order to prevent common accidents.

# Nappy-changing

Changing your baby's nappy is a frequent event in the first year and beyond. You will first need to give some thought as to whether you want to use disposable nappies or reusable ones. Getting to grips with changing a nappy can be a challenge to begin with, but you will soon develop your own technique.

The environmental impact of nappies has been the subject of much debate in recent years. Disposables and reusables each have their pros and cons, and it may be that you decide to use a combination of both, depending on your particular situation. Whichever type of nappy you choose, you will need plenty of them – in the early days you will get through around ten per day.

## What you need

✓ Nappies (disposable or reusable)
✓ Nappy sacks (optional)
✓ Wipeable changing mat(s)
✓ Changing stand or unit (optional)
✓ Disposable or cloth wipes/cotton wool
✓ Barrier cream
✓ Muslin squares
✓ Top-and-tail bowl
✓ Nappy bucket

Disposable nappies are undeniably convenient and reliably absorbent. However, they are a relatively expensive option, because you will be buying them for two to three years. Since you throw them away after use, they fill up your rubbish bin (and cause it to smell) and are a significant contributor to landfill. Even biodegradable ones are still toxic to the environment, as they can take many years to decompose.

In recent years, reusable cloth nappies, sometimes called 'real' nappies, have become increasingly popular with parents looking for a more environmentally friendly alternative to disposables that can also save them money. There are three main types: all-in-one, two-part and pocket nappies. There is a wealth of information on the internet about the different options, and you may also have a local a nappy 'library' or real nappy network, staffed by enthusiasts who will be delighted to demonstrate how to use the nappies and possibly even lend you a few to try before you take the plunge. Some local councils also offer incentive schemes to encourage parents to use reusables. While the initial outlay for reusable nappies can seem daunting, it is worth bearing in mind the huge savings that can be made in the long run, as you can reuse them as many times as needed, including for further children. In addition, there is a good market for buying and selling second-hand nappies online via cloth nappy forums and websites.

### Creating a changing station

You will be changing your baby's nappy many times every day – and possibly at night, too – so the more efficiently you can do this the better. It will help speed things up if you have a specific place in your home to do this, a 'changing station', with everything you need to hand. If you have a home over more than one floor, you may want to consider setting up two stations: one downstairs for the daytime and another one on the upper floors for the evening and night.

All you really need to create a changing station is a wipeable, padded changing mat with all the other paraphernalia to hand, but some parents like to buy a special unit. Here, the mat is integral to a stand and there are shelves underneath and compartments to the side for all the bits and bobs (some models come with wheels to allow you to move them from, say, bedroom to bathroom). Even more fancy are dressers with cupboards and drawers – these are naturally more expensive, but they can continue as an item of furniture long after your baby is out of nappies. The important thing to remember is never to leave your baby unattended on the changing mat or unit – they soon develop the skill of rolling and will surprise you the first time they do!

The items you will need to stock your changing station are listed in the Box opposite. Having some spare outfits to hand in case of leaks is also useful. A lidded bin or bucket is not essential if you are using disposable nappies (although it does save you from making repeated trips to your outside bin), but you will definitely want one if you have opted for reusable nappies, as you will need somewhere odour-proof to store dirty ones

until you can wash them or they are collected by the laundry company (see Box overleaf).

## Changing a nappy

Changing your baby's nappy regularly will help prevent their skin from becoming red and irritated. You should aim to change a nappy at least every four hours, or sooner if it is full and heavy or soiled; a newborn baby will need a clean nappy as often as ten to twelve times a day.

First, remove the dirty nappy and, if you are using a disposable, keep it to the side. If your baby does not like the sensation of the cold plastic changing mat, you could put a muslin square under their bottom. This will have the additional benefit of soaking up any urine, should they wee while the nappy is off – a surprisingly frequent occurrence! For a newborn, it is recommended that you clean the skin with cotton wool soaked in water, as a baby's skin is very delicate at this time. However, there is no medical reason why you cannot use

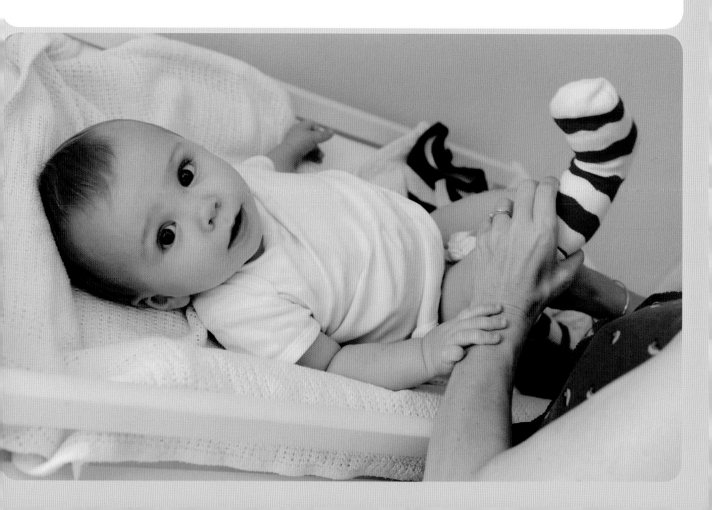

## Washing reusable nappies

There is no need to be put off using reusable nappies by the thought of all the washing and drying – it is easy! Simply pop the nappy and any liners, inserts and cloth wipes into a lidded bin or bucket – they do not need to be soaked or boiled. Heavily soiled nappies can be quickly rinsed into the toilet if necessary. Wash the nappies on a normal cycle at 60°C, with either a small amount of detergent (add an additional rinse, if possible, to ensure there is no product build-up) or an eco-friendly washing ball and then put out to dry. Some brands of nappies can be tumble-dried, but the environmental benefits will be reduced if you tumble-dry each time.

However, if the very thought of washing dirty nappies makes you pale, there are nappy-laundering services that will do this for you, collecting your dirties at the same time as they deliver a pile of fresh ones.

wipes – ideally, use the type for sensitive skin (without alcohol or fragrance). Hold your baby's ankles to lift the legs and wipe around the whole area. When cleaning, always wipe your baby's bottom from the front to the back. This is especially important for girls, as it reduces the risk of a urine infection from the bacteria in their poo. Never try to retract a boy's foreskin (see opposite). You need to clean in all the creases and skin folds, including under a boy's scrotum. This can be tricky and needs care, particularly when your baby is older and more wriggly.

Once the whole bottom area is clean, dry it well with the muslin or more cotton wool, again making sure that you get well into the creases. If you are using disposables, fold the used wipes and cotton wool into the nappy as you seal it up; otherwise put them in the bin. Reusable cloth wipes should be washed after every use, so leave them in the nappy bucket. Apply barrier cream if using to treat or prevent nappy rash (see opposite), slide a clean nappy under your baby's bottom and fit it

according to the manufacturer's instructions. You can use an additional liner (either disposable or washable) to help protect reusable nappies from heavy soil. If you are out and unable to dispose of the nappy immediately, seal it in a nappy sack. When you have finished, wash your hands.

### Care with boys

When cleaning a boy's genitalia, do not attempt to retract the foreskin in order to clean behind it, as you may cause damage to the delicate tissue. It can take many years for a boy's foreskin to be retractile: while this often happens by the age of three, it may not occur until they are much older. It is a good idea to keep the penis pointing down while you are changing him, so if he wees it goes into the nappy or muslin cloth. Similarly, when putting on the new nappy, point the penis downwards as you fit it; if the penis is pointing upwards or to either side, you could find that the wee escapes from the nappy.

## Monitoring the contents

A baby's first poo is an odourless black/green tar-like substance called meconium. It is made up of cells from the intestine, together with mucus and bile, which your baby ingested while in the womb. Although it looks strange, it is entirely normal. Over the next few days, the poo changes to a bright yellow, mustard-like consistency, containing what look like little seeds – again, this is normal and the poo will remain like this if your baby is breastfed. If your baby is formula-fed, the poos become brown. If you are mixed feeding (using both breast milk and formula), the poos are a combination of yellow and brown. Poos change in character again when your baby is weaned: typically, they become darker, thicker and smellier (see Box in Chapter 5, p.118). The number of poos that your baby passes can vary widely and still be considered normal. For example, a breastfed baby who is over two weeks old can poo at every feed or as infrequently as once a week.

Baby poo should always be soft and passing stools should not cause your baby any discomfort. Constipated poos are hard and you may notice your baby straining or grunting as they try to pass. A baby that is formula fed is more likely to become constipated than a breastfed baby. If the poos become runny or watery as well as more frequent than is usual for your baby, this might be diarrhoea, particularly if the colour changes to green or brown. If your baby is having iron supplements (e.g. because they were premature), their poo may be black. Blood mixed with the poo is *not* normal and you need to see your GP if you notice this. See Chapter 8, pp.164 and 176 for how to treat constipation and diarrhoea.

## Nappy rash

Your baby's bottom is continually exposed to wee and poo, chemicals and rubbing/friction from the nappy, as well as the warm, moist environment that a nappy creates. It is not at all surprising if their bottom gets sore from time to time. Nappy rashes are also extremely common. However, some babies are more susceptible to rashes than others and, if your baby gets one nappy rash, they are highly likely to get another.

Once your baby is out of the newborn period (i.e. after one month), it is a good idea to leave your baby's nappy off for periods of time whenever you can. This gives the skin some time in the air away from the nappy, which can help sore areas to heal and the skin to dry. Lay them on a changing mat covered with a muslin square or an old towel, so that if they do wee or poo it is easy to clear up. Babies seem to love the freedom this brings, and will often kick their legs around with excitement, so it is a good thing to do in any case.

There are some other things you can try to relieve nappy rash:

- change the nappy more regularly
- make sure you dry the skin completely before putting on the new nappy
- switch to a different brand of nappy, in case your baby's skin is sensitive to a particular component
- try using barrier cream.

Avoid using talcum powder to 'dry out' the skin, as this can cause further irritation. Most nappy rashes will clear up in four or five days with the above treatment. If the rash is very red and you can see multiple tiny red dots around the main area of the rash, this might be a fungal infection known

### Caring for the umbilical stump

Newborn babies have a mucousy stump on their belly button, the remnant of the umbilical cord (see Chapter 1, p.12). It is important to keep this clean by wiping it with cotton wool and water every time you change the nappy, making sure you allow it to dry completely. (It is fine to bath your baby even when the cord is still jelly-like.) The cord can sometimes be covered by the nappy, so fold over the top of it so that the cord remains exposed to the air (if you are using disposables, you can cut a semi-circular shape out of the waistband). The cord will shrivel and darken to a blackish colour (this is normal) before naturally dropping off within seven to fourteen days (or sometimes even sooner).

Your baby's skin, like your own, is covered with bacteria. If the area where the cord meets the skin becomes red, hot or swollen, or it starts to smell, see your midwife, health visitor or GP, as this may indicate an infection. The cord links to major organs inside the body, so any infection needs to be taken seriously. If it is minor, cleaning the cord with alcohol wipes, keeping it dry and using topical or oral antibiotics can be enough. Occasionally, the infection is more aggressive, in which case intravenous antibiotics are given. If you notice any bleeding of the stump, perhaps caused by an accidental knock, see a healthcare professional as soon as possible. See also Chapter 8, p.182 for information on umbilical granulomas.

as thrush. Typically, the rash is seen in the moist area, including in the creases. An over-the-counter antifungal cream should work well against this (you do not need a prescription). Apply it with every nappy change, and continue to use it for at least five days after the rash has gone. See Chapter 8, pp.165, 180 and 182 for more information on thrush and skin rashes. If you are unsure about the type of nappy rash your baby has, go to your GP.

# Clothing your baby

There is no doubt that baby clothes are one of the pleasures of parenthood. However, dressing your baby can be a tricky affair and you may feel differently about those cute outfits once you have struggled to get them on and off a few times. More important, however, is knowing how to dress your baby to keep them at the right temperature.

## What you need

✓ 5 vests
✓ 5 sleepsuits
✓ 2 cardigans
✓ Hat (winter/summer)
✓ 2 pairs of scratch mittens
✓ Outdoor coat or all-in-one suit (for winter)
✓ Gloves (for winter)
✓ Shoes (for older baby)
✓ 5 daytime outfits (for older baby)

Your baby's body and head should feel warm to the touch. Your baby should not sweat or be red; nor should they get cold. Newborn babies cannot regulate their body temperature very well; the older they get, the better they are at temperature regulation, but they have more surface area from which to lose heat, so you still need to clothe them appropriately. It is best to dress them in a vest, adding further layers, such as a sleepsuit and cardigan, as and when required. Hands and feet are likely to be colder than the trunk, but if they are tinged with blue, you should add another layer of clothing. By adjusting the number of layers, you will be able to maintain a steady temperature for your baby. Even during the hot summer months, you may be moving in and out of air-conditioned environments and should have another layer of clothing to hand.

Other than for the first few hours after birth, hats do not need to be worn indoors unless it is colder than 18°C. When you are outdoors, use a hat whenever your baby's head feels a little cold and, in the summer, a hat should always be worn for protection from the sun (see p.51).

Natural fabrics, especially cotton, are preferable for any items that are in direct contact with your baby's skin and it will be more convenient for you if they are machine-washable and able to be tumble-dried. Resist buying a lot of any one size, as you will find that your baby grows rapidly.

As your baby grows and develops, you may want to dress them in more interesting clothes. Remember that any articles of clothing must be flexible, so that your baby can wriggle and move about. As they begin to get mobile, you will find that your baby's knees get very rough and sore, no matter what surface they are crawling on. It is a good idea to put them in clothes that will protect their knees and be up to the wear and tear, yet still allow them to move freely – trousers and dungarees are ideal, but make sure they still give you quick access to the nappy.

## Dressing your baby

Newborn babies look so fragile that dressing them can be a little daunting initially. Do not be too worried, as babies are fairly resilient; they have withstood the birth process, after all. However, your newborn's arms and legs are very loose and floppy to begin with, so you need to be very

gentle when putting on their vest and sleepsuit. Babies can be very wriggly at any age, so preparation is key; make sure that you have the clothes to hand and that you never leave them unsupervised. My top tip is to ensure that their nappy is clean before you start – there is nothing more annoying than getting your baby dressed, only to find you need to change their nappy!

In general, babies do not like things going over their heads. Some vests can be put on like a shirt: lay it out on the changing mat, so that you can put your baby on top of it and simply slip their arms in. The same technique can be used for sleepsuits. If the item of clothing needs to go over the head, put the back of your baby's head into the head hole of the garment first; then, as quickly and smoothly as you can, move the remainder of the head hole over your baby's face. In this way, you are only having the clothes over their eyes for a moment and, if the material is stretchy, you will be able to keep it off their face entirely. Babies like the freedom of being undressed and often kick a lot: make sure you do up the legs of the sleepsuit before putting their arms in, so that they do not kick it off again.

### Older babies

You may be surprised to find that your baby soon learns to help – and hinder – you in the dressing process. Older babies are adept at, for example, lifting their legs for you when you are putting on their trousers and, conversely, refusing to allow their arms to be bent when you are trying to get them into a top. Your main concern, however, is that they are likely to try to get off the changing mat, so you may feel safer dressing them on the floor. If your baby is very mobile, you could dress them while they are sitting up on your lap.

### Footwear

Shoes are an important element for your growing baby. Before your baby is walking, there are wonderful, soft leather baby shoes that you can use to cover their feet. However, aside from providing a little warmth and perhaps a bit of protection if they are crawling, these are purely a fashion statement. Do not put your baby in

## Top Tips

Try to keep clothes as fuss-free as possible. The older babies get, the more inquisitive they become, and you will soon discover that they find buttons, zips, buckles and bows endlessly fascinating. You could spend your day constantly redoing their outfit – not so fascinating for you!

Once your baby is weaned, you may have to change their clothes after every meal (even if you use an all-encompassing bib), so it pays to have things you can easily mix and match and that are easy to keep clean.

structured shoes until they are steady on their feet and have been walking for a few weeks. The Society of Chiropodists and Podiatrists recommends the following: 'Ideally, a child should not require shoes until they are walking competently out of doors. In order for the foot to develop normally and naturally, the child should be barefoot for as long as possible and within the realms of safety to avoid injury.'

I love the idea of children being able to wander around barefoot, as this allows the bones and ligaments within the foot to settle into the correct position once they are bearing weight. I realise that it is not always practical, and protecting your child from injury must be your top priority. However, when you are safely at home, you can let them run around barefoot. Once your child requires a structured shoe, you must keep checking that the size and fit is correct. If the shoe is too small, the bones within the foot are not able to grow properly and this can cause your child pain and discomfort. They may start walking in such a way as to minimise pressure from the shoe, and this too will affect the developing bones of the foot as well as those of the leg. Tight-fitting shoes can also cause blisters and sores on the skin from rubbing. You may find that your child will not let you know that their shoes are too tight, so ideally you should get their shoe size checked every eight to twelve weeks.

# Bathing

Your baby will need a bath every few days and you should know how to do this safely. Bath time can be a good opportunity to play with your baby and many enjoy the sensation of the water and splashing around. Later on, a bath in the evening can let your baby know that bedtime is approaching and it is time to wind down.

Very young babies do not need bathing everyday: their skin is very delicate and can become very dry if washed too much; in any case, newborns do not really get dirty. 'Topping and tailing' every day (see Box on p.41) and a bath once a week can be enough. Since your newborn cannot support themselves, you will need to bath them using the technique described here. Bathing older babies is a very different affair and, as well as ensuring their safety, you main concern will be minimising the mess! However, if you are relaxed about this, bath time can be a fun learning experience for your baby.

## What you need

✓ Baby bath, or bath support for use in adult bath

✓ Baby bath thermometer (optional)

✓ 2 soft towels

✓ Flannel/sponge/soft cloth

✓ Baby bath products: bubble bath, shampoo, baby wash

✓ Moisturising cream (if necessary)

✓ Nail file, baby scissors

✓ Bath seat

✓ Non-slip bath mat

✓ Face shield (optional, for older babies)

✓ Cotton wool

## Before you begin

Bathing your baby is easier with a little prior organisation. Have all the items in the equipment list to hand, plus a fresh nappy and a set of clean clothes. Choose a time that suits you and your baby – it does not have to be the evening if you are both tired. Make sure that the room is warm and free from drafts, as babies lose heat rapidly. Fill the bath by starting with the cold water first, then adding the hot water until it is the right temperature, mixing it well to ensure there are no hot spots. If you keep the water to a shallow depth of 5–8 cm, it will make things more manageable. The important thing to remember is that the water temperature needs to feel neutral to your elbow (about 37°C) at the time you put your baby in the water – you can also use a baby bath thermometer to confirm this. This may mean making the water slightly warmer to begin with, as it will cool quickly while you are undressing them. Always check the temperature again before you put your baby in.

## How to bath your newborn

Start by washing your baby's face and hair. It can be tricky to do this while holding your baby securely in water, so it is better done before you put them in; doing this first also keeps them warmer, as they spend less time with a wet face and wet hair. Wrap your baby in a towel so that their hands are tucked away. To clean your baby's face, use the warm bath water and a piece of cotton wool. Wipe one eye from the corner nearest the nose to the outer corner. Discard this piece of cotton wool. Clean the other eye in the same way with a new piece of cotton wool – this stops the transfer of a possible infection from one eye to the other (see entries on

conjunctivitis and sticky eyes in Chapter 8, pp. 175 and 181). Using a third piece of cotton wool, wash the rest of the face and the neck. You can wipe around the outer ear, but never use a cotton bud to clean inside your baby's ear, as this may cause damage. Milk can get into the creases of the neck, so make sure you clean this area well. Dry your baby's face and neck with the second towel.

You only need to wash your baby's hair once a week or so. Keeping your baby wrapped in the towel with their arms carefully tucked away, position your baby with their head over the bath. Wet their hair and wash it using a small amount of baby shampoo. Rinse well and dry the hair thoroughly with the second towel.

Now you can take off the towel and bath your baby. A bath support cradles your baby in a semi-reclined position in the water, leaving you with both hands free to wash them. Otherwise you will need to hold your baby with one hand and use your other hand to wash the water over your baby's skin. A secure way of doing this is to place your arm

around their upper back and hold your baby under the armpit on the opposite side to you. This leaves your other arm free to wash them. Remember to clean the creases. Some people use a little baby bubble bath in the water and simply use the bubbly water to wash their baby. Alternatively you can put some baby wash on a soft sponge and use this. Either method is fine, but avoid soap, which is too drying for delicate skin. While some babies love the water, others enjoy it less, and most dislike being removed from the water – be prepared for crying!

Once you have dried your baby thoroughly, including their creases and in between their fingers and toes, rub moisturising cream on their skin (including the face) if necessary. Bath time can be a good opportunity to give your baby a massage (see p.52), but afterwards dress them quickly before they get cold.

### Cutting your baby's nails

You will need to trim your baby's nails regularly and this is easier to do after a bath, when the nails are much softer. Cut them with a pair of baby scissors – these have rounded tips, to prevent accidentally stabbing their skin – and use a nail file to smooth any rough or sharp edges. If you are too daunted by this idea, or your baby fidgets or resists, you could try cutting them when they are asleep or you can carefully tear or nibble them off instead.

### Bathing older babies

Once your baby can sit up reliably, bath time becomes playtime, particularly if you bath them with their siblings. You will still need to be in the bathroom, but you can allow your baby to splash around for a while before the serious business of washing takes place. A rubber bath mat will minimise sliding. Put some towels on the floor around the bath if you are worried about the mess and do not put too much water in the bath (just enough to cover their lower body). Give your baby some plastic cups and jugs, empty plastic bottles and squirty or floating toys, so that they can experiment

> *Never leave a child under eight unsupervised in the bath, even if you are using a bath support or seat – tragic incidents can happen in seconds.*

– but keep a close watch to make sure that they do not drink the bath water!

When you are both ready, wash your baby's face and body as described above. Washing their hair can be more of a challenge, as babies rarely find this enjoyable. You may have to encourage them to lean back into your arm so that the soapy water does not run over their face and into their eyes – a face shield may be useful, although many babies dislike these. You could also try using a shower attachment to rinse off, but remember to check the temperature of the water first. If all else fails, you can simply rub their hair clean with a damp sponge, cloth or flannel.

### Bathing with your baby

If your baby finds the bath experience frightening, it may comfort them to have a bath with you. Even when your baby enjoys the water by themselves, bathing together can be a wonderful way to bond (see Chapter 1, pp.18–19). While you can do this single-handedly, it makes it easier if your partner can hand the baby to you and take them from you to dry and dress them. Remember not to fill the bath as deep as you would if you were bathing alone and that the temperature of the water needs to be right for your baby (which may make it cool for you). When your baby is small, maintaining body contact by having them on your chest can help them feel secure. Later, bending your knees up and resting your baby on your thighs gives them reassuring eye contact throughout.

### Topping and tailing

Your baby's face, neck, hands and bottom need washing every day, but this can be done by 'topping and tailing' rather than giving a bath. You can top and tail at the changing station if you have a bowl of warm water close by. It is possible to buy a special two-section bowl, but an ordinary small kitchen bowl will do just as well, as long as you always clean your baby's face and hands before their bottom.

Undress your baby down to the vest/bodysuit. Clean your baby's face as outlined in the section on bathing your newborn. With a fresh piece of cotton wool, wipe around your baby's palm and in between their fingers (a newborn's hands are often tightly curled, so you may need to gently open them to do this). Finally, take off the nappy and clean their bottom in the same way as you do when you change them (see p.33).

# When your baby cries

Some babies cry a lot, others hardly at all and it is often felt to be the luck of the draw! However, crying is a baby's primary method of communicating with you before they learn to speak. Crying can be – in fact, is designed to be – concerning for parents and you will naturally want to understand what it means and what you can do about it.

However, before you eagerly read on for a 'quick fix' to your baby's crying, you should understand that not all crying has an identifiable reason and, by extension, that there is not a failsafe way to make it stop. Nor does crying necessarily mean that you have done something 'wrong'. If you can bear these two points in mind when your baby cries, it will go a long way to making you feel less anxious about it, which will help you to be more effective at soothing your baby.

## Why do babies cry?

This is not a trick question, I promise! Babies usually cry for one of the following reasons:

- hunger
- physical discomfort (including being in pain)
- being too hot or cold
- tiredness
- needing a nappy change
- illness
- just wanting a hug.

Older babies (three months or more) are more resilient and better at communicating, but they still cry for the above reasons, and also because of:

- boredom
- frustration (their desire to do things is greater than their skill)
- loneliness
- teething
- fear (of other people, of separation from you).

It is also worth considering what your baby may be thinking. I know that some parenting manuals will say that your baby is being 'demanding and manipulative' by crying, or that only a 'naughty' baby cries. I feel that babies do not have this agenda and only cry because they need something: principally food or love.

Some experts feel that all babies are programed to cry and it is perhaps how we as parents perceive and respond to their distress that accounts for the differences between them. They feel that babies cry more in the first three months, then settle and cry less as they get older. Might there be a physiological reason for this? We simply do not know.

## How you respond

Your particular parenting style will determine how you wish to respond to your baby's cries. Some people go to their baby the second they whimper, while others leave them to cry a little first, to see whether their baby settles themselves or persists and really needs their attention.

Again, some parenting philosophies will tell you that you are going to have a very 'spoilt' baby if you rush to meet their every demand. I do not know that there is a right or a wrong way to respond, but it may be of interest to you to know that babies who get a more immediate response do not grow up to become more demanding toddlers and children. You are not, therefore, making a rod for your own back by going to your baby immediately. Indeed, babies thrive when their needs are met, whereas those who are not attended to can become more dependant and demanding. There is also the possibility that if you leave your baby to cry until they are very distressed, it will become harder to 'read' what their cry may mean (see opposite).

Being attentive to your baby will not only make them feel loved and secure, but may actually prevent crying, as you will soon learn to spot the visual cues that babies give about their needs. For example, a tired baby will often fidget and rub their eyes before any crying actually starts. This means you can judge the most appropriate response, in this case, perhaps putting them in a quiet corner of the room to rest a little, as opposed to stimulating them with lots of toys on a playmat. It has been documented that babies from cultures where it is normal to carry them around for most of the day tend to cry less. This may be because, if their baby is physically very close, the parents are more responsive to their needs.

### Is doing nothing an option?

Science tells us that when babies cry alone and unattended they experience panic and anxiety, which floods their body and brain with adrenaline and cortisol stress hormones. Research has found that when developing brain tissue is exposed to these hormones for prolonged periods, the nerves in the brain fail to form connections and will degenerate. Is it therefore possible that infants who endure many nights or weeks of crying it out alone are actually suffering harmful neurological effects that may have permanent implications for the development of sections of their brain.

### Finding the reason

This is probably the bit that you really want to know, but I am afraid there is not one simple answer. Start by addressing the most common reasons that babies cry, as listed on p.42. Try not to always assume that they need food – instead, go through the list of problems one by one. Usually, by the time you have got to the bottom of the list all is well; if not, go back to the top and have another go.

While a newborn tends to have one type of cry, but with varying volumes and intensity, as your baby gets a little older, the type of cry will change according to the reason, allowing you to make the appropriate response:

## Thumb-sucking

It is very common for babies to suck their thumbs for comfort – more than 40 per cent of babies under a year do so. Most children can safely suck their thumbs without damaging the alignment of their teeth or jaws until their permanent teeth begin to appear at around the age of six. Not all thumb-sucking is equally damaging: some children merely rest their thumbs in their mouths rather than aggressively sucking on them. Prolonged thumb-sucking can cause a narrowing of the upper jaw, but this is very rare and happens in children who aggressively suck their thumbs for many years. Most children have stopped by the time they are two or three.

The main issue for thumb-suckers is that the skin on their thumb may become sore. The best way to help this is to put some moisturising cream on the thumb at night-time when they are not sucking it.

- gentle, low, 'on-and-off': bored, settling to sleep
- loud, rhythmic: uncomfortable, hungry/thirsty, dirty nappy
- intense, persistent, sounding angry or distressed: pain, illness – respond immediately.

I gather that you can get an app for your smart phone that decodes your baby's cries! However, I recommend that you trust your instincts instead. your feelings are likely to be in tune with your baby and, within a short time, you will be far better than any app at knowing exactly what is wrong.

## Common soothing methods

Sometimes all is well and yet your baby continues to cry. Soothing your baby is often the only way to stop the crying when you have drawn a blank with all the normal reasons. There are many tried-and-tested ways of doing this and you will find that some work better than others for you and your baby. In addition, remember that your baby will be easier to comfort on some days than others.

Always start with the simplest methods and only graduate to the more time-consuming ones if you really need to – you may also find that, given a bit of time to themselves, your baby will cease crying with the minimum of help from you. See also Chapter 4, p.104 for information about controlled crying.

### Holding your baby close

Skin-to-skin contact (see Chapter 1, p.18) is a lovely method of comforting your baby when they are very small. You could also try wrapping them snugly in a blanket and holding them close to you, which is a bit more practical if you need to be up and around doing things. For information about swaddling, see Chapter 4, p.95.

### Movement

Your baby may cry less if they are kept in motion. Easy ways to do this are to walk up and down the stairs, sit with them in a rocking chair, place your baby in a baby swing, bounce them gently on an exercise ball or in a baby bouncer or carry them around the house in a baby carrier or sling. If the crying is more persistent and you also feel like a change of scene, take them out for a walk using the carrier or their pram, or put them in their car seat and take them for a drive.

### Sounds and music

Babies sometimes stop crying when talked or sung to. If this has no effect, put on some relaxing music, as much to calm yourself down as to soothe your baby. Some babies are comforted by repetitive

Sometimes, babies cry because they are overstimulated, so try keeping the environment quiet and dark.

noises or vibrations: you could catch up on the vacuuming or expose them to the steady rhythm of a washing machine, a ticking clock, an un-tuned radio or a hairdryer.

### Sucking for comfort

Your baby may calm down if given a dummy to suck. If you are worried or embarrassed by this (see Feature opposite), you can encourage them to suck their fingers or thumb if they are not already doing so spontaneously (see Box on p.45). Avoid offering the breast or bottle if you know that they are not hungry, as this could lead to other problems.

### Comfort blankets or toys

A familiar blanket/muslin or a favourite soft toy can be of great comfort to babies, particularly if you have always placed something next to them from birth. Beware that disaster can strike if you lose or mislay it, so it can be a good idea to have an identical replacement, if only so that you can wash the original with it being missed!

## How much crying is normal?

Your newborn may have a sleepy couple of days before finding their voice. At this stage, babies usually cry for one to five hours per day, although anything up to twelve hours is still considered normal. After two weeks or so, you may find that your baby really starts to let rip, particularly in the evenings. Bouts of crying starting at around 5pm and lasting for three hours are known as 'colic' (see Chapter 8, p.175). Not all babies get colic, but if they do, your evenings may be spent singing, rocking, driving around …in fact, anything to make the crying stop. However, colicky babies will usually settle at around three months and you will start to get your evenings back. You may notice that your baby now cries in a different way, depending on how they are feeling at any given moment, and you have got better at knowing what they need.

## Coping with crying

Prolongued crying can be very frustrating when you have tried all the methods outlined above and nothing has worked, especially at the end of a long and tiring day when you may already be at a low

## Top Tips

**1** It is normal for babies to cry: it is not a reflection on your parenting nor on the type of person your baby will turn out to be.

**2** There is not always a reason or a solution to the crying! Be patient and hang on to the knowledge that this stage will not last forever …

**3** Other carers often seem to have the knack (and the patience!) for soothing babies, so you could ask them to come on a regular basis if your baby is crying for extended periods.

ebb. It is important not to blame either yourself or your baby: it is highly unlikely that you have done anything to cause the crying and your baby does not 'know' the effect that they are having.

However, if you start to feel tense or stressed, it will be more difficult to soothe your baby. While rocking and bouncing movements are fine, never shake your baby to try to 'bring them out of it' or to vent your own frustration. Instead, take some time to calm yourself in a place where you cannot hear the noise, taking a few deep breaths to help you relax. (If you have already checked for signs of illness, your baby will almost certainly be fine for a few minutes.) If necessary, ask your partner or a friend to look after your baby while you have a long bath or lie down in a quiet room – even just an hour away from the crying will give you the energy to go back to your baby. Dealing with persistent crying over a prolonged period can contribute to postnatal depression (see Chapter 7, pp.158–9). If you need further support, or are worried that you may harm your baby, contact the charity Cry-sis (see Useful Resources).

# Using a dummy

Variously called pacifiers, comforters or soothers, dummies can play a part in helping to calm your baby, although their use is not without controversy. This is because research has shown that they can cause issues with teeth; there have also been concerns as to whether they interfere with breastfeeding. However, on the positive side, dummies are considered to reduce the risk of Sudden Infant Death Syndrome. The following information may help you to decide whether or not your want to introduce a dummy to your baby.

The British Dental Health Foundation advises against using dummies because they can cause problems to your baby's growing and developing teeth. Common problems include a crossbite (when the upper teeth are behind the lower ones) or an overbite (when the upper front teeth project over the lower ones). The longer your baby uses a dummy, the more chance they have of being affected. You should therefore wean your baby off their dummy by the time they are about a year old – this can be done by gradually decreasing the amount of time it is used. Incidentally, you should never dip your baby's dummy into anything sweet or allow your baby to go to sleep with a bottle of milk/formula in their mouth, as this can lead to tooth decay.

In 2011 there was a review of evidence into whether there was a relationship between dummy use and unsuccessful breastfeeding. The outcome showed that in highly motivated women who are breastfeeding well, the use of a dummy was not detrimental to breastfeeding. In these instances, the dummy was introduced at around two weeks. Both the Lullaby Trust (formerly the Foundation for the Study of Infant Death – FSID) and the American Academy of Paediatrics (AAP) recommend that, for breastfed babies, you delay the use of a dummy until a month old, when breastfeeding has been properly established. You may want to consider using orthodontic dummies, which are flatter than the more traditional bulbous ones and are shaped to closely mimic the sucking action of breastfeeding.

The Lullaby Trust and the AAP also endorse the advice found from two separate studies that showed up to a 61 per cent reduction in the risk of SIDS with the use of a dummy. Nevertheless, they advise the withdrawal of the dummy by six months, as the risk of SIDS has reduced by this age. However, there have been no trials in the UK that have found the association of dummies and fewer cases of SIDS to be true. Indeed, most babies no longer have the dummy in their mouth if they have been asleep for 30 minutes and most SIDS babies are found after this time.

If you do decide to use a dummy as a means of comfort, there are some important safety aspects to remember. Never attach string to the dummy in order to hang it around your baby's neck, as this is a strangulation hazard. In addition, dummies will need to be sterilised until your baby is six months old.

# Safety in the home

It is important to make your home safe from the moment your baby is born. As your baby becomes more mobile, you will need to make further adjustments to make sure that they do not come to harm.

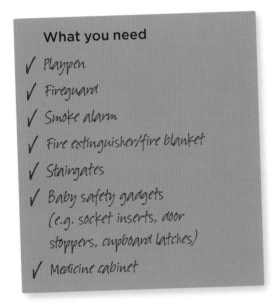

### What you need

✓ Playpen

✓ Fireguard

✓ Smoke alarm

✓ Fire extinguisher/fire blanket

✓ Stairgates

✓ Baby safety gadgets (e.g. socket inserts, door stoppers, cupboard latches)

✓ Medicine cabinet

Every parent wants to know that they are always doing their best to keep their baby safe. In general, it is better to foresee a problem and try to prevent it from happening than to have to deal with the consequences after it has occurred. Investing in some specific baby safety equipment (such as playpens, stairgates), as well as more general ones (e.g. smoke alarms, fireguards), will help to give you greater peace of mind. Nevertheless, there are innumerable potential dangers in any home and it is impossible to identify and safeguard against them all. Your baby also needs to learn that certain things are unsafe, so that they know to stay away from them when they are somewhere else. If you have 'wrapped them up in cotton wool', not only may you restrict their natural curiosity, you may also hinder their ability to protect themselves. You will therefore need to make some decisions as to which protective measures are sensible.

## General safety

Installing specific safety equipment will go some way towards keeping your baby free from harm in the home, but you will also need to adopt some safe practices. Make sure that anyone taking care of your baby while you are not around knows these, too.

## Fire and electricity

Fire is a fascination for young children, so always use a fireguard that is screwed to the wall and never leave your baby alone in the room. The standard safety features on UK sockets are relatively robust: in order to receive an electric shock, an infant would need to put one finger in the top hole and physically push down the safety switch inside, while a second finger was in another hole. Nevertheless, it is perhaps better not to take the chance – always turn the switch off. You can also use plastic inserts to cover sockets, but make sure that they fit properly and are not split or otherwise broken.

## Windows and glass

It is possible for a mobile baby to climb onto furniture in order to reach a window. Fit window locks and/or restrictors that limit how far the window can be opened and make sure that you tie up loose curtain or blind cords, as these are a strangulation hazard. If you have glass doors, check to see whether they are fitted with safety glass (it will display a kite mark). Attaching coloured stickers to the glass at your baby's eye level could save the odd bump, as they will be able to see that there is a surface there.

## Furniture

Most furniture is robust enough to withstand the weight of a toddler hauling themselves up, but you may want to pack away flimsier items while your baby is at this 'cruising' stage (see Chapter 6, p.135). Also beware of smaller, freestanding items, such as televisions and small bookshelves/cupboards, which your baby could pull onto themselves – screw these to the wall if possible. If a low coffee table, for example, has sharp corners, you could cover these with soft plastic guards. Some parents go further and swathe bubble wrap over chair legs and so on, but you may find this excessive!

## Bags and bins

Leave your handbag well out of reach: inquisitive infants can find small objects and pills to swallow. Similarly, be careful what you throw away into the bin. Again, small bits and pieces could be a choke hazard and your baby could easily put a discarded plastic bag over their head and suffocate. Hanging bags are a particular strangulation hazard.

## Plants and pets

Houseplants will create a mess if pulled over and some types also have sharp leaves. Others can be poisonous if eaten – the Royal Horticultural Society publishes a list of potentially harmful plants. Cat litter can also be poisonous and if your baby touches any faeces they could contract toxoplasmosis. Never leave a baby alone with a pet, even a trusted and well-behaved one, and keep an eye on the pets in any homes you visit.

## Kitchen safety

Keep flexes out of reach. This is most important for things like kettles and irons. Ideally, you should have a short kettle flex that sits against the kitchen surface and wall. Never leave the iron standing on the ironing board – store it somewhere safe when cooling and always make sure the flex is out of reach. When cooking, keep pan handles pointing in towards the wall. Store sharp knives, graters and so on in a drawer that is fitted with a child-resistant catch. Similarly, make sure cleaning liquids are kept in a secure cupboard. Place hot drinks in the middle of the table or up high out of reach and do not hold your baby at the same time as having a hot drink (they can be very wriggly when you least expect it). If you have not done so already, invest in a smoke alarm and a fire extinguisher or fire blanket.

### Cupboard love

If your baby is fascinated by your kitchen cupboards, you could rearrange things so that they have one that is 'theirs'. Fill it with plastic bowls and wooden spoons, empty cereal packets, sealed plastic containers filled with rice and so on, so that you satisfy their curiosity and yet be sure they can come to no harm. It will keep your baby amused for ages while you get on with the cooking!

## Medicines

Wherever you keep your medicines (e.g. kitchen, bathroom), make sure that they are stored in child-resistant bottles out of reach. Better still, invest in a locked medicine cabinet, so that you have got into good habits by the time your child is older.

## Preventing falls

One of the very common reasons why babies need to go to hospital is because they have had a fall. You must therefore take care as soon as your baby learns to roll. In addition, there are measures you should take to prevent falls:

- Never leave your baby unattended on a changing mat, the bed, the sofa … They will surprise you the first time they roll and you do not want to find them on the floor having rolled off the surface that you left them on.
- Do not use a bouncy chair on a table or high surface – always put them on the floor.
- Hold the handrail when carrying your baby up and down the stairs.
- As well as using stairgates at the top and bottom of each flight, ensure that the gaps in the banisters of your stairs are not wide enough for your baby to fall through.
- Always use the straps/harness on your baby's bouncy chair, swing seat and high chair, even if you only put your baby there for a moment.
- Do not leave anything in the cot that your baby could stand on to climb out.

# Out and about

Getting out of the house with a young baby can often be a challenge. A little preparation and some careful planning will help to make a trip to the shops or a longer journey much easier.

## What you need

- ✓ Car seat
- ✓ Car sun shield(s)
- ✓ Child-view mirror (optional)
- ✓ Pram/pushchair/buggy
- ✓ Parasol
- ✓ Rain cover
- ✓ Changing bag
- ✓ Baby carrier or sling/papoose (optional)

## Planning a trip

Whether it is a quick trip to the park or a longer journey, preparation is key. You need to be able to transport your baby reliably and safely whenever you are out of the house – in fact, it is a legal requirement to use an age-appropriate infant car seat whenever you transport your child by car.

Think about whether it is more sensible to use a pram/pushchair/buggy to get to your destination (e.g. you have other things to carry) or whether it will be easier to put your baby in a sling or baby carrier. I found a baby carrier indispensable in the first few months: I loved having my baby close to me when I went for walks and, when I was shopping, it not only freed up both hands but saved me from trying to negotiate obstacles in shops with the pram. Pack all the essentials in your nappy-changing bag (see Box, right), but add another bottle or snack in case you are delayed.

## Travelling by car

When making a journey by car, take care as to where and how you pack items inside. For example, an umbrella may become a spear under the forces of an emergency stop. Similarly, any object within your baby's reach could be thrown at you while you are driving. Plan your route in advance, allowing for more frequent stops than usual, so that you can feed and change your baby. This will also give them a break from the car seat, as it is not good for the development of your baby's back and spine if they spend longer than two hours at a time in a 'bucket'-type seat. If it is a long journey, have an overnight bag handy with all the things that you will need

## What's in the bag?

A nappy-changing bag is a must-have for any trip. It has several compartments in which to store all your bits and bobs, but the best thing of all is that it comes with a handy small changing mat. Depending on the nature of your journey, you could stock your changing bag with the following:

- nappies, wipes, nappy sacks and barrier cream
- scarf or cover for discrete breastfeeding
- muslins cloths for possets (and just about anything else!)
- change of baby clothes in case of a nappy explosion or sickness
- a blanket/extra layer of clothing
- sunscreen or protective clothing
- dummy (if your baby uses one)
- entertainment: a toy and book.

immediately on arrival – that way, you can leave the unpacking until later. A sun shield for the car window will make things more comfortable for your baby and you may also find a child-view mirror useful for monitoring your baby while driving.

### Travelling by coach, train or plane
Using public transport needs some thought. For example, are there any stairs or tight spaces to negotiate with your pram? (Remember that most people are willing to help if asked.) If you are making a long journey by coach, train or plane, it is wise to book an aisle seat (your baby does not need a seat until they are two years old), so that you can get in and out easily without disturbing other passengers. Allow plenty of time before your departure to find your seat and get organised.

### Sun protection
It is very important to get the right balance between exposure to and protection from the sun. Babies need some sunlight in order to make vitamin D, which is important for their growth and bones. However, the sun's rays can be harmful, burning their delicate skin. Babies under six months old should not be in direct sunlight and no baby should be out in the midday sun. Once they are six months and are in direct sunlight, they need to be covered either by clothing or high-factor sunscreen (ideally Factor 50), as well as a hat.

Half an hour before they go outside, apply sunscreen thickly to every area of your baby's skin not covered by clothes or a hat, including their hands and feet. This will need to be reapplied at least every couple of hours, especially if they have been playing in water (even if the bottle says it is waterproof). If your baby has eczema or very sensitive skin, check the ingredients to look for any that you know they are sensitive to and test any new sunscreen on a small area before applying to the whole body.

Sunglasses are good protection for your baby's eyes. They should meet the British Standard BSEN 1836:2005 and carry the CE mark on the label.

# Things to do with your baby

There are likely to be numerous groups for new mothers and their babies in your area. Activities may range from coffee mornings and exercise sessions through to music classes and other things designed specifically to aid a baby's development.

In what can often seem like a never-ending cycle of feeding, winding, washing and changing nappies, groups and classes provide a way for you to have structured, quality one-to-one time with your baby. That said, if you are not a 'groups' person, your baby will be perfectly happy being stimulated at home by you. Joining a class should also not be seen as a way to get ahead of the pack in terms of your baby's development.

Your council will often have a list of activites for young families and you could ask your health visitor whether there are any particularly good groups nearby. Check your local paper and notice boards in the park, corner shop, church hall or nursery.

## Breastfeeding groups

Aside from getting one-to-one support from a lactation specialist or breastfeeding counsellor, you may find it helpful to go to a drop-in breastfeeding group (you do not need to make an appointment). These may be held in a Children's Centre, health clinic or local café and they provide a good way to discuss any issues you may be having with breastfeeding in a relaxed environment with other mothers and trained volunteers.

## Mother and baby groups

Run by volunteers for a small fee (some may be free), mother and baby groups are a great way to meet other new mothers (and fathers, too!). They also give your baby an opportunity to play with new toys surrounded by other children, while you have a chat over a cup of coffee and a biscuit. They usually take place in a community or church hall and you may have to try a few out before finding one that suits – look for one that seems friendly and well run, with clean, up-to-date toys.

## Mothers' fitness groups

One of the hardest things is to regain and maintain your level of fitness while looking after a baby, and a tailor-made mothers' fitness group can be the ideal solution. Variously involving running round the park with your baby in the buggy to jigging around to Latin beats while wearing a baby carrier, these classes avoid the need for childcare while you exercise and are a good way to stay motivated and to meet other new mothers. Check that the instructor has a recognised qualification in postnatal exercise. See Chapter 7, pp.149–50 for when it is safe to start exercise after birth.

## Baby massage

Performing massage on your baby is a wonderful way to show a loving touch and is particularly beneficial to building confidence in first-time parents who are unused to or nervous about handling their small babies. Techniques that have been developed over a number of years are demonstrated by a qualified instructor on a doll, while you learn to perform the strokes on your baby. Although there are a number of baby massage videos on the internet, it is usually best to attend a class in person, so that the instructor can adjust your technique if necessary. A course usually runs for around six weeks, with a new sequence added each week until you have covered the entire body. Baby massage classes can be started at anytime (ideally when your baby is six weeks), but are best begun before your child begins to crawl.

Never wake your baby up to be massaged and do not persist with the routine if they fall asleep, are crying or unhappy in any way. You will be provided with a handout of the strokes, so you can continue at home if necessary.

### The benefits of baby massage

Baby massage is relatively new in the Western world, although it has long been practised in India and Africa. The positive effects on both babies and caregivers have been widely researched and documented, with a number of studies focusing on the benefits for babies born prematurely.

Babies find the massage calming and relaxing and many parents report improved sleep patterns. Those babies who are hyper-alert and hypersensitive become more accustomed to being touched and held. Baby massage also stimulates the circulatory system, and the clockwise, circular motion of the abdominal massage routine appears to aid flow in the digestive tract, reducing wind and constipation.

One of the biggest benefits of baby massage, however, is the strengthening of the bond between you and your baby. This is particularly significant, as babies today spend a lot of time in chairs and pushchairs, with the result that we tend to hold our babies less than our ancestors did. Touch is the first sense to develop in the womb and the last sense to leave us when we die. The skin is our largest organ, and positive and nurturing touch plays a vital part in your child's development.

### Massage oils

The type of oil you use for the massage is very important and your instructor will tell you which brand they prefer and will probably provide you with the oil for the class. If you are practising at home, use a simple, cold-pressed, preferably organically grown vegetable oil. Avoid products with more than one type of oil in, and steer clear of mineral and synthetic oils, as these are difficult to absorb, making it difficult for the skin to breathe. Essential oils are very concentrated and are best avoided when massaging babies.

## Baby music classes

Music classes suitable for babies are led by trained musicians and offer a more structured approach to

music than the nursery rhyme sessions that often take place at mother and baby groups. Do not be fooled into thinking that attendance is a guarantee that yours will be the next musical prodigy! Nevertheless, music classes can be hugely enjoyable and will introduce your baby to a new range of songs and sounds, as well as giving them the chance to play some basic instruments.

### Baby swimming
Being in the water from an early age can help children to learn the life-saving skill of swimming. Classes take place in a warm pool under the close guidance of an instructor. Your baby learns some core skills and get a gentle workout, which strengthens their muscles, heart and lungs and can help establish a healthy routine throughout childhood and

beyond. Being in the water with your baby offers plenty of opportunity for eye and skin contact and so is a good way for you to bond. However, courses are relatively expensive and bear in mind when you sign up that there may be weeks you will have to miss because your baby is unwell.

### Baby and toddler gyms
With programmes designed according to age (from four or six months onwards), baby and toddler gyms aim to develop children's skills in balance, agility, coordination and spatial awareness, using a variety of pieces of equipment. There are a number of franchises and you may also find that your local leisure centre runs a similar class (although this will be unstructured and supervised by you rather than an instructor).

## Baby yoga/mother and baby yoga

Classes for baby yoga and mother and baby yoga are becoming more popular, as more and more people appreciate the benefits of doing gentle movements, breathing exercises and positioning.

### Baby yoga

Baby-specific yoga classes usually involve your performing gentle movements on your baby. Your teacher will also instruct you on how to place your baby in the various positions, such as lying on their abdomen (see also Feature on 'Tummy time' in Chapter 6, p.136). You will also be encouraged to continue to do your own yoga with your baby at home, too. Classes often involve singing and soothing words and the relaxation sessions at the end of each session provide a wonderful time for you to truly unwind and connect with your baby – the stillness that comes over the class is incredible.

### Mother and baby yoga

Yoga classes for mothers and babies can either be structured primarily for the mother (with your baby incorporated into a few of the postures) or aimed at including both of you in all the postures. Either of these are a great way for you to get into or back into yoga in an environment where your baby can be with you. As your baby becomes more mobile, the class adapts and progresses to encourage your child to explore more of the poses and breathing techniques independently. The postures are wonderful for strengthening core muscles and calming the mind and sensory system. Ensure your teacher is qualified to teach postnatal yoga.

# A new baby in the family

A new arrival changes the dynamic of the family unit for your other children and needs to be handled sensitively. Some thoughtful preparatory measures and time spent exclusively with them will go a long way to helping them adjust.

You can start preparing your child for the situation before your new baby is even born to give them plenty of time to adjust. For example, you could put the baby's car seat in the car, so that they get used to sharing their space, and allow them to fasten one of their dolls or teddies in it. However, it is wise not to tell your child that there will be a new baby too early on in your pregnancy. Nine months is a long time for a child and they will probably soon forget about it, meaning that your careful preparatory work was for nothing. In fact, you will be surprised at how long it will be before you child notices your bump and starts asking questions!

As the time of birth approaches, your child can help you chose a new toy for the baby as a welcome gift and perhaps decide which sleepsuit they will wear first. However, avoid making everything about the new baby. Your child should know that they are still important to you and are not being 'replaced'.

*Be patient and allow your child to accept and get used to the new baby in their own time – they will soon enjoy the benefits of a having a sibling.*

## The first meeting

It is important that your baby's siblings are involved from the very beginning and it is great if they can spend some time with you and the new baby soon after the birth. Carve out some space from other visitors for this first meeting so that you can give them your full attention. Try to look as much like your old self as possible – be up and dressed if you can – and have the new baby in the cot rather than in your arms. Give your child your full focus to start with and only introduce the baby when they are ready. Have a gift for them from you and/or the baby and arrange for them to give the baby their present or a card they have made themselves as well. If they want to, let them hold the baby (supported by you). Do not force an engagement, though, and be prepared for your child to lose interest very quickly. When you do have other visitors, try to make sure that they acknowledge your child's presence as well as the new baby, perhaps by bringing them a gift as well or making a fuss of them.

## Stepchildren

It can be particularly hard for stepchildren to deal with a new sibling. The new baby makes you and your partner's commitment to each other very clear. The disruption that a new baby inevitably causes may also remind them of the time when their parents broke up, causing feelings of upset and confusion to resurface. Try to encourage them to talk through their feelings (if they are old enough) and reassure them that there is always a place for them in the new family unit, emphasising the positive aspects of having another sibling to have fun with.

## Getting back to normal

After the new baby arrives and things have settled down a little bit, try to keep up as many of your child's previous routines and activities as you can. This will help them to cope with the changes that are happening in their family. For example, keep your child's bedtime routine the same and go to their playgroup or visit friends so that they can play with familiar children. Getting them involved with caring for your new baby can be really helpful. Older children often love having a job and feel really important that they are the only ones to perform a certain task; getting the nappy ready, finding the wipes, handing you the towel at bath time, and so on. Remember, though, that you should never leave your baby under the supervision of your older child, even for a minute – it is not uncommon for them to 'accidentally' hurt the baby when your back is turned.

## Special time

Having two children (or more) is a very different experience from having only one and dividing your time and energy between them can be tricky, particularly if your first child is still very young and needs your constant care and attention. However, it is important that you try to keep some time special for you and your older child – they have to adjust too, no matter what their age.

Your older child may instantly love their new sibling and want to help you care for them but, unfortunately, this is not always the case. Be prepared for extra demands and try as hard as you can to give them appropriate attention. You also need to accept that this is not always possible; you can only do so much, and getting stressed about this will only make you less able to take care of your tribe. If you are struggling, ask close family members or friends whom your older child knows well to spend some one-to-one time with them. This phase of family life is also a good opportunity for your child to have fun outings and treats with Dad, which can be billed as special, 'grown-up' time, leaving you able to get on with looking after your baby.

# Feeding

Everyone wants to have a
happy, well-fed baby. This can
be achieved whether you
exclusively breastfeed, formula-
feed or give your baby both
breast milk and infant formula.
All babies are different from birth,
so feeding strategies need to
be flexible enough to suit each
individual baby as well as
the whole family.

# Breastfeeding

Breast milk is nutritionally perfect for babies. It is designed to exactly meet their dietary needs and it adjusts constantly, depending on their age. This makes it suitable for babies from prematurity all the way through to over one year of age.

## Why breastfeed?

Not only is breast milk the perfect food for babies, it is also easy for their immature system to digest. In addition, your baby receives transferred immunity from you (i.e. immunity to the diseases you have been exposed to) while breastfeeding and your milk helps to develop their own immune system. Because it is tailor-made to meet your baby's needs, few by-products are produced, so there is little waste and the poo smells sweet and inoffensive. Breast milk is the correct temperature and requires no preparation. Incidentally, it is also the most environmentally friendly option: there is no processing involved, no packaging to dispose of and no superfluous milk to throw away. Most importantly, however, it provides very significant health benefits to you and your baby, in both the short- and the long-term.

### Benefits for your baby

Many trials have been conducted to find out the true benefits of breastfeeding. Unfortunately, the picture is still not 100 per cent clear; it is also not known how long you need to breastfeed your baby for in order to guarantee these beneficial effects (and, indeed, those for your health, too). Nevertheless, we can be fairly certain that there are several benefits to a baby's health that can be attributed to breastfeeding:

- less chance of being constipated
- less chance of developing asthma/wheeze and eczema
- reduced obesity and fewer cases of type 1 and 2 diabetes
- small reduction in the risk of childhood leukaemia and lymphoma

- fewer diarrhoea and vomiting bugs, coughs and colds and middle ear infections (otitis media)
- significant reduction in the mortality rate among premature and low-birthweight babies from necrotising enterocolitis
- less fussiness when weaning
- possible reduction of the risk of Sudden Infant Death Syndrome.

### Benefits for you

Breastfeeding has physical benefits in the immediate postnatal period and some positive effects on your future health. These include:

- quicker return of your uterus to its normal size, which helps reduce blood loss
- reduced incidence of premenopausal breast cancer and some types of ovarian cancer
- increased bone mineral density, which may help to prevent osteoporosis.

There is also one significant benefit to your pocket: breastfeeding is cheaper than paying for bottles, teats, sterilising equipment and infant formula!

However, you need to remember that you may not be able to choose the way you feed your baby: some mother and baby combinations just simply do not work as a breastfeeding team. Try to remain open-minded and always think about what is best for you as a family.

## What does breast milk contain?

Human breast milk is primarily made up of water, fat, protein, carbohydrates (mainly lactose), vitamins, minerals and trace elements. It also contains other substances, such as hormones, enzymes, growth factors, essential fatty acids, immunological properties and protective factors. Interestingly, it is not sterile: it contains hundreds of bacteria! Many of these are thought to be beneficial, especially the Bifidobacterium species (see below). Breast milk is a dynamic fluid that adapts to your baby's changing needs and environment, so the exact composition will vary from day to day and even between feeds. Initially, it is called colostrum; feeding your baby regularly over the first few days sets in motion the hormone cascade that prepares your body to make mature milk.

## Colostrum

Your first milk, colostrum, has a thick, creamy texture and is yellow (it contains betacarotene). You baby needs very little of it: nutrients are present in a very concentrated form. It has an anti-infective role, as it contains antibodies – predominately Immunoglobulin A – which protects your baby from infections that you have previously been exposed to and to which you have become immune. Beneficial gut bacteria are supported by Bifidus factor, which protects against e-coli, listeria and other bacteria that cause diarrhoea. Colostrum has high levels of epidermal growth factor (EGF). This seals the gut to prevent large molecules from penetrating the gut wall and passing into the blood circulation, potentially causing food allergies and intolerances (see Chapter 5, pp.122–3). Colostrum also has a laxative effect, so your baby is unlikely to become constipated (a common side effect of formula – see Chapter 8, p.176).

## Mature milk

Two to five days after the birth, your milk changes to mature milk. There is a dramatic increase in the volume that is produced, often referred to as your milk 'coming in'. Women report knowing their milk has come in with some of the following symptoms:

- breast swelling/fullness/tingling
- milk leakage
- change in the consistency of the milk
- their baby swallowing more frequently.

The terms 'foremilk' and 'hindmilk' were introduced years ago in research that helped define the thinner milk at the start of the feed and the fat-rich milk at the end. We now know that the fat content changes gradually throughout a feed, making it difficult to define when foremilk would end and hindmilk start.

Both the thinner and thicker milk are crucial elements of the feed and it is important to make sure that your baby feeds for long enough to get enough calorie-rich milk at the end (see section on feeding from one breast or two on pp.68–9).

### Breastfeeding at a glance

Here is an overview of breastfeeding to help you understand how it works in practice:

- In order to produce the best milk that you can, you need to be rested, calm and well hydrated.
- The milk you produce for the first few days is called colostrum. Only very small amounts are required. You will need to feed every two to three hours (day and night) during this time in order to make mature milk.
- Mature milk starts to be produced after two or three days if you had a vaginal delivery or after four or five if you had a Caesarean section. Your breasts swell and may be painful.
- Once your milk has come in, aim to feed your baby every three to four hours during the day, stretching the interval overnight as guided by your baby or you.
- The body makes milk on the basis of 'supply and demand'. This means that the more your baby feeds, the more milk you will make; conversely, if they only feed a little, you will only produce a little.
- It takes about six weeks for your milk supply to stabilise.
- Newborn feeds can take up to one hour, including breaks for winding and changing the nappy; frequent feeds are better than fewer, longer feeds.
- Older babies feed much more quickly than newborns and need fewer feeds per 24 hours.

# Breastfeeding techniques

Breastfeeding may be natural, but it is a technique that you and your baby have to learn. Problems arise when your baby is poorly positioned or has not latched on properly, so it is essential that you are shown the correct way to breastfeed from the beginning.

While I have given details on the various techniques, nothing can beat a bit of practical instruction. Your midwife will help you to get started. Many hospitals also have a specialist lactation consultant on the postnatal ward, so ask to see them if you require further information or support. Once your midwife has discharged you, you will still be able to call on your health visitor for help or see a lactation consultant privately. Many women find the early stages of feeding a challenge and this is where breastfeeding support organisations come into their own (see Useful Resources). They have helplines so that you can get in touch with a breastfeeding counsellor, who can give advice over the phone and may be able to arrange a visit to your home.

## What you need
- ✓ Feeding chair (specialised type optional)
- ✓ Breastfeeding pillow
- ✓ Feeding bras
- ✓ Nipple cream
- ✓ Breast pads

## Preparing to breastfeed

A supportive chair and breastfeeding pillow can help you maintain a straight, supported position when feeding. If you are twisted and taking your baby's weight in your arms, your baby may slip from a good latch to a bad one, causing you pain or resulting in less transfer of milk (see overleaf). In addition, not being fully relaxed can inhibit the production of the hormone oxytocin, which is needed for the 'let-down' (flow) of your milk.

## Feeding chair

Unless you are lying down to breastfeed (see p.66), you will need to sit in a comfortable chair, with pillows for back support. Your lap should be flat or slightly raised, so that your baby tips towards not away from you (which would result in your supporting the weight of your baby). Most chairs are too high, so consider putting a few books or a footstool under your feet. If you buy a special feeding chair, make sure it is low and supportive in the right place for you to maintain this position (tipping back can prevent a good latch at the start).

## Breastfeeding pillow

It important that you bring your baby up to nipple height rather than stoop to bring your breast towards them. A good, firm pillow will enable you to support your baby at the right level for the duration of the feed without having to take their weight in your arms. At the beginning, this can really help you to feed your baby well. When your baby is older, most ordinary pillows work just as well and you may even find you do not need to use one anymore. See Useful Resources.

## Having everything to hand

Arrange a small table near you with a large glass of water, a notebook and pen to record the feeds (see p.68), nipple cream and breast pads (see Feature opposite), a muslin cloth for mop-ups, the phone and a magazine/book or TV remote control.

# Breast care

The success of breastfeeding partly depends on taking good care of your breasts. Nipples can get sore, particularly in the beginning, so nipple cream is a good investment. There are many different types of cream on the market, but the best ones are more of a thick ointment than a thin, liquidy moisturiser. You can test the cream by putting some on your lips. If they stay coated for about 15 minutes, this is a good product (many will have soaked in after a few minutes). Use one that does not need to be wiped off before feeding, as this can cause further soreness (read the information leaflet that comes with the product to check).

Once your milk comes in, you may find that your breasts leak some milk as the time for the feed approaches. For the first few days, the feeds are small and the breasts rarely leak during this time, so you will initially be using your breast pad as a protective dressing to protect sore nipples (see below). Thereafter, using breast pads to soak up the milk prevents unsightly stains on your clothing. Some women's breasts do not leak milk, so when the nipples are no longer sore, it may not be necessary to wear pads.

There are many breast pads to choose from: disposable thin or thick ones and washable cotton or wool ones. The disposable, thin ones are made of a material similar to nappies, containing beads that swell and hold the moisture. The thicker ones can be more comfortable, but also have a much higher chance of leaking. Try them both! Initially, use disposable pads and replace them at every feed to prevent infection (bacteria may not be eliminated by washing). Once the nipples are healed, you can move on to washable pads if you prefer.

## Moist wound healing

It is important to take care of your nipples from the start in order to avoid damage. The first step is always to make sure you are getting the best latch possible, so that they do not become sore through poor technique. However, there can still be some rubbing and a little soreness even with a really good latch. Sore, dry nipples can crack and bleed and this can lead to a series of other problems with breastfeeding (see pp.72–7). Just as you apply lip salve regularly to moisturise sore lips and prevent or heal any cracks, using lots of thick nipple cream and a breast pad after each feed will prevent dryness and help to keep the skin supple, so that it can stretch when feeding. This strategy is called 'moist wound healing'.

After each feed, apply a large pea-sized amount of cream to the tip of the nipple and over a few millimetres of the areola closest to the nipple – try not to cover the entire areola, as this can block the surrounding sebaceous glands (Montgomery's tubercles) that lubricate the nipple. Leave the cream as a thick layer rather than rubbing it in. Place a breast pad over the nipple before you put on your bra or the cream will just rub off; the pad will also protect the nipple from being grazed by the bra material. After an hour, check the nipple: if all the cream has been absorbed, apply more.

Repeat after the next feed, using a new breast pad. Do not reuse the same one, as bacteria can build up on the pad, causing an infection such as thrush (see p.74). If the nipple sticks to the pad as you try to remove it, wet the pad to help separate it … and apply more thick nipple cream next time. Continue with moist wound healing until the nipples have healed and are pain-free.

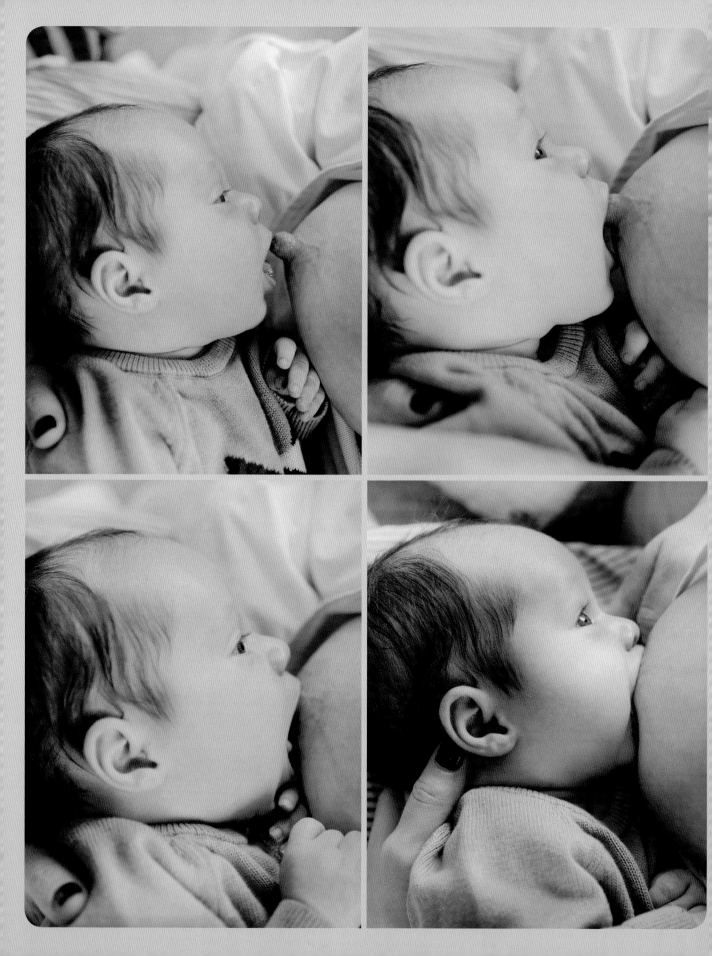

## How to achieve a good latch

A good latch is the key to a successful feed. Most breastfeeding problems occur as a result of a poor latch, so it is important that you know when your baby is correctly latched on to the breast and when you have a poor latch and need to take them off and start again. At first, you may have to have two or three goes at latching before you are successful, but in time you and your baby will learn how to achieve a good latch straight away.

Hold your baby in the cross-cradle position (see overleaf). Align them so that their nose is opposite the nipple and bring them close to the breast. Brush their nose/top lip against the nipple to stimulate a response (see top left picture). Wait for them to lift their chin and open their mouth wide, like a huge yawn, then bring them quickly to the breast by putting pressure between the shoulder blades (not by pushing the head). The nipple should enter the mouth by the top gum (see top right picture). Try to get your baby's bottom lip to make contact 2–3 cm away from the nipple – this is called an asymmetrical latch (see bottom left picture). When latched correctly, more areola should be visible above the nose than below the chin and the lips should be flanged out wide (see bottom right picture). This way, the nose remains free to breathe.

The initial sensation of the latch may feel a little painful. If this decreases after about ten seconds, check for deep, steady sucks with swallows to confirm that the latch is good and that milk transfer is taking place. If you feel increasing pain, you have a poor latch, so de-latch your baby from the breast (see below) and start the process again. Some women feel a mild, tingling sensation or even an almost painful spasm, as their baby begins to suck and, perhaps, several times during the feed. This is the 'let-down' of the milk and does not indicate a poor latch.

### De-latching your baby

Babies often clamp down on the nipple with their gums as you try to take them off the breast. To release the nipple in a pain-free way, insert your little finger into the side of your baby's mouth while they are still latched on and bend it so that it is between the gums. They will then 'bite' your finger instead of your nipple, allowing you to slide your nipple out unharmed.

### Comfort-sucking

With a new baby, it is very important to ensure that they are transferring enough milk. Sometimes babies suck on the nipple without extracting milk, known as 'comfort-sucking', either because they need a rest mid-feed or they have finished and are enjoying the calming effect. Comfort-sucking is fine, provided your baby resumes the feed or has already transferred enough milk. However, it must be balanced with your need to rest and keep your nipples from becoming sore – if you are tired and in pain, you will very quickly give up breastfeeding.

### Winding your baby

It is always a good idea to wind a baby during feeding, as they may swallow air at the same time. If you do not help your baby to get the air out, they may burp and vomit the milk when you lie them down and all your hard work with feeding will have to start again!

How often you wind and at what stage in the feed is often down to individual babies – as is the success of the process. One strategy is to wind when they have slowed down or become sleepy. This will stimulate/wake up your baby, giving you the opportunity to put them back on the breast for more milk, which will hopefully help them settle and sleep well afterwards. There are various positions in which to wind a baby:

- sitting your baby upright on your lap, supporting their chin with your hand (until they have gained head control)
- lying your baby over your shoulder
- lying your baby on their front on your lap, keeping their face free so that they can breathe.

Rub or pat your baby's back gently but firmly. This releases trapped air in their stomach, resulting in a burp. This can sometimes be accompanied by a small amount of regurgitated milk – known as 'possetting' – so have a bib or muslin cloth handy so that you can protect your clothing and mop your baby's mouth.

## Positioning your baby

Effective positioning for breastfeeding ensures that your baby is held close to your breast with their nose free (so that they can breathe) and their chin up (so that they can swallow milk – termed 'milk transfer'). To help remember this position, imagine you are a soldier standing to attention: have your head facing forwards in line with your body, not looking over one shoulder or tipped sideways so that one ear is closer to the shoulder than the other. Now imagine you want to drink water from a glass: you lift your chin to create an open angle (a little more than 90 degrees) between your chin and your chest, so that you can swallow the water. This is the position your baby must be in when on the breast. The particular hold you use – cross-cradle, cradle, underarm or side-lying – must include supporting your baby close to you so that you can maintain this position.

### Cross-cradle hold

I recommend that you start breastfeeding using the cross-cradle technique (see top left picture). This position will enable you to get the best latch possible while your baby's head is very wobbly. The instructions given are for the right breast. When you start with the left, use the other hand and reverse the directions:

- Hold your right breast with your right hand, with your thumb where your baby's nose will be (on the side of the breast near your armpit) and your fingers where the chin will be (near your cleavage). Ensure that your hand is well back towards your rib cage, so that your baby does not bump into your fingers on the approach.
- Hold your baby with your left hand, with your index finger by their lower ear, three fingers around their bottom shoulder and your thumb resting at back of their neck; your palm should be between the shoulder blades.
- Bring your baby towards you so that their abdomen faces yours and line up their nose with your nipple, making sure you keep your back straight and the breast still.
- Move your baby closer to the breast and latch them on as described previously.

### Cradle hold

If things are going well in the cross-cradle hold, you can now switch to what is called the 'cradle hold' by taking your right hand out from under the breast and putting it between your baby's shoulder blades (see top right picture). Points to remember are:

- your hand should be on your baby's shoulders not on their bottom, as this may cause them to put their chin down, thereby reducing the amount of milk transferred
- you need to keep your elbow close to your body
- your baby's head should be resting on your forearm, not in the crook of your elbow.

These elements will help you to maintain the 'nose free, chin lifted up' soldier position.

### Underarm hold ('rugby ball' or 'football' hold)

If you have had a Caesarean and your abdomen is sore, you may want to adopt the underarm hold (see bottom picture). Your baby is positioned so that their body is tucked under your arm, which means that there is no pressure on your abdomen from their weight. This hold is also useful for when feeding is going well on one side, but you are unable to master the same technique on the other. For example, feed on your 'easy' right breast using the cross-cradle technique; change to the 'difficult' left breast and use the *same* instructions but with your baby's body tucked back under your left arm.

### Side-lying hold

While it can be a very restful way to feed a baby, I only recommend side-lying in bed after about three weeks, when your baby has gained better head control, unless there is a second person to help. This is because it can be hard to latch/re-latch your baby in this position. Lie in the bed on your right side, with your shoulder on the mattress and your head on two pillows. This will enable you to look at your baby when latching and feeding without straining your neck. Place your right arm so that your hand is tucked up between the pillows almost under your head and your elbow is raised up and out of the way. Help your baby to latch on with your left hand, making sure their nose is free.

# Managing the feed

Knowing when your baby is properly hungry and how long you should feed them for will help you both to get the most out of the feed.

Feeding a newborn once your milk has come in takes up to one hour, with about 40 minutes for actual milk transfer (usually in two sittings) and an optional period of comfort-sucking. Any longer than this and your baby will probably become too tired to maintain a good latch or suck hard enough to get any more milk. Prolonged feeds may also make your nipples sore. Staying calm and relaxed will allow the hormone oxytocin to be released, which stimulates your 'let-down' reflex.

## Feeding cues

Babies give out many signs to indicate that they are hungry, known as 'feeding cues'. It is best to feed your baby when they show early feeding cues, which include:

- licking or sucking fingers
- 'rooting' – turning their head towards the breast (or anything else that comes into contact with their face) and opening their mouth in anticipation of a feed
- wriggling hands or other hand movements
- restlessness.

Crying is a late feeding cue and can result in your baby becoming distressed at the breast or falling asleep exhausted. Both make it hard to get a good latch, so calm them before trying to breastfeed if you have not managed to spot the earlier cues. Your own body will also let you know when it is time for a feed, as your breasts will be full. It is always best to follow your baby's feeding cues rather than the clock.

Your baby will usually settle into good, slow, rhythmical sucking and will swallow frequently and quite regularly for the first ten minutes of the feed. You will notice that for the next ten minutes or so of the feed your baby's sucking pattern changes, with more pauses and periods of comfort-sucking, interspersed with periods of good swallowing. After about twenty minutes, it is a good idea to wind your baby and change the nappy before feeding again, as this will help to stimulate them to feed again, particularly if they have fallen asleep on the breast. Remember, though, that every baby is different, so ask your midwife or breastfeeding specialist to help you with assessing this.

This second part of the feed will follow the same pattern. When your baby appears to have had enough and has had a period of comfort-sucking that feels right for you both, gently wind them again, but in the early days, try not to wake them up. Your baby will then usually sleep for two to three hours, show feeding cues (see left) and then need another feed.

At the early newborn stage, frequent feeds are better than fewer, longer feeds. The feed duration will usually get shorter as your baby gets older and stronger. For example, some five-month-old babies may be able to complete a feed in about fifteen minutes. By this time, you may be feeding only four or five times in 24 hours. Older babies will stay awake after the feed has finished and will want to play or to be stimulated before they need a nap.

## One breast or two?

You should start each feed on a different breast from the one you started with previously (make a note of this if you think you may forget), as babies always feed best at the beginning of a feed and it is important to stimulate both breasts equally.

In the first few days of breastfeeding, use both breasts at each feed to transfer colostrum, following this pattern:

- about twenty minutes on the first breast
- wind
- change the nappy
- about twenty minutes on the second breast
- wind
- help to settle
- start the next feed on the second breast.

When the mature milk first comes in, use one breast per feed to increase the likelihood that your baby will drink the fat-rich milk. This will also allow your baby to drain the breast to prevent blocked ducts and mastitis (see pp.76–7):

- about twenty minutes on the first breast
- wind
- change the nappy
- about twenty minutes still on the first breast
- wind
- help to settle
- start the next feed on the second breast, following this pattern.

When your supply steadies (or if you feel you have a low milk supply), feed predominantly on the first breast, but consider offering the second as follows:

- about twenty minutes on the first breast
- wind
- change the nappy
- about twenty minutes still on the first breast
- wind
- consider offering the second breast for a short additional feed if your baby is not settled at this stage
- start the next feed on the second breast.

As your baby gets older and their suck gets stronger and more co-ordinated, the time spent transferring milk can get shorter and the comfort-sucking can get longer. Remember that all timings are approximate and that every baby is different, so it is important to follow your baby's feeding cues.

## How much will my baby drink?

The very first milk, colostrum, is produced in very small quantities, roughly 1–10 ml per feed (although for some women it may be as high as 100 ml). However, this is plenty to fill your newborn's stomach, which is only the size of a small marble. This amount gradually increases until the mature milk comes in at around two to five days:

- **Day 1:** 7 ml (just over one teaspoon)
- **Day 2:** 14 ml (just under three teaspoons)
- **Day 3:** 38 ml
- **Days 4–5:** 50–70 ml
- **Days 6–7:** 80–120 ml.

Thereafter, the quantity of milk your produce rises dramatically and your baby will take greater volumes at each feed, although by the tenth day their stomach is still only the size of a ping-pong ball. The amount you produce will stabilise at around six weeks from the estimated delivery date at 750–1,500 ml per 24 hours and, if milk is removed from the breast, the same quantity will be produced to replace it. Mothers who make milk with a low energy content may produce larger volumes, and their babies will feed more to satisfy their needs. However, increasing the number of times that you breastfeed or express milk enables you to produce

## Top Tips

To help achieve the aim of having a contented, well-fed baby, you need to surround yourself with people who share your feeding philosophy. Remember that you do not have to justify your chosen method to anyone.

One of the breastfeeding hormones, oxytocin, makes you feel sleepy – very handy when you want to catnap in between your baby's feeds!

When you feel it is time to stop breastfeeding, try not to feel guilty – it is a wasted emotion and you are being a fabulous mother just by being there for your baby.

more milk over a 24-hour period. You may need to do this if your baby is having a growth spurt and seems hungrier than usual. However, bear in mind that there can be a 24-hour delay in the response of your milk supply. So, for example, if your baby has fed a lot on one day, they may feed less the next, but your breasts may produce more milk as a response to the previous day.

Once supply has been established, all that changes from now on is the precise constitution of the milk, which adapts to meet the nutritional needs of babies as they grow. Breast milk is sensitive to the environment, too: if the weather is hot, the milk will naturally become more diluted and your baby will need to feed more frequently. So exclusively breastfed babies do not need to be given additional drinks of water from a bottle.

The majority of mothers produce enough milk for their babies for at least the first six months. The quantity of milk naturally decreases once solid foods are introduced. This should be done by six months, as breast milk alone is no longer sufficient

nutrition for a growing baby after this time – although it is still a very important part of their diet. See Chapter 5 for more information on weaning.

All the amounts of breast milk listed are, of course, approximate, as it is not possible to measure exactly how much your baby is taking from the breast. Even expressing (see pp.78–81) is not an accurate measure of how much milk your baby takes – merely an indicator of how much milk a pump can get out of the breast for you – and a baby will drain the breast more effectively than any machine. In any case, a baby that feeds from the breast will need less volume than if they were given a bottle of expressed breast milk or formula to achieve a comparable weight gain and to be satisfied until the next feed. This is because, when breastfeeding, a baby's stress levels decrease and their heart rate slows. So try to resist comparing the amounts your baby drinks from the breast with the volumes of formula that are normally recommended (see Box, p.85) – it is the quality not quantity of breast milk that is significant here.

## How do I know if my baby is getting enough milk?

This is one of the most common concerns of breastfeeding mothers. If only there were gauge saying 'full' and 'empty' on a baby's stomach, life would be a lot easier! However, there are some ways to tell that your baby is getting enough milk.

To start with, you can assess whether there is an effective sucking pattern with audible swallows. Then monitor the nappies. Colostrum is an anti-diuretic (it prevents dehydration), so there may only be one wee in the first 24 hours, two in next 24 hours, increasing to five wees per day by the fifth day, when the mature milk should be in. Colostrum is also a laxative, so expect lots of poos! As your baby gets older, they should still have plenty of heavy, wet nappies, but the poos can become less frequent.

Babies are satisfied by their feeds if they settle and sleep in between (i.e. they are not constantly crying) and wake for feeds (i.e. are not 'hibernating' and needing to be woken up). Your baby will probably be feeding six to eight times in 24 hours until they are sleeping through the night or have been weaned onto solid foods.

As time goes on, weight gain will be an important indicator that your baby is getting enough milk. Babies can initially lose up to ten per cent of their birthweight (e.g. for a 3,500 g baby, this is 350 g) before starting to put weight on again. When they are back to birthweight (which should be by two weeks), babies gain an average of 30 g per 24 hours until they double their birthweight at about four to five months. Growth slows down dramatically after this. (During illness, a baby's weight can become static or even drop, but it is important that they gain weight steadily once the illness is over.)

If your baby seems generally content and is gaining weight, then they are getting enough milk, but if you have any concerns, you can always ask your health visitor or GP.

## Stopping breastfeeding

At some stage you will be ready to stop breastfeeding. The World Health Organisation recommends breastfeeding exclusively for six months, but in the end it has to be a personal decision. All I can say is that it needs to be right for the whole family and it does not matter what everyone else does or thinks you should do.

The more time you can take to stop breast-feeding the better – a minimum of two weeks is ideal. This allows your body to adjust to the decrease in demand and so produce less milk, reducing both the discomfort of fullness that the missed breastfeeds may cause, as well as the risk of mastitis that may result due to insufficient milk removal. This strategy gives you time to adjust emotionally, too.

When you feel ready to begin the process, alternate breast- and bottle-feeds for a few days, then progress to missing two consecutive feeds, and so on. However, try to start and end the day with a breastfeed. If you experience growing discomfort at any stage, reintroduce a breastfeed until the symptoms stop, then cut back the feeds again, but this time more slowly. Using a breast pump to remove a small amount of milk will also help to make you comfortable. You can stop cutting back at any stage of this pattern and continue to mix-feed your baby with as many or as few breastfeeds to suit you and your baby's needs. For example, many women continue to breastfeed their baby in the morning and at night well beyond a year, or give just one feed per 24 hours, depending on their daily routine. This prolongs that special bond with your baby and the breast milk they receive continues to provide all the health benefits, including boosting their immune system to protect them when crawling around or mixing with other children. See also the Chart in Chapter 5, pp. 120–1 detailing a baby's milk requirements in the first year.

# Breastfeeding problems

Most breastfeeding problems start with sore nipples or breasts or an unsettled or sleepy baby who is not transferring enough milk. If help is sought early, small issues can be nipped in the bud and breastfeeding can then continue successfully. If left too long, they can cause a series of complications that require more extensive attention.

The key is to first ensure efficient milk removal before trying to determine and address the cause. Many problems are relatively straightforward to sort out and you have many ports of call should you need help in identifying the issue or support in dealing with it (see p.62). Never feel that you have to struggle on alone if you develop problems with breastfeeding or that you simply are not any good at it and should give up.

## Sleepy baby

Newborn babies can be very sleepy and tend to take short feeds before going back to sleep again. You may need to take steps to wake your baby mid-feed (e.g. change their nappy, wash their face). Try to feed your baby when they show feeding cues (see Box, p.68), not according to a rigid time schedule. This way you will know that they are properly hungry and more likely to stay awake and achieve milk transfer rather than just comfort-suck.

If your baby still seems sleepy, check that they are medically well – your healthcare professionals will help you to monitor jaundice (see Chapter 8, p.178) and weight gain, as well as general health.

## Unsettled baby

Breastfeeding helps calm your baby and makes them feel safe and nurtured. Sometimes, however, your baby may be hungry, but seems to fuss at the breast, only achieving a poor latch (see opposite). In the early days, this unsettledness can be part of the difficulty some babies have in adjusting to the outside world after birth.

Try to feed your baby as well as you can by ensuring there is good milk transfer, not just comfort-sucking (listen for their swallows). After a feed, spend time with your baby skin-to-skin (see Chapter 1, p.18) or adopt other calming strategies, such as loose swaddling (see Feature in Chapter 5, p.95), putting your baby in a sling/baby carrier or singing to them (see Chapter 2, pp.45–6). If they are still unsettled, consider other possible reasons, such as a stomach ache or being overtired/lonely/frightened and take the appropriate measures. In time, babies do naturally adjust to life, allowing normal feeding to take place. If the above strategies do not work contact your health visitor or a breastfeeding specialist. For older babies, see also the section on nursing strikes opposite.

## Poor latch

A poor latch is one of the most common early breastfeeding problems. Often, the most obvious sign of a poor latch is sore nipples (see opposite). However, if your baby falls asleep on the breast, this can indicate that the nipple has remained in the front of your baby's mouth, where they use it like a dummy, comfort-sucking before eventually falling asleep. This example of a poor latch can result in repeated cycles of unsettled behaviour: your baby falls asleep for a short time, wakes again crying because they are hungry, latches to the breast but falls asleep again very quickly without having a full feed. Aside from causing difficulties with settling, a poor latch may mean your baby gains weight more slowly than expected. In addition, because the breasts are not being drained adequately, they can become engorged (see p.75) and this can eventually result in a decrease in your milk supply. You may also become exhausted by frequent feeds.

Start by working through the correct latching technique, focusing on achieving the asymmetrical latch (see p.65). It is important to get as much nipple and areola in your baby's mouth as is necessary to take the nipple to the junction of the soft and hard palate, as the sensation of something touching this part of the mouth stimulates them to continue to suck and so transfer milk. You will also need to manage any engorgement (see overleaf) in order to prevent frustration for your baby and to preserve your supply by preventing the build-up of excess milk.

## Sore nipples

The main causes of sore nipples are a poor latch (see above), incorrect use of a breast pump or pulling your baby off the breast rather than safely de-latching (see p.65). First, revisit the position and latch techniques and ensure your baby has an asymmetrical latch. It may be necessary to have help to correct this. Before you start feeding, check that the breast is not too engorged for your baby to achieve a good latch. If your breasts are very full, you could express a little first (see section on engorgement management overleaf).

If you have not been taking care of your nipples in the way described in the Feature on p.63, start doing so now. Even though it may feel painful, it is important to continue to feed your baby regularly to meet their nutritional needs and to prevent your breasts from becoming too full, which could lead to blocked ducts and mastitis (see pp.76–7). Begin by feeding on the least sore side. This will take the edge off your baby's appetite and encourage the 'let-down' reflex, which will get the milk flowing freely – both actions mean that they will not suck quite so strongly when transferred to the sorer side.

If your nipples become very dry, they may develop fissures or cracks, which can bleed while you are feeding. While this may be very distressing for you, blood in the milk will rarely bother your baby. See also Box on nipple shields overleaf. With time, the elasticity of the nipple tissue will improve and your baby will be able to get a better latch, but until that happens, it may be necessary to consider expressing (pumping milk by hand or machine) and giving your milk in a bottle

(see pp.78–81). This is not only so that your baby receives enough nutrition to thrive, but also so that the breast knows to produce increasingly more milk for the next feeds. Do not feel as if you have 'failed' at breastfeeding – the most important thing in this instance is to have a positive experience for you and your baby.

Even though you are expressing, it is important to attempt to breastfeed at each feed for a short period of time before giving the bottle in order to practise the technique. Do not force your baby onto the breast too many times, however, as this can cause frustration, lethargy and even a breast aversion, where your baby refuses the breast and cries every time you attempt to breastfeed. With time and (if necessary) with specialist help, you will be able to latch your baby.

## Biting the nipple

The first teeth that babies grow are their bottom front teeth (see Chapter 6, p.142) and, as they put their tongue over their bottom gum to breastfeed, mothers usually do not even notice a difference. Once the top two front teeth come through, your baby may bite your nipple by mistake – this is usually momentary and they will release very quickly. Although biting can be painful, the way you react is very important. If you cry out in pain or shock, this could frighten your baby and they may not want to breastfeed at the next feed, as they associate this fright with feeding.

The best strategy is to de-latch your baby from the breast and firmly say 'no biting'. Stop the feed and move on to the next part of the daily routine, even if your baby has only fed for a short while; some mothers reinforce the 'no biting' warning by putting their baby down in a safe place and walking out of the room for a minute. The idea is to let your baby know that it is not acceptable to bite and that the consequence is that the feed ends.

## Nursing strike

Some babies, particularly older ones, may feed really well for ten minutes, then push themselves off the breast and scream when you try to put them back on. There can be many reasons for this 'nursing strike'.

First, babies sometimes get bored: there is nothing to see when breastfeeding, so they push away in order to have a look at what is going on around them. Try feeding in a quiet place where there are fewer distractions, put a picture in their line of sight to look at it or wear a chunky necklace, so that they can reach up and play with it while they are feeding.

Similarly, an older baby may want to move on to more interesting things, such as crawling around or playing with their toys, so the minute they feel like they have had enough, they come off the breast. To counteract this, focus on getting good milk transfer at a time when they are sleepy, for example, just before or after a nap or in the morning/at bedtime. In addition, monitor their weight gain and their general level of contentment.

If your baby is having a few bottles of expressed milk or formula, they may get to like the faster flow and not want to put the effort in to work at the breast. In this instance, babies often complain until you offer them a top-up from a bottle. One solution is to stop the bottle-feeds and go back solely to the breast, hoping your baby will re-establish breastfeeding – be careful that their weight is not affected, otherwise they will become more unsettled because they are hungry. Another is to let them feed until they complain, then give them a top-up before offering them the breast again at the end of the feed. If your baby starts to refuse the breast or cries shortly after the beginning of the feed, consider giving them the top-up first, continuing the breastfeed when you have taken the edge off their appetite. You should also consider that perhaps it is the time to stop breastfeeding – your baby can still have breast milk if you wish: you can express your milk and give it to them via a bottle, training beaker or ordinary cup, depending on their age.

### Thrush
Thrush is a fungal infection caused by the yeast-like fungus Candida albicans. It can affect both mother and baby. Breastfeeding mothers may get the infection around their nipples after an episode of cracked nipples; it is also common to get thrush following a course of antibiotics.

## Nipple shields
Made from very thin, clear, soft plastic, nipple shields are shaped like a Mexican hat and rest on your nipple. For some babies, they help them maintain the latch and drink breast milk. Nipple shields are marketed as helping sore nipples but, in reality, they often exacerbate the problem, as babies can take the shield into their mouth and then bite the nipple between their gums, causing more pain.

Women who have very flat or inverted nipples, or have a baby with tongue-tie (a condition where there is a tight piece of skin between the underside of the tongue and the floor of the mouth), can find them helpful when their baby is not managing to latch at all. Nipple shields are particularly useful for premature babies, who are not strong enough to suck for very long. When they release suction, the shield remains in their mouth; when they are ready to suck again, they can then successfully draw the shield and breast back into their mouth and achieve some milk transfer.

While there is a time and a place for everything, there are many problems that result from using the shield, mostly resulting from the fact that babies often do not take a full feed. These include excessive windiness, long feeds, a baby who is still hungry after a feed or is not gaining weight, as well as breasts that are not drained (leading to engorgement and mastitis and, ultimately, a decrease in milk supply). However, the biggest issue is that babies can get a version of nipple confusion (see p.81) and refuse to breastfeed without the shield.

To overcome most of these problems, almost all babies will need a top-up and you should express to ensure your milk is removed. The use of nipple shields should therefore be viewed as a short-term solution (one week only), while you continue to try latching your baby throughout this time, getting expert help if necessary.

Your principal symptom is a burning/stinging sensation from the nipple to the ribcage that is often described as feeling like needles stabbing into the breast. This pain usually intensifies between feeds, which distinguishes it from the pain of sore nipples (which usually gets slightly better between feeds). Visual signs are a pink and shiny areola and nipples: you may notice that the areola is pink near the nipple, and then becomes darker in colour further away from the nipple (a thrush-free areola is uniform in colour). Thrush usually occurs on both breasts.

Babies often have a white tongue after a feed from the milk, but if this is present before a feed, particularly on the back of the tongue with a normal, pink or clear area at the front, it could be a sign of thrush. When a baby is heavily colonised, thrush also appears on the insides of the cheeks, lips and around the anus as a nappy rash.

It is very important to treat both yourself and your baby, even if one of you only has mild symptoms, as it is easily transferred between you. Although you can use an antifungal cream on your nipples, this can cause young babies to gag, so your GP may prescribe oral medication. See Chapter 8, p.182 for details on how to treat thrush in babies.

## Engorgement

When your milk comes in at between two and five days after the birth (see p.61), it is normal for your breasts to become heavier, larger and tender as they begin to produce larger amounts of mature milk. At this stage there is too much milk – enough for twins! The body takes a few days to adjust to the volume your baby actually requires. It is important that you take steps to ensure this happens without too much pain or a detrimental effect on the overall supply of milk, and this is best done by removing milk regularly over the next 48 hours (usually by putting your baby to the breast).

If the milk is not removed frequently and the breast drained well at each feed, this can progress to engorgement, a term used to describe when the breast is swollen with extra blood supply and fluid (oedema) as well as with the extra milk. The milk can become trapped in the breast, making it hard for your baby to get out without help and causing your breast to become very painful. Some of the possible signs of engorgement are:

- swollen breasts with tight or shiny skin
- generalised redness of the breast
- increased breast tenderness/pain/heat
- difficulty latching your baby effectively, as the breast and the skin around and including the nipple are tense
- difficulty removing milk from the breast
- mild fever.

Engorgement can cause blocked ducts and possibly mastitis, an infection of the breast that may require antibiotics (see sections overleaf). After a few days of engorged breasts, the body thinks the milk is not needed, so cleverly reabsorbs it. Your milk production will decrease, meaning that you may not have enough milk for your baby to be exclusively breastfed in the weeks and months ahead. It is therefore essential to treat the condition promptly. It is best to seek help from your midwife, health visitor, GP or breastfeeding specialist, but there are also a few self-help measures to help you manage breast engorgement:

- Apply a warm, wet compress to encourage blood flow to the area.
- Gently massage the breast to stimulate the 'let-down' reflex.
- Hand-express for a few minutes immediately before the feed to soften the areola, as this will help your baby to latch. Focus on the area where your baby's nose and chin will be – usually by your armpit and cleavage.
- Ensure your baby gets a good latch, focusing on the bottom lip making contact with the breast 2–3 cm from the nipple (asymmetrical latch).
- Help your baby to obtain milk by massaging the breast from armpit to nipple as they feed.
- Offer only one breast per feed to improve drainage and ensure your baby gets enough of the fat-rich milk (see the section on feeding from one breast or two, pp.68–9).
- When your baby has finished the first part of the feed, assess the breast with your hands to feel if any part has lumps or is sore. When you put your

baby back on the same breast for the second part of the feed, focus your massage on that area to help the milk flow from there.

- After the feed, check the breast again. If it still has lumps or is sore, express a small amount of milk, either by hand or by pump, to make it more comfortable.
- Also check the other breast: if it is very lumpy or sore, express a small amount of milk (not more than 30 ml).
- Apply a cold compress (a flannel soaked in cold water) to both breasts for up to twenty minutes after the feed.

At the next feed, swap breasts and repeat these steps. Breastfeed your baby throughout the day and night to ensure that your breasts are drained regularly. Anti-inflammatory medication (such as ibuprofen) is also very effective (although it usually takes a few days to take effect) – talk to your GP first before you take anything.

## Blocked ducts and blebs

Blocked ducts can occur when you are busy and so may give your baby a shorter feed than usual, when your baby is older and distracted and does not feed for so long, or when there is a change in the feeding pattern (e.g. going on a journey). Poor drainage may also be the cause, due to a poor latch, pressure from clothes, fingers gripping the areola or from large, pendulous breasts where the milk cannot drain evenly from the breast. As well as performing the self-help measures for engorgement, try to feed your baby in a different position (e.g. using

the underarm hold if you usually use the cradle hold) to get their chin to press on the blocked section.

An obstruction at the tip of the nipple, visible as a white spot or blister, is called a 'bleb' and is much less common. Blebs must be physically removed and you can do this quite easily yourself: gently scratch the top off the bleb with a sterilised needle to pierce the skin (trying not to stab the nipple and cause bleeding). Once the bleb has been removed, allow your baby to feed in order to relieve the blockage. You may need to repeat this before several consecutive feeds before the blockage is completely cleared.

## Mastitis

When milk stays in part of the breast, either because of engorgement or a blocked duct, it is called milk stasis. If the milk is not removed, under pressure it will leak back into the surrounding breast tissue, where it will cause localised inflammation, seen as a red area on a section of the breast. This initial stage is called 'non-infective milk stasis mastitis'. If this continues, the tissue becomes infected with bacteria, and you will very quickly develop a fever and flu-like symptoms (e.g. achy limbs, shakes). This can be called 'infective mastitis'.

It is not possible to tell from the symptoms alone which type of mastitis it is. You can clear it up yourself if you remove the blocked milk from your breast, but if the symptoms are severe, you are likely to need treatment with antibiotics – see your GP as soon as possible. Throughout the problem, it is important to keep removing the milk from the breast as well as treating the symptoms.

# Expressing

Removing milk from the breast by hand or by pump is called 'expressing'. You may need or want to do this so that someone else is able to give your breast milk to your baby. Expressing can also be used while trying to overcome some breastfeeding problems.

## What you need
✓ Breast pump (manual or electric)
✓ Breast milk storage bags
✓ Small cool bag and freezer blocks

I recommend exclusively breastfeeding your baby from the breast for the first three weeks. This allows time for you and your baby to learn the technique and helps your breasts adjust to the 'supply and demand' mechanism, ensuring that you have a good milk supply for your baby. After this time, you can give your baby your expressed breast milk from a bottle to give you greater flexibility with feeding. For example, having someone else give your baby a feed will allow you to have some time to yourself; and, if you return to work and want your baby to continue having breast milk, you will need to express during your working day.

If you think you may want to give expressed milk to your baby at some point during the first year, it is a good idea to introduce the bottle when your baby is between three and six weeks old. After six weeks, babies develop a stronger gag reflex (see Box in Chapter 5, p.115) and can refuse the teat if they are not used to it. This can be very distressing for you both, so please get help from your health visitor, GP or breastfeeding specialist, as they can give you some helpful tips. See also the section on nipple confusion overleaf.

Hopefully, breastfeeding will go smoothly for you and you will not need to express earlier than three to six weeks. However, if early breastfeeding problems develop or your baby is unable to feed directly from the breast (e.g. because they are being cared for in the neonatal unit), you will need to express using the best pump available in order to drain the breast (so that you are not in pain from engorgement), maintain your milk supply and provide your baby with the important nutritional benefits of breast milk.

It is worth renting a hospital-grade electric double breast pump initially, until you know how much you are going to use it (see Useful Resources). These top-of-the-range pumps are extremely efficient at expressing, which will save you time in the early days and ensure that your baby is getting as much of your milk as possible. Efficient pumping

*Your employer is legally obliged to provide a private, safe and hygienic environment for you to express at work. This should include a place to store your milk, as well as somewhere to rest.*

## Storing and transporting expressed breast milk

Special sterile bags (bought from chemists) can be used to freeze breast milk for later use. Simply pour your milk into the bag from the bottle you used while expressing and label with the date and the volume expressed. Freeze the milk as soon as possible after pumping.

A small cool bag can be used to transport cooled expressed breast milk in bottles, with the lid sealed tightly to prevent leakage, until it is ready to be heated and used. Breast milk should only be kept at room temperature for four hours – any longer or warmer and germs will grow – so use a freezer block inside the bag. Avoid transporting frozen milk: after it starts to defrost, it needs to be used within 24 hours, whereas fresh milk can be stored in the fridge for four to five days. Nevertheless, I would recommend using this fresh milk as soon as possible, as it will have warmed slightly on the journey.

Advice differs in the amounts of time that you can safely store breast milk for, but a conservative amount of time is:

- **room temperature:** four hours
- **fridge:** four to five days
- **freezer:** three to four months.

also ensures maximum breast drainage, which helps protect the milk supply. After six weeks from your estimated delivery date, you will have a better idea of your pumping needs, and can either continue to rent or can buy a different pump that suits your needs. If you are only going to express occasionally, you may find that a (cheaper) manual pump is sufficient; however, for regular expressing, an electric one is the better bet, particularly one that allows you to pump from both breasts at once. Make sure that whatever you buy fits your breasts properly. The funnel part of the pump is called the 'breast shield' and there should be 3–5 mm between your nipple and the edge of the funnel

to prevent rubbing and pain. To achieve this, you may need to get a large (27 mm) or extra large (30 mm) breast shield.

## Hand-expressing

If you need to express before your mature milk comes in, perhaps because your baby is in the neonatal unit or is having difficulty latching on, you will need to do so by hand. This is because colostrum is present in very small volumes and, if you use a manual or electric pump at this time, most (if not all) of the colostrum collected will be caught in the mechanism and therefore wasted. When you get 10 ml after about ten minutes of hand-expressing, you can move on to pumping.

If you need to hand-express, you should be getting support from a breastfeeding specialist to help you learn the technique. However, here is the basic method:

- First wash your hands.
- Place your thumb and index finger (or second finger) on either side of breast, about 3–5 cm away from the nipple. Ensure there is a straight line from your thumb through the nipple to your other finger.
- Hold a sterile container close to the nipple with your other hand.
- Press gently back towards the rib cage and compress your finger and thumb together in a slight downward motion, taking care not to move along the skin (which may cause a friction burn)
- Hold for five seconds and you should start to see the milk drip. Release and repeat several times.
- When the milk flow appears to slow, rotate your hand to compress in a different place and repeat as necessary.
- When milk flow ceases, swap to the other breast.

Stay as relaxed as you can, as this will help your milk flow. You usually need to hand-express for two minutes at a time on each breast, swapping between the two breasts for a period of about ten minutes. Hand-expressing eight times in 24 hours should be enough to stimulate your milk supply and to collect at least some milk if you are unable to breastfeed your baby.

## Pumping

Expressing by using a manual or electric breast pump allows most women to extract milk more quickly and in greater volumes. If you are using a double pump (which allows you to pump both breasts at the same time), you will also need a hands-free pumping bra. See Useful Resources.

Start by sterilising the parts of the pump and bottles that will come in contact with the milk (see overleaf). Apply some nipple cream to the inside of the funnel (the part that will touch the areola), which will reduce the friction and prevent sore nipples and damage to the areola. Make sure that the nipple is as central as you can get it inside the funnel and is able to move freely and not catch on the edge.

Turn the pump on, increase the strength until the sensation feels about the same as your baby's suck, then possibly turn it down a little – it needs to feel comfortable. If you are pumping both breasts at once, put the other funnel on the second breast at this stage. Try to resist watching the milk as it comes out, as this can make you tense. Your milk flow is enhanced when you are relaxed, so you are better off distracting yourself (e.g. reading). When the milk stops flowing, take a short break, then pump again until the milk flow ceases once more.

I do not usually recommend having the pump on for more than fifteen minutes in total. Any longer than this and you may damage the breast tissue, all for a very small increase in yield. Once you get the hang of it, you can try varying amounts of time (e.g. pumping/resting in five minute intervals), but I suggest pumping for ten minutes, resting for a few minutes, then pumping again for five more minutes.

Do not be alarmed if your expressed milk has a pink tinge. It may be that your nipples are cracked, hence a small amount of blood is in your milk, or the blood may be coming from inside your breasts. Either way, the milk is fine for your baby to drink. If you are in pain and your milk is pink, then you should check with your midwife, health visitor or GP whether you have an infection.

## Nipple confusion

Does the introduction of a bottle or dummy while still continuing to breastfeed cause nipple confusion? Breastfeeding experts are divided on this topic. The concern is that if a baby has a teat or dummy too early, then they may develop breastfeeding problems, such as difficulties with latching or even refusing the breast altogether. However, it is likely that, rather than being confused by the physical difference between a teat and a nipple, your baby is actually unsettled by the differing practices that surround a bottle-feed. The answer is probably to treat every baby as an individual and, if you are using a dummy or feeding from a bottle, to follow the four guidelines outlined below.

### Mimicking the breastfeeding technique

If you have a favoured hold when breastfeeding, place your baby in the same way and in the 'soldier' position outlined on p.66. Bring them close to the teat just as you would to the breast, and wait until their mouth is open wide. This will allow a smooth connection with the teat. If your baby pushes the teat out of their mouth, remove it and repeat the process rather than wiggle the bottle around in the mouth until they start sucking.

### Matching the length of the feed

Try to make the bottle-feed the same length as the breastfeed – this may mean elongating the bottle-feed. If you allow your baby to drink the entire contents of the bottle in five minutes, they may still show feeding cues (see Box, p.68), which may tempt you into feeding more. Overfeeding a baby can result in stomach ache or your baby sleeping past the time of their next feed, meaning that your breasts are not stimulated at the time expected. This can lead to engorgement or problems with the milk supply. Feed your baby half of the feed, then stop and wind them. Cuddle and soothe them for five minutes, then give another 25 per cent of the feed. Repeat the five-minute winding/cuddle break, then give the remainder of the feed.

### Volume control

Because bottle-feeding allows you to see the exact amount of milk your baby is taking, you may feel the need to continue feeding until they have consumed the 'correct' volume (see p.69 for estimates for breastfed babies). However, breast milk is a dynamic liquid, which means that it changes according to the environment and your baby's needs. Instead of following generalised guidelines, feed your baby the volume that they actually want at that time. If they slow down and stop drinking, by all means wind them and try to keep them awake to encourage a re-latch, just as you would when they sleepily breastfeed. However, if your baby stays asleep, do not push the bottle into their mouth. If your baby sleeps for longer than expected or, conversely, wakes early for the next feed, use this information at the next bottle-feed in order to gauge the amount required more precisely – this, importantly, will protect your milk supply (see below).

Also check that you are using a teat that is appropriate for your baby's age (see overleaf): if you are using a teat for an older baby, the flow may be too quick, which will result their taking too much milk too quickly.

### Protecting your milk supply

Unless it is planned carefully, giving your baby a bottle of expressed milk at the time when they would normally feed from the breast can interfere with the 'supply and demand' mechanism that is essential for successful breastfeeding. This can lead to your baby becoming 'fussy' at the breast, as there is not enough milk for them. In order to maintain the correct balance, pump the same amount of milk (or slightly more if you can) that your baby takes from the bottle within 24 hours of the 'missed' breastfeed, ideally as close to the usual feed time as possible. If you cannot collect this amount in one pumping session, try an additional session after the next breastfeed. If you keep expressing throughout the time you are away from your baby, you will ensure that there is sufficient milk for your baby.

It is very tempting to miss a pump session, as this is, of course, more work for you. Try to think that the milk from the missed feed is still in the breast and, if you do not express it, your body will think that the milk is not needed and will reabsorb it, ultimately causing your supply to decrease.

# Formula-feeding

Some mothers choose to feed their baby infant formula from birth or move on to formula at some point in the first year. Others do a mixture of breast- and formula-feeding, known as 'mixed feeding'.

**What you need**

- ✓ Steriliser
- ✓ 6 bottles (glass or BPA-free plastic)
- ✓ 6 teats in each type of flow to fit your brand of bottle
- ✓ Bottle brush
- ✓ Bottle warmer (optional)
- ✓ Infant formula (powder or ready-made liquid)
- ✓ Powder dispenser (for powder formula)
- ✓ Thermal flask/thermal travel bag (for powder formula)

The particular approach you take should be determined by whatever works best for you, your baby and your individual family situation – any combination is fine, as long as your baby is gaining weight. Although infant formula cannot provide your baby with everything that breast milk can, it is still an effective alternative that has been shown over many years to be a great substitute. So you can be sure that, when it is prepared safely, your baby is being well fed and will thrive.

Based on cow's milk, infant formula has been modified so that it is suitable for babies under one year. It comes in two forms: ready-made liquid formula in sterile cartons or bottles and powdered formula in non-sterile tins (to which you need to add water – see overleaf). Check that you are using an appropriate formula for your baby's age and needs. Any leftover ready-made formula must be kept in the refrigerator for a maximum of 24 hours, after which it needs to be thrown away. Powdered formula is a cheaper option and is the type you are more likely to use if you solely formula-feed. The current advice is that you need to make up each bottle at the time it is needed. This means that if you are away from home, you will need to take powdered formula with you to mix with hot water. An ordinary flask can be used to transport hot water or you can put some into a sterilised bottle to keep in a thermal travel bag until you are ready to make up a feed.

There are an enormous variety of bottles to choose from. Some are designed to reduce colic (see Box opposite) and others aim to mimic the shape of the breast, supposedly to promote a baby's natural latch and to make it easier to switch from breast to bottle. A lot of this is clever advertising and I do not think that it really matters which size or model you go for, provided they are made from glass or BPA-free plastic. Bisphenol A (BPA) is the chemical used to make plastic clear and is present in bottles made from polycarbonate. BPA is known to leach into the fluid in the bottle. Animal studies show that low levels of BPA affect the development of the brain, the reproductive system and the immune system. In laboratory rats, exposure to BPA has been linked to an increased risk of some cancers, decreased sperm counts and reduced fertility, and hyperactivity. BPA exposure has also been linked to obesity, diabetes and the early onset of puberty, but there is on-going international debate about the degree to which BPA affects humans. In 2009, six major manufacturers stopped making their baby bottles with BPA. Look for bottles labelled 'BPA-free' or ones made from polypropylene or polyethylene, which are usually opaque or coloured rather than clear.

Most new bottles come complete with a teat (often a teat suitable for newborns). Teats come in different flow speeds for when your baby gets older and their suck is stronger and more co-ordinated. Start with the teat that provides the slowest flow, so that there is minimal milk leaking from the side of your baby's mouth. Your baby's swallow is not fully coordinated initially, so too fast a flow can cause them to choke. However, if you hear your baby sucking air down the side of the teat or the feed is taking a long time, consider a faster flow teat. As your baby gets older, you may need to keep switching to ever faster-flowing teats. However, if you find that a lot of milk dribbles out, revert to the slower flow teat for a while.

## Sterilising feeding equipment

Breast milk and formula are breeding grounds for bacteria, so it is really important that you sterilise all containers, teats, breast pump parts and so on until your baby is six months old, otherwise they could become ill. There are several different types of sterilising system:

- boiling in water for ten minutes (no special equipment required)
- cold-water sterilising with tablets
- microwave or electric steriliser (steam).

Start by washing your hands thoroughly with hot, soapy water and cleaning the area that you are going to be working on. Take the bottles apart so that the teat, collar, lid and bottle are separated. Wash with hot, soapy water – use a bottle brush to make sure all milk residue is removed – then rinse well in cold running water. You can put things in the dishwasher, but they will still need to be sterilised afterwards. Sterilise according to the instructions of the particular system you are using. If you are using a microwave or electric steriliser, remember that the steam is generated from the bottom of the machine, so make sure that you put the parts in so that the steam will clean everything

## Which bottles should I use to reduce the chance of colic?

When babies are bottle-fed, air needs to enter the bottle in order to balance the displacement of the breast milk or formula they drink. If air does not return successfully, a vacuum is created inside the bottle, which disturbs the flow of liquid, making it harder for the baby to drink. This may cause them to take in and swallow air between their mouth and the side of the teat rather than just the milk/formula from the bottle. Excess air or wind in the intestine is thought to be one of the possible causes of colic (see Chapter 8, p.175).

Manufacturers are working hard to achieve a successful return of air and all do it in a slightly different way. The best thing is to try a brand of bottle and see how your baby gets on with it. If your baby feeds smoothly without fussing and does not appear to take air in when feeding (the air will be heard as a sucking sound going in between their mouth and the side of the teat), then that is the best type of bottle for your baby.

Even if the bottle is working correctly, you need to make sure that the teat is always filled with liquid – feeding with the bottle in a horizontal position creates a mixture of air and milk/formula in the teat. In addition, add an extra 30 ml of the feed to your baby's bottle so that they never drain the bottle empty and are then left to suck in air, even if this milk is wasted at the end of the feed.

on the inside. Let the machine run its course – do not be tempted to stop it before it has finished, as this may not allow enough time for all the bacteria to be destroyed. Check the instructions for how long things will remain sterile without opening the lid. Alternatively, assemble the bottles and lids straightaway (wash your hands thoroughly again first). Take care not to burn yourself on the steam – allow it to cool down first.

### How to make up powdered formula

Powdered formula is not sterile, so it needs to be mixed with hot water in order to kill any bacteria. First make sure that all equipment has been sterilised and that surfaces are clean. Boil at least 1 litre of fresh, cold tap water in the kettle – do not use water that has been boiled before or left in the kettle for a while, or bottled water (as it often contains too much sodium and sulphur). Allow the boiled water to cool slightly, but for no more than 30 minutes, so that it remains above 70°C. Wash your hands and remove a bottle, teat, cuff and lid from the steriliser. Add the required amount of water into the sterilised bottle. Following the instructions on the container, put the appropriate number of scoops of formula into the bottle. Assemble the rest of the bottle and shake well to mix. If you are not using it immediately, you can keep the bottle in the refrigerator for four hours – after this time, it needs to be thrown away.

While making up bottles of formula is straight-forward, there are some important points to bear in mind:

- Manufacturers' instructions vary as to the exact proportions of water and powdered formula to use, so follow those given for your particular brand very carefully.

*Be wary of warming up bottles of formula in a microwave: they heat unevenly and 'hot spots' in the feed may burn your baby's mouth.*

- Do not add extra powder when making up a feed, as this can make your baby constipated and may cause dehydration (see Chapter 8, pp.163–5 and 176).
- In hot weather, do not be tempted to dilute the feed by using less powder, as your baby may not get enough nourishment; instead, make up the feed as normal, then add more water.
- Do not add sugar or cereals to the feed.
- Do not warm a bottle more than once.

## Warming a bottle

When using ready-made formula or expressed breast milk that has been stored in the fridge (see Box, p.79), you may need to warm the milk before giving it to your baby. This is particularly important for newborns, as introducing a cold liquid into their core will reduce their body temperature. Stand the bottle in a bowl or pan of hot water. After a few minutes, take the bottle out of the hot water, shake it and then put it back. Take it out again a few minutes later and shake once more. Alternatively, use a bottle warmer for the amount of time recommended by the manufacturer.

Always test the temperature of the liquid before giving it to your baby. Do this by dripping some onto the inside of your wrist – it should be body temperature and therefore should feel neither cold nor warm. If it is too still too cold, repeat the above steps. If it is too hot, hold the bottle under a cold running tap or stand in a bowl of cold water and recheck the temperature a few minutes later.

## How to give a bottle

You need to find a comfortable, supported place to sit and your baby needs to be held in a reclined sitting position (i.e. more upright than they would be if breastfeeding). Hold them on your lap, cradled in the crook of your arm, you will both enjoy the closeness. Brush the teat against your baby's mouth to encourage them to open wide, and then allow them to draw the teat in. Hold the bottle at an angle, so that the liquid always fills the teat, otherwise they will be taking on air (see Box, p.83). Also listen for signs of air being taken in from the side of the teat and adjust the position of the bottle if necessary. Babies can feed more quickly from

### Average volumes for formula-feeds

As a general rule, babies require more volume of infant formula than they do of breast milk – typically 150–180 ml per kilogram of their bodyweight per 24 hours.

For example, by the end of the first week, a 3 kg baby will consume between 450 ml (i.e. 150 ml x 3) and 540 ml (i.e. 180 ml x 3) per 24 hours. Divide this volume by the number of feeds in 24 hours (usually six to eight) and this will give you a rough guide as to the volume a baby will consume at each feed. Add an extra 30 ml to the volume in case your baby is having a growth spurt and suddenly requires more feed, and to ensure that the teat is always filled with liquid.

As your baby grows, so does the volume of feed that they need. For example, a three-month-old baby may need five or six feeds each of 150–180 ml, a four-month-old the same number but with increased volume of 210–240 ml. Once you start weaning your baby, they will need less formula (see Chapter 5).

Some babies are hungrier than others. Note also that your baby will not always take the same amount at each feed. This is normal and often balances itself out by the end of the day.

a bottle than from the breast, so take some breaks in the feed so that you can help them to bring up wind (see p.65 for winding techniques).

## Mixed feeding

Some mothers feed their babies with both breast milk and formula, a method known as 'mixed feeding'. This practice can be done in various ways to suit you both. For example, you could breastfeed for one feed and give formula the next, or breastfeed during the day and give formula at night. Bear in mind that if you are not exclusively breastfeeding, your milk supply will be affected, and so you will still need to breastfeed or express regularly to make sure that your baby's nutritional needs are being met.

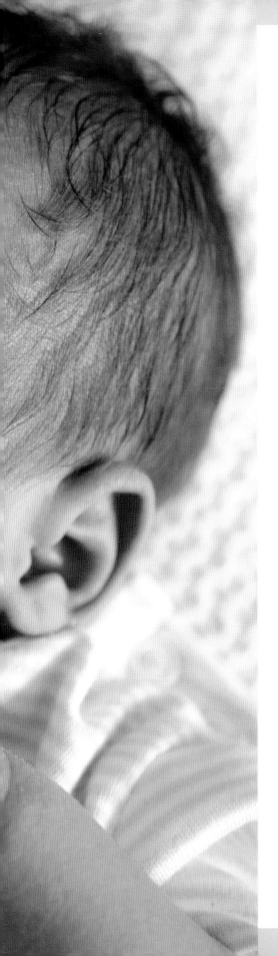

# Sleep

Sleep is essential to
well-being, so it is important
for both you and your baby.
Understanding your baby's
sleep requirements will give
some stability and structure
to your days and nights,
allowing you both to get
the rest you need.

# What is sleep?

We still have so much to learn about sleep, but we do understand the different stages of sleep that need to occur in order to feel refreshed. These are similar for babies as for adults, the main difference being that babies need more hours of sleep and some have to learn how to get to sleep by themselves.

Sleep is required for normal development and for the ability to function properly. In fact, it is just as important as food. More specifically, when people sleep, the following processes occur:

- hormones are released, enabling tissue repair, muscle growth and the regulation of appetite
- the immune system is strengthened
- the brain processes events and memory and concentration are improved
- energy is restored to the body.

Poor sleep can affect mood, concentration and energy levels. Good-quality sleep therefore enables your baby to thrive and you to cope with the challenges of looking after them. We do not really know why babies need so much sleep, but we assume it is because they are going through such rapid growth and brain development.

## Types of sleep
There are two types of sleep: rapid eye movement (REM) and non-rapid eye movement (NREM).

### REM sleep
Sometimes termed 'dream sleep', REM sleep occurs when the eye's movement is rapid but most other muscles in the body are paralysed. You may see your baby's eyes moving beneath the closed lid and their breathing pattern can also quicken.

### NREM sleep
Little eye movement occurs in NREM sleep. Dreaming is rare and the muscles of the body are free to move (hence, people can 'sleepwalk'). NREM can be further divided into three stages:

- **N1:** light sleep; your baby is just drifting off and still wakes easily.
- **N2:** a slightly deeper state; your baby is more difficult to wake.
- **N3:** the deepest sleep, also known as 'slow-wave' or 'delta sleep'; your baby may be totally unresponsive to stimuli.

About half of the sleep of a newborn is REM sleep. By the time they are five years old, children spend just over two hours in REM sleep.

## The sleep cycle
Sleep proceeds in cycles throughout the night, with each cycle consisting of three stages of NREM sleep and one stage of REM. Usually, once sleep is established, there are four or five cycles over the course of the night, each of 90–110 minutes. There tends to be more deep sleep (N3) in the early part of the night and more REM sleep before waking in the morning (see Chart opposite). Although we tend in go up and down in the depth of our sleep in a step-by-step way, it is random as to whether we get lighter or deeper in our sleep at each step.

The light sleep (N1) stage is when babies are most likely to wake up rather than progress to deeper sleep and another sleep cycle. When this occurs in the middle of the night, we as adults know to roll over and go back to sleep again. However, babies do not always naturally do this and, when they no longer need to feed at night, this can often be the reason that they wake up again and again.

## How much sleep do babies need?
Children need more sleep than adults. However, just like adults, one may differ from another in the exact

## Typical sleep pattern of a newborn

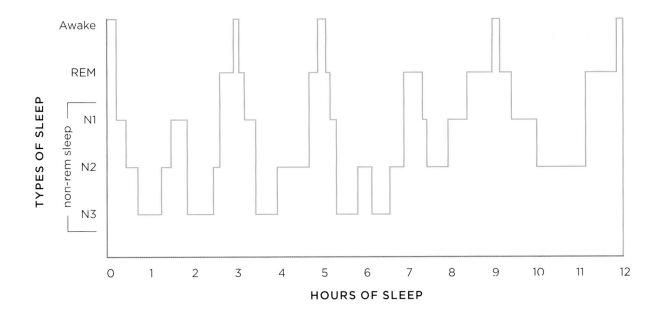

TYPES OF SLEEP

non-rem sleep

Awake

REM

N1

N2

N3

HOURS OF SLEEP

0  1  2  3  4  5  6  7  8  9  10  11  12

amount of sleep they need. For example, some babies sleep through the night for ten hours from the age of six weeks, while others never sleep for more than eight hours in one go; smaller and premature babies need more sleep than average-weight or full-term ones. It is therefore important that you do not compare your baby's sleeping with that of others, as all babies are different. Nevertheless, it is possible to make some generalisations about the amount and nature of a baby's sleep.

### Newborns to three months
On average, newborn babies will sleep for between sixteen to twenty hours per day, broken up into a series of short naps and longer sleeps split equally between day and night. They are unlikely to sleep for more than three or four hours in one stretch (their small stomach means they fill up easily and therefore need to spread their feeding over 24 hours) and rarely stay awake for more than two hours at a time. Babies will spend more time in REM sleep than in NREM sleep and this light sleeping state can be easily disturbed.

Over these first three months, the overall amount of sleep needed will gradually decrease

by two or three hours, the daytime naps will become shorter and less frequent and the length of the night-time sleep will increase (although babies will continue to wake at night to feed).

### Three to six months
Some babies will be sleeping for ten or eleven hours at night, with two or three separate naps during the day. At three months, they may still wake up once or twice in the night for feeds, but by six months they should be sleeping through the night.

### Six to nine months
As babies grow, they need less and less sleep and by six months they will be sleeping for only about fifteen hours in total. They may need only two naps during the day and should be sleeping for eleven or twelve hours at night.

### Nine to twelve months
By now, a baby may need only fourteen hours of sleep in total. They may just have one long sleep after lunch or, if this is not enough for them, a short nap in the morning as well. At night they may sleep for eleven to twelve hours at a stretch.

# Getting into good habits

Establishing sensible practices from the beginning may help avoid some common sleep problems and will ensure that you are doing all you can to keep your baby safe and well-rested.

## What you need

✓ Moses basket/crib and mattress (optional)

✓ Cot/cot bed and mattress

✓ 3 cotton sheets to fit chosen size of bed

✓ 2 cotton cellular blankets to fit chosen size of bed

✓ Baby sleeping bag (optional)

✓ Baby monitor

✓ Curtains or blinds to reduce the light

✓ Night-light (optional)

The primary safety concerns are to keep your sleeping baby at the right temperature and to ensure that air can fully circulate around them – a very young baby can overheat and is not able to move their head away from anything that has fallen on them. Teaching your baby about the rituals of sleep plays a large part in helping them to settle themselves, both at the start of their sleep and if they happen to wake during the sleep cycle.

### The sleep environment

Although the aim is for your baby to learn how to get themselves to sleep in a variety of environments (see Box, p.97), the night-time sleep hormone, melatonin, is triggered by darkness. So, the room in which your baby is put to sleep at night should be darkened by curtains or a blind. When you need to attend to your baby in the night, using a dim night-light will help to maintain the night-time atmosphere.

The recommended temperature for a baby's room is around 18°C. At this temperature, a cotton sheet and two cellular blankets, which trap heat, should be enough to ensure that they are warm. You could consider a baby sleeping bag as an alternative. These are particularly useful when your baby gets more mobile and is able to kick blankets off or roll over and get in a tangle – both actions may result in your baby waking up. Make sure you use the size that is appropriate to your baby's age and that is a suitable tog – 2.5 tog is generally recommended for standard conditions.

Babies are unable to control their temperature and can easily overheat or get too cold. Ideally, they should be dressed for bed in a vest, nappy and sleepsuit. Do not put a hat on them, as an uncovered head is an important way for them to lose heat if they are overheating. If you find your baby becomes too hot, remove a blanket; if their hands and/or toes are cool and tinged with blue, you can add an extra layer (in either instance, recheck them twenty minutes later to see that they are comfortable).

The cot should not be near a radiator or a sunny window, because this increases the likelihood of overheating; in addition, curtain tie-backs and blind cords are a strangulation hazard. It is recommended that your baby's cot is as clutter-free as possible. This means no pillows, duvets or toys, which could cover their face. Cot bumpers should also be avoided, as these trap heat and can be used to climb on when your baby becomes more mobile.

Toys in the cot are not only a hazard, but may also encourage your baby to play; similarly, mobiles above the cot can be a distraction and keep your baby awake.

## Sleeping with your baby

Current thinking is that you should have your baby in your room until they are six months old. This provides reassurance for you, allowing you to hear if your baby gets into difficulty. There are three main options for sleeping in the same room as your baby:

- a separate Moses basket/crib/cot in the room
- sleeping alongside your baby (made possible with recent modifications in cot design)
- co-sleeping (sharing a bed).

### A separate cot

Your baby can sleep in a full-sized cot from birth, as long as you place them with their feet at the end of the cot (see Feature overleaf). A cot will last until your baby is about two years old and ready to go into a proper bed. Not every bedroom can accommodate a full-size cot as well as a double bed so, if you are finding it a bit of a squeeze, use a Moses basket or crib for the first few months. Moses baskets have the advantage of being light and very portable, so that you can keep your sleeping baby close to you wherever you are in your home. A Moses basket will last until your baby is about two months, a crib for possibly up to four. When your baby has outgrown this bed, consider moving a piece of your bedroom furniture to another room for a short while to give you space to install the full-size cot.

### Sleeping alongside

A bedside cot with a side that lowers completely allows you to sleep alongside to your baby and touch them without moving from your own bed. Sleeping close to your baby means you are both likely to get more sleep, and reduces the risks posed when your baby shares a bed with you (see below). It can also make breastfeeding easier if you have had a Caesarean section, as you do not have to twist so much or carry your baby far.

### Co-sleeping

Sharing your own bed with your baby is known as 'co-sleeping'. Around half of all mothers in UK co-sleep with their babies at some point. However, there are times when it can be dangerous to do so:

- you and/or your partner are smokers (even if you never smoke in bed or at home), have been drinking alcohol, take medication or drugs that make you drowsy or are feeling very tired
- your baby was born before 37 weeks (i.e. was premature)
- your baby weighed less than 2.5 kg at birth.

Currently, you are strongly advised against co-sleeping with your baby because of the risk of smothering them (see also the Feature on Sudden Infant Death Syndrome overleaf). If you are keen on co-bedding, take some precautions to make things as safe as possible. First, you must ensure that the mattress is firm, so your baby is not enveloped by it, and that they will not be accidentally covered by the bedding or pillows, which may cause them to suffocate or overheat. Your baby must not be able to fall out of bed or get trapped between the bed and the wall, nor should they be sleeping next to other children. If you are sharing the bed with

*If you have been given a second-hand cot, invest in a new mattress, as a previously used one will have moulded to another baby's shape and may not offer your baby the best spine support.*

# Sudden Infant Death Syndrome

Sudden Infant Death Syndrome (SIDS), also known as 'cot death', is the sudden, unexpected and unexplained death of an apparently well baby. This is a very emotive and difficult issue and, although a lot of research has been done in this area, the answers to why some babies and infants suddenly die without any warning are not always there. Here is a summary of the findings from the research and what this means for you and your baby.

One in 3000 infants dies suddenly and unexpectedly without an obvious cause – this is only 300 babies per year in the UK, so the risk that it will happen to your baby is extremely small. SIDS usually occurs between two and four months and while your baby is sleeping in their cot at night. It can also happen when they are asleep during the day, as well as, rarely, when they are awake. SIDS is more common in the winter months, in boys, in premature babies, in babies whose parents smoke, in a baby whose sibling has died of SIDS, in babies who sleep on their fronts and in babies who sleep in their parents' beds.

Smoking is one of the greatest risk factors for SIDS. If you smoked between one and nine cigarettes a day during your pregnancy, the risk of SIDS will have increased by four times compared to not smoking. When your baby is exposed to a smoky environment after birth, the risk increases by nine times compared to babies who are not exposed to smoke. If you or your partner is a smoker, consider getting help to give up, as this can make a huge difference to both your own and your baby's health. Your midwife, health visitor or GP should be able to tell you what support is on offer in your local area. It takes a lot of will power and determination, but the health benefits to you and your family are huge. Regardless of whether you or your partner smoke, do not let anyone smoke in the same room as your baby and do not wear smoky clothes around them if you have been in a smoking environment yourself. To reduce further the chances of SIDS:

- always put your baby on their back to sleep
- place your baby with their feet to the bottom of the cot, with the bedding well tucked in and no higher than their armpits; or use a baby sleeping bag
- do not let your baby get too hot and keep your baby's head uncovered while they are asleep
- never fall asleep with your baby in a chair or on the sofa, as you may drop or roll over onto them
- if you are co-sleeping (i.e. they are in your bed), good safety advice needs to be adhered to (see p.91)
- breastfeed if possible, as this has been shown to slightly lower the risk of SIDS
- consider using a dummy for the first few weeks, as research suggests this may have a positive effect on the reduction of SIDS
- if swaddling your baby (see Feature overleaf), use a light material only.

While you should always place them to sleep on their back, please do not worry if your baby rolls onto their stomach later on. If they are able to roll over like this, they will also be able to move themselves if they are getting too hot. See Useful Resources for further information about safe sleeping and SIDS.

your partner, they need to be aware that the baby is in bed – this is particularly important for when you bring your baby into the bed when your partner is asleep. Finally, always place your baby on their back to sleep.

## Teaching babies the difference between night and day

Babies begin to differentiate night from day within the first two to three weeks and there are a number of ways in which you can help your baby to understand the difference. During the day, play with and talk to them as much as possible, make feeding social, surround them with everyday noises, create a light and bright home and wake them if they fall asleep during a feed. At night-time, have a pre-sleep routine (see below), stay quiet and calm when feeding and keep lights and other noises/stimulation low.

By three months, your baby's daytime sleeps become shorter and night-time sleep is longer. However, this sleep pattern can also be affected by exposure to daylight. Some research shows that time spent in daylight, especially in the afternoons, will help babies sleep longer at night.

## Recognising the signs of sleepiness

Babies (like adults) can become overtired. When overtired, the body's response is to release hormones (e.g. cortisol, adrenaline) to fight fatigue, and this can make it difficult to relax, settle down and stay asleep. Babies also tend to wake up earlier if they went to bed overtired and irritable.

You will come to recognise when your baby is starting to get tired and should go to bed. Signs of tiredness include:

- yawning
- crying/whining/becoming irritable
- nodding off
- becoming quiet and still
- staring into space
- rubbing their eyes
- pulling their earlobes or twizzling a lock of hair (older babies).

If you spot any of these signals, you know that it is time to put your baby down to sleep.

## Establishing a bedtime routine

We all benefit from winding down at the end of the day and, just like you, your baby will find it easier to settle if they know what is coming next. A series of relaxing steps will soothe your baby and prepare them for sleep. These can include:

- a calm/quiet game
- a bath and/or a massage
- changing into sleepwear
- saying goodnight to everyone
- a story
- a lullaby and a goodnight kiss.

Whatever works for you is fine, but try to keep your activities to the bathroom and bedroom, rather than going into other areas of your home.

### Baby monitors

Monitors allow you to hear (and some versions allow you to see) your baby when you are not in the same room as them. Some models come with a thermometer to measure the room temperature, a range of songs and nursery rhymes to settle your baby and the facility for two-way communication. Advanced types can send a video relay to your smartphone.

If you are able to hear your baby cry from the room that they are put to sleep in you do not really need a monitor. Monitors accentuate the entirely normal small noises and cries that all babies make in their sleep – ones that do not require your attention. If you are aware of all these noises, you may be tempted to keep checking on your baby. This may prevent them from learning to settle themselves or even cause them to wake up properly, and you could end up picking them up for a cuddle or feeding them when they really did not need either! However, a monitor can be useful for peace of mind during the daytime and for the evening when you are out of earshot, as your baby's louder, persistent cries do need a response.

The important thing is that you carry out the routine at the same time – and stick to the same pattern (whenever possible) – every night. Do not leave it too late in the evening to go through these steps or your baby will become overtired and will find it harder to settle.

## Letting your baby settle themselves

Throughout the ages, parents have rocked, soothed and patted their babies to sleep. However, if this is routinely done at every bedtime, babies come to associate this activity with falling asleep, which can become a problem if they will not settle without it. I fell into this trap with my daughter, who for many months would not go to sleep without being patted on the back. This became difficult to sustain and there are many other examples of babies needing to be comforted for hours each night to get in order to sleep. Such associations are particularly problematic when your baby wakes during the night and is unable to get themselves back to sleep without your assistance.

At one to two months old, you can begin to teach your baby how to settle themselves to sleep. The best way to do this is to introduce a regular bedtime routine (see p.93) and to put them to bed when they are sleepy but still awake. Leaving your baby to settle themselves can be hard at first, particularly if they cry a little, but once they have become used to the environment – and provided you stick to your own particular bedtime rituals – they will soon learn that this is a cue for them to go to sleep on their own. See also pp.99–102 for how to deal with common sleep problems.

# Swaddling

Swaddling – wrapping babies securely in fabric – is believed to go back as far as the ancient Greeks and Romans. It is thought that it gives babies a feeling of security by mimicking the experience of being in the womb and is also considered to induce sleep and minimise colic. There has been a recent trend for swaddling, increasing the demand for special swaddling clothes by about 60 per cent. However, the practice is not without controversy and there is also a range of differing advice from midwives, nursery nurses and doctors. No wonder it is hard to know the right thing to do!

The principle reason that swaddling hit the headlines is an article in a British paediatric journal by Professor Nicholas Clarke, a consultant orthopaedic surgeon and professor at the University of Southampton. He wrote that, for the hips to develop properly, the legs need to be able to bend up and out at the hips. Tight swaddling extends and presses the legs together, forcing the hips of a baby into a straightened position. This can lead to a condition called developmental dysplasia of the hip (DDH).

DDH occurs when the bones of the hip joints are not aligned correctly. This prevents the hips from developing in the right way, which can lead to difficulties with walking when children are older and early hip replacement in later life. Checking for the condition forms part of your baby's routine neonatal assessment (see Chapter 1, p.14), with a simple test that involves moving the legs of your baby, while feeling over their hips. If a 'click' is detected, this may indicate that the hips are not fully in the joint and this will need to be confirmed by ultrasound scan. Twenty per cent of babies are born with mild DDH, which resolves of its own accord. However, tight swaddling puts these already weakened joints under pressure and may interfere with the body's ability to repair itself. It may also cause this mild version to progress to severe DDH. Professor Clarke also noted that an education programme in Japan advising against swaddling saw the prevalence of DDH halve.

Other orthopaedic and paediatric specialists endorse Professor Clarke's research, adding that in countries such as Nigeria, where women carry their babies with their legs splayed around their waist, DDH is extremely rare. For this reason, baby carriers or slings that support this 'frog' position are thought to be more beneficial than those that leave the legs dangling straight down and unsupported.

The Royal College of Midwives has given advice not to swaddle your baby, but supports parents from cultures where it is the norm by giving information about safe practices (e.g. allowing the baby to have some movement in the swaddle). The Lullaby Trust, a charity which advises on safe sleeping and conducts research into Sudden Infant Death Syndrome (see Box, p.92), points out there are other risks from swaddling your baby, such as overheating. They add that you must not put your baby on their stomach while swaddled. If you do swaddle your baby, their advice is to use a thin material and not to cover your baby's head at any point.

So where does that leave us? I feel that loose swaddling definitely has a role to play in soothing and settling a baby and, provided their legs are free to move into a 'frog' position and the material is sufficiently lightweight to prevent overheating, their development will not be harmed.

# Managing life and sleep

Whether you are a stickler for routine or are happy with a 'go-with-the-flow' approach, being aware of the broad sleeping patterns of babies in the first year will help you maximise the time you have for other things.

You may not be able – or even want – to arrange everything around your baby and their sleep patterns. Events, siblings and day-to-day life are some of the reasons we often have to improvise. If you are the sort of person who prefers structure, try not to worry about this: simply go back to your normal routine the following day; if you are not in a routine, the odd disruption is unlikely to bother either you or your baby.

To some degree, your ability to manage your life and your baby's sleep will depend on your baby. I remember my first baby would sleep anywhere – including in a noisy coffee shop! – whereas my second baby did not enjoy sleep in the same way, needing to be in a calm environment. Either way, you will still want to go out to the shops, meet friends and so on at a time that may not particularly suit your baby, so flexibility is vital. I suggest that you try to allow your baby to sleep when they need to, but recognise that this does not always have to be in their bed at home (see Box opposite). Be mindful, however, that when you move your baby to a different place after they have fallen asleep, they may sense a change in their surroundings, causing them to fully wake up in the lighter stages of the sleep cycle.

In the first year, a baby's sleeping pattern is closely interlinked with feeding. For instance, a baby who is not feeding enough in the day will naturally wake more at night. You may want to consult the chapters on Feeding and Weaning in order to consider sleep and food in tandem, before working out the most appropriate sleep pattern for your baby.

I should say upfront that the sleeping patterns outlined below and in the Chart overleaf are only a guide. As I mentioned before, all babies are different, so you may have to adapt certain elements so that they are more suitable for your little one. Similarly, if you have other family commitments (e.g. you have to pick your partner up from the station at 6.30pm, another child has a playgroup in the early afternoon), you will need a different bedtime and nap times from the ones I have suggested.

You will also notice that your baby may be in an established sleeping pattern one minute, then, due to illness or any other change from the norm, the pattern is suddenly disrupted (e.g. they nap more during the day and wake more during the night). It is not worth trying to keep to normal timings when they are ill. I do recommend, however, that you try to stick to the same bedtime routine to give you the best chance of settling your baby.

If you find that things are going awry for no apparent reason, be patient and logical. Patterns and routines can usually be reinstated if that is what

> Rigid sleep schedules do not always give you freedom or flexibility and may cause you stress and anxiety if you or your baby are not able to stick to them.

you want, but may require minor adjustments. For example, if your baby is starting to wake up earlier and earlier each morning, you may want to cut short one or two of the daytime naps. In all cases, however, do what feels natural and works for you and your family.

## Newborn to three months

Newborn babies initially spend most of their time asleep and their wakings are dictated by hunger. After each feed, they may stay awake for a short time before going back to sleep (or sometimes fall asleep while feeding!). During those early days you will be establishing a feeding pattern too, whether it be with breast milk or formula, so your baby will be feeding frequently throughout the day and night. This may be as much as every two hours (timings are taken from the beginning of the last feed). The first week of this can be very tough, so try to nap at the same time as your baby if you can. It is difficult to develop a sleep routine at this stage, so it is probably best to leave your baby to sleep as much as they need to, while you get to know them and understand their requirements.

After a couple of weeks, your baby will be able to stay awake for slightly longer periods and you may find that the gaps between feeds also become longer. From five to eight weeks old your baby may only need three naps a day (one or two of these may be in the pushchair or car seat if you are out and about), and the naps become consolidated and begin to follow more of a pattern. Roughly, this consists of a nap of about an hour in the morning, an after-lunch nap of about two to two-and-a-half hours and a short late-afternoon nap of about half an hour to get them through to bedtime. This allows a bedtime routine to start at 6–6.30pm and for them to go to bed at about 7pm. The aim is to have them sleeping through from 7pm (waking them up for a late feed at about 10pm) to about 7am the next day by twelve weeks.

## Three to six months

Babies usually drop one of their daytime naps (usually the late afternoon one) in the three-to-six month period and you may find that you have to bring forward their bedtime for a while in order to avoid overtiredness. However, as the weeks pass, you can begin to gradually push it back again. At three months, your baby may still need a late evening feed, but you should work towards dropping this as time progresses. By the time babies are ready to be weaned at six months, most are sleeping through the night for at least ten or eleven hours. Your baby will become increasingly active in their sleep, and may wake themselves up as they move around the cot. Try not to dash straight to them (not always easy when they are sleeping in the same room) – given a little time, they may settle themselves again.

### Napping anywhere

If you have a busy life or have older children, you will not want to be tied to the house for your baby's daytime naps. In order to achieve this flexibility, it can be very helpful if, right from the word go, you have your newborn sleeping wherever you happen to be in the house. Try to vary what they are sleeping in (as long as they are safe and secure), for example, the pram, Moses basket, bouncing seat or your arms. If you are chatting, watching television, cooking or doing any number of other things at the time, your baby will learn to sleep in a busy environment from the start.

From about a month old, it is a good idea to let your baby have some of their daytime naps in the pram or car seat. They will then get used to being able to sleep when you are out and about, which will make shopping, visiting friends, going on holiday and so on much easier. However, try to avoid moving your baby from cot to pram/car seat and vice versa while they are asleep, as the change in their environment may cause them to wake. Also make sure they get a proper rest in their bed at night. As they grow, you may want to limit this napping strategy to their shortest daytime nap only, making sure that their longer one – and certainly their night-time sleep – is somewhere quiet.

## Sleeping patterns for the first year

| AGE | TOTAL SLEEP PER 24 HOURS | NAP TIMES |
|---|---|---|
| Newborn–4 weeks | 16–20 hours, with a maximum of 4 hours at a stretch | As and when, frequently throughout day and night |
| 1–2 months | 14–17 hours, with two wakings for a feed at night | **Three naps:**<br>• mid-morning (approx. 1 hour)<br>• after lunch (2–2.5 hours)<br>• late afternoon (short) |
| 3–6 months | 14–17 hours; 10–11 hours at night, with one or two wakings for a feed at night | **Two/three naps:**<br>• mid-morning (short)<br>• after lunch (2–2.5 hours)<br>• possible very short nap in late afternoon |
| 6–9 months | 15 hours; 11–12 hours without waking at night | **Two naps:**<br>• mid-morning (short)<br>• after lunch (2–2.5 hours) |
| 9–12 months | 14 hours; 11–12 hours without waking at night | **One/two naps:**<br>• after lunch (2–3 hours)<br>• possible very short nap in mid-morning |

### Six to nine months

Babies who have still needed three naps up to now will probably drop one. Two naps per day – usually a short nap in the morning and a longer one after lunch – will give you even greater flexibility to get on with life. Babies of this age can wake up due to separation anxiety: they miss you, worry that you are not there and that you will not come back. Teething can also cause disturbed sleep during this stage, and sometimes even earlier (see Chapter 6, p.142). They should have worked out how to settle themselves, but if not, do not worry – see pp.104–5 for suggestions on how to help your child learn how to get to sleep.

### Nine to twelve months

Your baby may no longer need a morning sleep or be satisfied with just a short catnap in the pushchair or car seat. This could mean that the lunchtime nap becomes slightly longer and it may be better for this to be in their cot at home to allow for a thorough rest. Try to resist cutting back on the daytime naps too much: the aim is for your baby to sleep well at night and not become overtired. If you are going back to work after maternity leave, you may want to gradually adjust the timings of your baby's sleep, so that they are up slightly later in the evenings to allow you some time with them.

# Common sleep problems

As many as 40 per cent of children experience sleep problems at some point in their childhood. Nights of disturbed sleep can be challenging for parents and will also impact on your baby's well-being if they are left to continue indefinitely. However, there are some ways to help solve a number of common sleep issues.

I should add that perceptions of what constitutes a 'problem' are subjective. If you are happy to spend ten minutes rocking or singing your baby to sleep, after which they sleep through the night without disturbances, then do not let other people tell you that you have a problem. Conversely, healthcare professionals are unlikely to consider that a very young baby who 'only' sleeps for five hours at a time at night has any sort of problem at all! Remember that no advice is failsafe and it may just be a case of riding out the particular behaviour until your baby has reached another stage in their development.

## Persuading your baby to have a daytime nap

Some babies seem to survive on very little daytime sleep. If your baby is sleeping well at night and seems happy and rested on short naps or even none at all during the day then you do not need to worry: this is simply normal for your baby – although perhaps a little frustrating for you, as you do not have so much time during the day to get on with other bits and pieces! However, if your baby seems irritated and unsettled during the day, you may need to help them settle for a nap. This is not always easy, but here are a few ideas to try.

### Having a naptime routine

To all intents and purposes, the naptime routine is a shortened version of the bedtime routine outlined on pp.93–4. Create a calm environment, feed in a dimly lit room with minimal stimulation, give your little one a cuddle to settle them after the feed and then put them down to sleep while they are drowsy. With luck, they will begin to know that this is their cue to sleep.

### A stage-by-stage approach

Working towards the end goal of a daytime nap in stages can be very successful, especially if you are not keen on controlled crying (see pp.104–5). However, you may need the patience of a saint and to accept that, initially, the end aim is all you want to achieve, no matter how! So, if your baby needs rocking or pushing in their buggy in order to sleep, this is what you need to do for the length of time you want them to nap. Once you have done this successfully for a few days and your baby is getting used to sleeping during the day, you need to move on to the next stage: to have them sleeping in their bed. Again, this might mean that you help them by patting their tummy, humming a lullaby or stroking their head. Gradually, you can try to reduce the time that you doing this and, slowly, slowly, you will get what you want: a baby that naps on their own during the day!

### Getting tough

If you do not have the required patience or simply do not have the time for a staged approach, you can try either the 'gradual withdrawal' or the 'controlled crying' sleep-training technique. A tougher stance is not for the faint hearted: you need to be very sure that you can be consistent and that this effort for a daytime nap is really worth it.

## Difficulty getting to sleep in the evening

The principle reasons that babies find it difficult to settle in the evenings are three-fold: they are overtired; they have had too much sleep in the daytime and are not tired enough; they do not like being separated from you. Advice therefore varies according to the particular circumstances.

### Overtiredness

As discussed earlier, it is a mistake to significantly reduce the daytime naps in the hope that it will make it easier for your baby to sleep at night. Try reinstating a short nap in the late afternoon for a time, while also making the other daytimes naps earlier to compensate. Make sure that the last sleep in the day is not too close to bedtime or for too long, as this may have the opposite effect: they may now not settle because they are not tired enough!

Alternatively, ask yourself if your baby's bedtime is actually too late for them. It may suit your family schedule, but if you are missing your baby's sleep cues, you may have to rethink your routine, at least until they are a little older.

### Not being tired enough

First, think about whether your baby's bedtime is at a sensible time (i.e. not too early) – a rule of thumb is 7–7.30pm – and whether they have had enough activity in the day to stimulate them, particularly in the afternoon. Try having a short activity time just before the bedtime routine begins (but take care not to overexcite your baby). Use a bedtime routine as described on pp.93–4, keeping the room quiet and dimly lit. Give your baby a chance to settle on their own, perhaps with some soothing music to go to sleep to. Employ some of the settling methods, such as loose swaddling or a dummy.

> Do not be tempted to let your baby 'sleep in' after a disturbed night in order to catch up on rest, as this will have an impact on the daytime naps, which in turn will affect the next night's sleep.

If your baby still resists sleep after you have consistently applied the above approach, look at the overall number of hours they are sleeping. Has this inadvertently crept up, either because you have been out and about or using the time at home to catch up on outstanding tasks? If you are satisfied that the amount of sleep is fine, you may want to try moving the lunchtime sleep a little earlier in the day or gradually reducing the length of the morning nap. If all else fails, it could be that your baby just needs less sleep than others or is a 'night owl'. Remember, though, that you baby still needs to have some sleep in the daytime or they will become overtired.

### Missing you

Babies who are used to their mothers being around when they go to sleep can find it hard to adjust to a more formal bedtime. If you want to change this, start by moving slightly further away from their cot each time until eventually you are able to leave the room before they fall asleep. Although you are still a presence in the room, keep eye contact and engagement to a minimum. This process of gradual withdrawal will help ensure that there are no feelings of abandonment. See also the section on teaching your baby to sleep, pp.104–5.

### Night-time waking

It is totally normal in the first few months for your baby to be waking repeatedly at night to feed, but once your baby is three months old they should be able to manage a good stint throughout the night, provided they have had a feed at around 10pm. When hunger is no longer the cause, a baby may wake because:

- they are too hot or too cold (more often cold, as their temperature drops in the middle of the night)
- they are thirsty
- their nappy is dirty
- they want a hug.

If they seem to have no physical needs, you may need to help them to settle by gently putting your hand on them or speaking to them in a low voice to reassure them that you are there. Try not to pick them up or feed them, otherwise they will associate crying in the night with cuddles and food and you may find it really hard to get them back in the cot to sleep. From about six months, you may want to start to teach your baby that they can settle themselves back to sleep, using the more stringent measures described on pp.104–5.

## Inconsistent sleep patterns

Your baby was sleeping beautifully and now they have gone back to waking in the night. What is going wrong? I am sorry to say that this can be normal: babies do not always do what the books say! Just because your baby was sleeping through the night does not mean that this will be an every-night event.

For example, your baby may sleep perfectly for a few weeks, regress for a while, then just as suddenly, start sleeping through again. It is important not to change the things that were working for you when they were sleeping through. Continue with your bedtime routine and do not be tempted into thinking that they are now waking for food – if they had been sleeping through the night, are still feeding well through the day and are putting on weight, they do not suddenly need a midnight feast! In all likelihood, this inconsistent sleep behaviour is a blip in their normal pattern and you simply need to get through it until they go back to sleeping through the night. However, certain things can upset a regular sleeping pattern and to help to clarify whether there might be a particular reason, ask yourself the following questions:

- Has your baby's daily routine been disturbed (e.g. are you staying with friends or family and in unfamiliar surroundings)?
- Are they unwell or teething?
- Are they afraid of the dark or seem alarmed in another way (e.g. a nightmare)?

Sleeping patterns are often disrupted by these sorts of events. Survive as best you can and, once they are better or your circumstances are back to normal, your baby will probably get back into their

*Keep a sleep diary to see if there is a pattern to your baby's wakefulness. At the very least, it may help you to see that the interruptions are not as often as you think they are!*

old pattern with a little help and guidance from you. Nightmares are not common in children until they become toddlers. All you can do is to reassure them that all is well and help them to go back to sleep in their own bed.

## Early waking

Babies commonly seem to think that the day starts far earlier than you think it should! Some babies are simply 'early birds' and need less sleep. Sometimes there is very little that you can do about this, but the following measures may help:

- cut down the daytime naps (either the number or the length, depending on what works best for you)
- gradually make their bedtime later, by up to an hour – do this in stages so they can adjust and not get overtired
- hang blackout blinds or thick curtains to block out the early sunrise
- leave them to see if they settle.

Failing this, if you are sure that they are fully awake but you really need more shut-eye, put a board book or small, hand-held toy in their cot (without giving them too much eye contact or stimulation), go back to bed yourself and hope that they amuse themselves for a while.

### The 'wake-to-sleep' method

A more structured approach to solving the early waking problem is the 'wake-to-sleep' method. However, you need to be feeling brave for this one! I have no experience with this technique personally, but friends have said that it worked for them. The idea is that you set your alarm to one hour before the usual time that your baby wakes. For example, your baby is waking at 5am, so set your alarm for 4am. Go to your baby to try to wake them – not fully, but enough to rouse them. Then let them settle themselves back to sleep, while you go back to bed yourself. You may find that this causes your baby to sleep through their normal 5am wake-up, finally rousing to start the day at a much more reasonable time. By continuing to do this for four or five nights, you may break the habit entirely.

### Standing up in the cot

At around nine months, babies become increasingly mobile and are able to pull themselves to standing using furniture, known as 'cruising' (see Chapter 6, p.135). Babies love to haul themselves up on the cot bars, but until they know how to get down again, it can cause problems after you have put your baby to bed. The best way to deal with this is to teach them how to lower themselves down in the daytime. However, at night, simply pop them back down again yourself and leave the room as quickly as possible – make the movement efficient and purposeful, rather than incorporating a cuddle. Repeat as often as needed until your baby falls asleep. If your baby resists, do not struggle with them. Just step away and either wait for a short time or come back a little later.

# Flat head syndrome

Some babies develop a flat head in the first few months and one of the causes is from lying on their back while asleep. There are two main types of flat head:

- **plagiocephaly:** one side is flattened, which causes the head to look asymmetrical
- **brachycephaly:** the back of the head is flattened and the face can appear wider

Some babies are born with a congenital torticollis, which means that their ability to turn their neck is limited. This can also lead to plagiocephaly, as their head is turned or angled more to one side. Another cause of a flat head is craniosynostosis, a rare condition but very serious condition caused when two or more of the sections of the skull fuse together early and are unable to grow and develop normally, leading to an asymmetrical head – this is corrected with surgery.

Premature babies often have altered head shapes, as they may have spent many weeks lying on their back or side in an incubator. This corrects as they grow and spend more time in other positions. Usually, the flattening of the skull is a mild, cosmetic issue and does not cause any problems with a baby's development. Severe cases of flat head will become more moderate over time and when the hair grows thicker and the skull increases in size, the flattened area will become less obvious.

In some instances, a baby with a flattened head will also have a preference for the direction they have their head turned. This may be the effect of gravity making their head fall frequently to the flattened side, with the result that the baby becomes more accustomed to looking that way. Over time this can lead to a shortening of the neck muscles on the side towards which the baby usually looks, and the child can then lose the ability to look all the way to the other side. This is known as an 'acquired torticollis'. It is important that you monitor this and some of the advice below will help you to prevent this from occurring.

Babies do need to sleep on their backs, as this significantly reduces their risk of SIDS (see Feature on p.92), but when they are awake you can alter their position. They can spend time in your arms, in a sling or baby carrier and on their stomach (see also the Feature on 'Tummy Time' in Chapter 6, p.136); when they are older they can sit up supporting themselves. If your baby has already developed a flat head, it may take six to eight weeks of employing these practices for you to notice a change. If you have any concerns regarding your baby's head shape or head-turning preference, you should ask to see a paediatric physiotherapist, who will advise a positioning and exercise programme.

You could also try using a helmet and skull band (cranial orthoses), which aim to reduce pressure on the flattened area and to put pressure on areas of bone that bulge out. However, these are fairly expensive (they are not available on the NHS) and there is limited evidence to show exactly how effective they are. Helmets or bands are used on babies between six to twelve months old, when the skull is growing at its fastest. Your baby needs to wear the device for up to 23 hours per day for between six weeks and six months, and it must be resized every six weeks to allow for normal growth and to prevent sores. Helmets and bands can be uncomfortable and hot, especially in the summer months, but some parents have reported very successful results.

# Teaching your baby to sleep

Some babies are not natural sleepers and or go through periods of very disturbed sleep when all normal measures for settling are not working. In these instances, they may have to be taught or to relearn how to settle themselves to sleep. There are many different ideas and strategies as to how to do this.

Sleep training provokes different reactions from parents, essentially because most involve leaving your baby to 'cry it out'. Some hate the idea of leaving a baby to cry and think that it is verging on barbaric to do so. Others take a deep breath and give it a good deal of thought, often as a last resort for getting their baby to sleep through the night. I am not going to comment on the rights and wrongs of sleep training, except to say that constant interruptions at night are exhausting and likely to be unsustainable; the same applies for a baby who will not sleep without you.

If you decide to give sleep training a go, you need to feel comfortable with whichever particular method you are about to embark on. Make sure you have got a few clear nights in the diary ahead of you – success will not happen overnight. Once you have started upon a plan, be prepared to continue with it in a consistent fashion, rather than trying it for the odd night here and there.

Sleep training is all well and good in theory, I hear you say, but what if it does not work? A word of caution: there is no 'magic wand' or 'money back guarantee' with any sleep-training method, although they are definitely worth a try. However, if the strategies outlined below have no effect on your baby's sleeping, seek help via your health visitor or GP, as they may be able to tailor-make a plan to suit your particular case or discover an underlying medical issue that may be affecting your baby's sleep. In addition, there are support organisations that can put you in touch with specially trained sleep practitioners (see Useful Resources).

## Gradual withdrawal

It may be worth beginning with the gentlest sleep training approach. Put your baby in their cot while they are still awake and try to settle them with minimal stimulation (e.g. patting their tummy, stroking their head, humming a lullaby). Keep lights and sounds low. Once they have stopped crying, try to leave the room. If your baby starts to cry again, go back and settle them again and continue this cycle until they have fallen asleep. The key to this approach is to avoid picking them up to comfort them: it is important that you leave them in their cot. As one friend said, 'You don't want them to have the "I've just woken up in the night and need a hug syndrome"'.

## Controlled crying

Another way to help your baby to sleep is to gradually increase the interval of time before you go to settle them. This technique is known as

> No matter how frustrated you feel at your baby's wakings, try to stay calm. Your tension will only make it harder for them to go back to sleep.

## Top Tips

Accept that nothing can really prepare you for the sleep deprivation caused by having a young baby, but that it is a stage that will pass.

When sleep-training, keep in mind that you are helping your baby to learn how to get themselves to sleep – an important skill that they will need for the rest of their lives.

Take turns with your partner in dealing with your baby in the night. If they protest that they have to go to work the next day, let them know that a long day spent looking after a tired baby is no picnic either!

Be wary of keeping your baby up for longer in the day in order to encourage them to sleep through the night. This causes overtiredness, which will actually make it harder for them to settle at bedtime.

'controlled crying'. It is not recommended for babies under six months and you must make sure before you start that your baby is well and not suffering from reflux, colic or any other condition that might cause them to cry when they are lying on their back (see Chapter 8, pp.180 and 175 for further information on reflux and colic).

Using a clock to help you keep time, leave your baby to cry for five minutes before you go to settle them. On the second night, leave them for ten minutes, then continue increasing the gap by five minutes on each subsequent night. Again, resist the urge to pick your baby up or interact with them (it is very hard not to crack when going in for the umpteenth time!), as you may give your baby the message that the harder and longer they cry, the more likely it is that you will pick them up. Remember that, unless your baby is ill, most crying is normal (see Chapter 2, p.42).

It can be distressing for you as a parent to know that you are deliberately leaving your baby to cry, so if this methods sounds too traumatic, some experts suggest that you modify the approach by helping your baby to sleep by rocking or nursing, while still increasing the time intervals. The theory is that your baby will create positive associations with going to sleep. However, the downside is that it can be difficult subsequently for your baby to settle themselves, which, after all, is the ultimate goal.

### The goal-orientated approach

If either of the above methods feels like too much of a leap, you could adopt a goal-focused, stage-by-stage approach, similar to what is described on p.99 for encouraging daytime naps. The aim is first to establish the *habit* of sleep before moving on to where and how your baby falls asleep. So, Goal 1 is to get them to sleep, either for the first time in the evening or after they have awakened in the night. For a few nights you can do anything it takes: feeding, cuddling, rocking, even having them in bed with you (provided you are practising safe co-bedding). Be careful not to make any of these a 'fun' experience. Once they are good at going to sleep, you need to work towards Goal 2, which is for them to settle in their own cot. Put them down in their cot while they are drowsy but still awake or, if they have woken in the night, let them stay in their cot. Pat, stroke or otherwise comfort them, but do not pick them up. The theory is that because they now are used to going to sleep, they should be able to settle in their own cot with you as their constant factor. When this practice is successful it is time to move on to Goal 3, which is for them to settle themselves to sleep in their own cot without any help from you. Start by reducing the amount of comforting while they are in their cot. Perhaps go in and pat their tummy a few times, then leave them to do the rest themselves or follow the method of 'gradual withdrawal' described above. Continue reducing the comfort you give until you are able to simply wish them goodnight and leave the room.

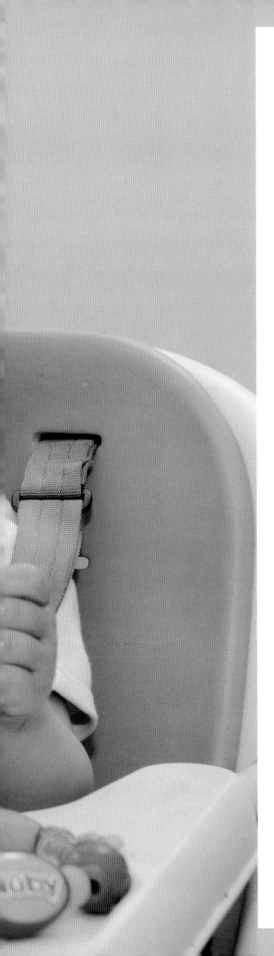

# 5

# Weaning

About halfway through their first year, babies start to require more nutrition than that provided by breast milk or formula alone. Introducing your baby to solid food – known as weaning – begins to complement their liquid diet. By the end of the first year, nearly all your baby's nutrition comes from solid food.

# When to wean

Until the age of six months, your baby gets all the nutrients they need from breast milk and/or formula. Between six and nine months, babies start to need additional nutrients from other souces, although breast milk/formula still continues to be an important part of their diet.

Initially, solid food is an addition to, not a substitute for, milk/formula. At this stage, weaning is mostly about getting your baby used to the different technique needed for eating solid food and exposing them to different tastes, textures and consistencies. However, from nine months onwards, babies really start to absorb the nutrients from what they eat and so solid food becomes an ever more significant part of their diet. Consequently, the milk volume they drink gradually starts to decrease and, by the end of their first year, your baby will be eating three meals a day, with a couple of snacks in between.

### When should weaning start?
The World Health Organisation and the Department of Health recommend introducing solid foods to your baby at around six months (26 weeks). You may start earlier than this and you can wean your baby at around four months. There is an ongoing debate about the ideal age to wean, mainly because each baby has slightly different needs. The important thing is not to feel pressured into weaning until you feel it is right for your baby and their developmental needs.

However, there are good reasons for not weaning much later than six months. By this time, a baby's iron reserves can become low and may require supplementation from other food sources. In addition, babies have greater requirements for protein, thiamine, niacin, vitamins B and B12, magnesium, zinc, sodium and chloride. Older babies can also occasionally have difficulty accepting solid foods and struggle to move on to lumpy food.

Weaning before four months is not recommended, as a baby's intestines and kidneys are still immature at this stage and not designed to cope with anything other than breast milk or formula. The right time to wean a baby born prematurely needs to be discussed with your health visitor, GP or a dietician.

### Signs that your baby is ready
While six months is the recommended age for weaning, you nevertheless should recognise your baby's individual needs. Signs that your baby is ready to be weaned include:

- needing extra milk/formula feed and/or seeming hungry a short time after good quantities of milk/formula
- not sleeping as well as they did, possibly waking at night when they had previously been sleeping through
- showing interest in the things you are eating and even trying to help themselves
- bringing things to their mouth and possibly chewing
- mimicking you when you eat (e.g. opening their mouth)
- teething.

If your baby is displaying this behaviour – and provided they can hold their head up well and sit stably with or without support (e.g. using pillows or cushions to prop them up) – you may want to begin the process of weaning.

# Healthy eating

Although ready-made baby food is widely available, many choose to give home-made food to their baby.

While jars of food are undoubtedly convenient at times, it is often better to make your own. It is cheaper, particularly if you batch cook, and fewer nutrients are lost in the cooking process. The textures of ready-made baby food are uniform and the tastes bland, which may delay your baby's transition to home food. Commercially prepared foods often have a high water content and contain additives. In addition, there are very few 'single' flavours available – these are the ideal ones to start weaning with, as it makes it easier to detect whether your baby has an allergy or intolerance to a particular food (see pp.122–3).

## The basis of a good diet
A healthy diet for babies is much the same as it is for adults; it should contain proteins, fats, carbohydrates, fibre and vitamins and minerals from a wide variety of sources. Remember not to let your personal likes and dislikes affect what foods you offer your baby. Weaning is also a good opportunity to review the diet of the whole family – in the not-too-distant future your baby will be eating many of the same meals as you.

### Bread, cereal, rice, noodles, potatoes, pasta
Carbohydrates and starchy foods are a great source of energy and fibre. Try to use wholemeal products and keep the skins on potatoes, as they are high in vitamins and minerals.

### Fruit and vegetables
We are advised to eat five portions of fruit and vegetables per day. These can be fresh, tinned, dried or frozen and can be drunk (e.g. juice, smoothies) as well as eaten (raw or cooked). This food group is high in vitamins and minerals. Try to offer your baby the 'colours of the rainbow' every day – something red, orange, yellow and so on – as this will ensure they get the variety of nutrients they require for growth and general health.

### Meat, fish, eggs, beans, nuts, pulses
Protein is vital for growth and development. Lean read meat is a great source of iron and will help to replenish your baby's iron stores (see also Box overleaf). Animal products are not the only source of protein: beans, tofu and pulses are all excellent providers, too.

### Dairy products
The dairy food group provides fat, protein and calcium. Calcium (together with vitamin D, the 'sunshine' vitamin) is vital for the growth and development of teeth and bones. Milk, cheese and yogurt are ideal sources.

## Vitamin supplements
The Department of Health recommends that all children from the ages of six months to five years are given an additional supplement of vitamins A, C and D. This is because it is sometimes difficult to get everything the body needs through the diet alone. The exception to this is if your baby is consuming at least 500 ml of formula per day (formula has these vitamins within its mixture) or has a good, varied diet and is exposed to sufficient sunlight. Supplements can be bought over-the-counter, but you maybe entitled to free vitamin drops – check with your health visitor. Only give the stated dose, as too much of certain vitamins can be harmful; also check the contents of any other supplements you are giving your baby so that you do not double up (e.g. cod liver oil also contains vitamins A and D).

### Fats

Babies grow very quickly and need lots of calories to fuel this rapid development. Fats are an excellent source of energy. Not all fats are 'bad'; some have an important role in transporting vitamins A, D, E and K throughout the body.

Essential fatty acids are unsaturated fats and must be obtained from the diet, as the body cannot make them. The two that are required by the human body are omega 3 and omega 6. Omega 3 is important for the brain, eyes and skin. It is found in oily fish such as salmon, herring, sardines, mackerel, halibut and tuna; boys can have up to four portions of oily fish per week, whereas girls need only two. Omega 3 is also present in shellfish, hemp seed, soya oil, sunflower and pumpkin seeds, leafy green vegetables and walnuts, and is often one of the things added to fortified eggs, drinks and cereals. The body needs omega 6 for many reasons (e.g. maintaining brain and nerve functions, building healthy cells). Good sources are palm oil, soya beans, rapeseed and sunflower seeds.

### Vegetarian and vegan babies

Many parents choose not to eat meat and to bring their baby up on a similar diet. When making this decision, it is particularly important to ensure your baby obtains enough iron, protein, calcium, zinc, omega 3 and vitamin B12 and to research the best way to ensure absorption of nutrients. For example, the body needs bile salts to absorb vitamin A; fat is essential for the production of bile salts. So, when serving orange and green vegetables (which are good sources of vitamin A) you could lightly fry them in vegetable oil or add them to an omelette.

Foods that are dense in the essential nutrients mentioned above include milk, cheese, well-cooked eggs and yeast extract. However, vitamin B12 does not occur naturally in non-animal forms, so a fortified adult breakfast cereal or an infant vitamin supplement may be necessary. Zinc is particularly important for the immune system and cell growth and repair and is present in high levels in soybeans, cashews, sunflower seeds, beans, whole grains and nuts. Iron is contained in pulses (particularly lentils), chickpeas, beans, leafy green vegetables (e.g. broccoli, spinach) and dried fruit (e.g. apricots,

### The importance of iron

Iron is particularly crucial for babies, as it enables good growth and development. The body is able to store iron for a period of time, but by six months, your baby's stores are extremely low and need to be topped up. It is more difficult for babies to absorb iron from vegetable sources than from meat (where it is present in high levels), but vitamin C helps absorption, so try to give your baby foods rich in this vitamin (e.g. citrus fruit, tomatoes, strawberries) at the same time as the iron source; conversely, calcium, zinc and magnesium diminish absorption. Good sources of iron are: meat (especially lean red meat), fortified breakfast cereals, dark green leafy vegetables, bread, wholegrains (e.g. brown rice), beans and lentils, dried fruit and soya bean flour.

figs, raisins, sultanas, prunes), fortified cereals (check for low salt and low sugar varieties) and egg yolks. Iron absorption is enhanced by vitamin C (see Box), so make sure you also include this at the same meal. Protein can be obtained through fish, pasteurised dairy products and well-cooked eggs (if your diet permits), as well as tofu, lentils, beans and chickpeas. Try to vary the type of dairy you give and limit the amount of cheese, which has a high salt content. Two or three portions of vegetable proteins or nuts per day will be needed to ensure your baby has enough protein and iron. However, do not give whole nuts, as your baby could choke (see Box, p.115) – grind them finely or use smooth nut butter instead.

Too much fibre in a baby's diet can cause digestive problems and may also inhibit the absorption of iron and other nutrients, so only serve moderate amounts of brown rice and wholemeal pasta.

Most vegetarian and vegan parents have a very good understanding of nutrition. If you are unsure how to provide these nutrients when weaning your baby, seek advice from your GP or a nutritionist.

# Getting started

You will need to have a few pieces of equipment in order to feed your baby with ease. In addition, understanding how to prepare and store food safely will ensure you getting weaning off to a good start.

## What you need

✓ High chair
✓ Portable baby seat (optional)
✓ Bibs
✓ Plastic floor mat (optional)
✓ Bowls and weaning spoons
✓ Training cups
✓ Infant cutlery
✓ Food processor or blender
✓ Steamer
✓ Ice cube trays
✓ Freezer bags, containers and pen

## Kitchen hygiene and food safety

It is really important to prepare the food for your baby in a clean area and to know how to store it safely, as babies are vulnerable to bacteria and infections. Always start by washing your hands with soap and wiping the surfaces that you are going to prepare the food on. Wash fruit and vegetables thoroughly, ensuring you get rid of any soil, and remove seeds or anything that could cause choking (see Box, p.115). Do not prepare raw meat or fish near other food to avoid cross contamination; use a different chopping board and wash your hands and equipment (e.g. knives) thoroughly before moving on to prepare fruit and vegetables.

After the meal, throw away any left over food rather than keeping it for the next meal, as saliva from your baby's mouth will have contaminated the food and means that bacteria is more likely to grow.

## How to make puréed baby food

Unless you are following the baby-led method of weaning (see overleaf), you will need to make special puréed food to feed to your baby. Initially, you should prepare your baby's food separately from your own, both for consistency and also for nutritional reasons – adult food can contain too much sugar and salt and, as a rule, babies need more fat and less fibre than we do.

You are spoilt for choice when it comes to baby food recipes: there are many books on the subject and you will also find a plethora of recipes on the internet (see Useful Resources). In general, try to use the freshest ingredients available and, if you can, steam or bake the fruit and vegetables instead of boiling them. This keeps more of the vitamins and minerals in the food and afterwards you can use the water from the steamer for making a stock or thinning purées (see below). Although it is true that vegetables need to be soft, beware of overcooking them, as this will also reduce their nutritional content – the food should retain both its colour and structure. Bake fish in foil then flake it off, taking care to remove any bones, and cook beef or chicken in your usual way, then shred it. Remember to add more fat than you would if you were cooking for yourself and never to add any salt or sugar (see Box overleaf).

## Getting the right consistency

Once the food has been cooked so that it is soft, make it into a purée using a food blender/processor or sieve. You may need to add water (cooled boiled water if under six months, tap water if older) or

## A word about salt and sugar

Salt is present in very small quantities in most foods and plays a part in the healthy functioning of the human body. However, until the age of two, your baby's kidneys are not mature enough to cope with too much salt in the diet. In addition, consuming high levels of salt can cause health problems in later life (e.g. high blood pressure leading to heart disease, osteoporosis, kidney disease). For this reason, you should never add salt to your baby's food to give it flavour. Babies of between six and twelve months should have no more than 1 g of salt per day, one- to two-year-olds 2 g per day. Salt can be listed on food labels as sodium (Na). To work out how much salt is in a particular food, multiply the sodium value by 2.5. For example, if there is 1 g of sodium in a food, this equates to 2.5 g of salt.

Similarly, there are many foods that are naturally high in sugar (complex carbohydrates) and that are important for your diet, fruit and vegetables being the obvious examples. However, excessive sugar in your baby's diet will damage the enamel of their teeth, causing decay, and may contribute to their developing type 2 diabetes. It can also cause disruptive behaviour in older children and is linked to heart disease in later life. In addition, large amounts of sugary foods and drinks can lead to obesity. When checking food labels, bear in mind that sugar is often listed as carbohydrate; it can also be called fruit syrup, glucose, dextrose or sucrose. Low-sugar foods have less than 5 g (one teaspoon) of sugar per 100 g of the food.

Homemade meals can be sweetened naturally with food such as carrots or sweet potatoes and, after one year, honey. Offer your baby sugar that is natural rather than refined, as the latter is depleted in vitamins and minerals. Also avoid food that contains artificial sweeteners (e.g. aspartame), as these may cause digestive problems. Try not to ban sugary food completely, as this may make it more desirable to your child. Instead, teach good eating practices, such as having a small amount of sweet food at the end of a meal.

breast milk/formula to achieve the appropriate thickness – initially, about one part food to five parts liquid to so that it is the consistency of runny yogurt. In fact, it is a misnomer to call these first foods 'solids', as they are extremely liquid! As your baby gets more used to the food, you can gradually add less liquid and leave in more lumps. By the end of your baby's first year, they can eat food that has just been chopped up with a knife.

### Freezing and defrosting

As your baby will only eat very small amounts, it will save you a lot of time if you make larger amounts of food in one go and freeze it in batches for later use. First let the cooked food cool to room temperature, then transfer into a container. Ice cube trays filled with purées of single flavours are ideal to start with (use about half a tablespoon in each section) and, once the contents have frozen, you can tip the cubes into an airtight freezer bag and return to the freezer in order to free up the tray for the next batch. Then you can take out cubes of different food to mix together for your baby's next meal. Alternatively, you can freeze ready-mixed food in meal-size portions in larger containers.

Food expands when it freezes, so only fill the containers to about two-thirds full. Do not forget to label the bags/containers with their contents and the date you made it. Food can be stored at –18°C or below for up to six weeks – you can freeze for up to twelve weeks, but it will not retain so many nutrients and may lose some of its taste and colour.

Once removed from the freezer, food should be stored in the fridge, be used within 24 hours and never be refrozen. Avoid defrosting for long periods of time at room temperature. If you have time, defrost in the fridge for four hours before a meal; otherwise submerge the container in hot water to defrost for immediate use. After defrosting, heat the food until it is hot throughout the dish, stir thoroughly to make sure there are no hot spots (particularly if you have heated it up in the microwave) and then cool to the right temperature for your baby to eat.

# Feeding your baby

There are two principal methods of introducing solid food to your baby: puréed food and baby-led weaning. You do not need to prescribe to just one method – many parents find that a bit of both works well. Whichever way you choose, by the end of their first year your baby will have progressed from very simple foods to eating the same sort of meals as you do.

## Puréed food

The concept of weaning that most of us are already familiar with is the one in which you feed your baby puréed food from a spoon. Many parents feel comfortable with this method, as it allows them to monitor how much food their baby is eating and there is generally less waste and mess. Remember that, if you are starting to wean earlier than six months (but ideally not before four months), all feeding equipment (e.g. bowls, spoons) needs to be sterilised and any water added needs to be boiled before use.

Put a small amount of warmed food on the baby spoon – over-filling will make things more messy! – and brush it against your baby's top lip. This may cause them to open their mouth and, if so, place the spoon in the mouth and tip the food out by lifting the spoon upwards as you withdraw it. Your baby's top lip will also help to transfer the food as you remove the spoon. Wait until they have swallowed the food, then offer another spoonful. Go slowly at first while your baby gets used to the sensation.

Do not be put off if your baby pulls a funny face. They are just getting used to the new sensation and taste, so persevere by offering another spoonful. Equally, they may get upset when you do not offer them more quickly enough! Be prepared for your baby to spit out some food – this is not a sign that they do not like it, but more that they are using their tongue to move the food around in their mouth and may push the food out by mistake.

## Baby-led weaning

Another method of weaning is one that encourages babies to feed themselves 'finger food' at a pace that suits them. This is known as 'baby-led weaning' (BLW). It differs from the other method described in that there is no puréeing and no spoon-feeding by parents. At the heart of the philosophy are two elements: babies eat what they like and stop when they have had enough. Because BLW is started at six months (rather than between four and six months), babies can cope with lumps, as the tongue-thrust reflex is less pronounced (see Box overleaf) and they can chew food in their gums. As a result, the purée stage can be bypassed. For many parents, BLW is the natural extension of breastfeeding, where the baby feeds as often as they want, taking as much milk as they need. In fact, breastfed babies are perfectly suited to this method of weaning, as they have already been exposed to different flavours through the breast milk, which changes depending on the food you eat. BLW may, however, be an unsuitable for premature babies, who often need extra nutrients and who may, at six months, lack the physical

### Taste sensations

Taste buds are situated all over the tongue and detect the five elements of taste sensation; salty, sour, bitter, sweet and savoury. Contrary to popular belief, taste buds are not divided into different regions on the tongue – in fact, the various tastes can be detected by any area of the tongue.

development needed to feed themselves – discuss with your health visitor first, who may advise you to wait until your baby is age-adjusted six months (see feature on Prematurity in Chapter 6, p.129).

People who use the BLW method feel that their baby integrates with their family mealtimes easily. They also find it easier to get out and about, because they are not limited by having to feed their baby themselves; in fact, those with other children or busy working lives often find that they follow this approach by accident!

The principle of BLW is not to put the food into your baby's mouth, but instead to place it in front of your baby and let them help themselves. You can just put it on the high chair tray, as a bowl is likely to be played with or flung off. Your baby will start by picking up the food, putting it into their mouth and exploring the textures and flavours. If your baby does not have teeth, they will chew the food with their gums, and they may spit it out until they can coordinate swallowing. Babies may take only a few mouthfuls at first, chewing the top off what

they are holding in their hand; for example, they will hold a broccoli floret like a bunch of flowers and just eat the head. They eventually build up to eating substantial amounts of food, especially as they

Weaning should be a positive experience for you and your baby, so pick a time in the day rather than the evening to start, so that neither of you is too tired.

## Gagging and choking

It is important to follow some simple practices to ensure that your baby is weaned safely. Many parents are concerned and upset when their babies gag: this is a reflex that is triggered when food (or another object) goes too far back in the mouth. Babies can go bright red in the face, their eyes start to water, and they open their mouth wide and dribble and spit or cough out the food; they then breath faster than normal and sometimes start to cry. However, gagging is a natural process – it enables babies to try food and not choke. Your baby will naturally push the object to the front of their mouth with their tongue before spitting it out (this is known as the tongue-thrust, or extrusion, reflex). Gagging happens only once or twice for some babies; for others, it happens at every meal. Try to stay calm, as your baby will look to you for reassurance and may need encouragement to persevere with more food.

Choking is different from gagging: it occurs when an object blocks or partially blocks the airway so that breathing is compromised. This rarely happens in babies, but it is dangerous and must always be dealt with promptly by following basic first aid techniques for removing the blockage and, possibly, restarting breathing (see Chapter 8, pp.170–1). To reduce the risk of gagging and choking:

- supervise your baby at all times when eating and ensure they are sitting upright, not reclined
- offer only small amounts of food at a time so that they do not put too much in their mouth at once
- avoid foods that may block the windpipe (e.g. whole grapes).

become increasingly dexterous and can open their hand to push food into their mouth. Once they develop a good pincer grip (at between nine and twelve months), they can pick up quite small pieces of food. When weaned in this manner, babies quickly move on to using a spoon and other cutlery, as they are already used to feeding themselves.

### What to give

There are some who say that you should make your baby's first foods vegetables rather than fruit, as they may develop a sweet tooth and therefore not want to eat vegetables when they are older. However, there is no real evidence to support this.

Suggestions for food are given in the Chart on pp.120–1. It is important to introduce one food at a time and continue with it for three days. This is so that you can determine that there are no allergic reactions or sensitivities – it helps to give it in the morning, so that you can observe any changes in your baby. Move on to another food for three days until you have several that can be combined during the same meal to offer mixed flavours rather than just one. When your baby is enjoying one meal per day, move on to two meals, giving a tried-and-

tested food at the second meal, as you know there will not be a reaction to this food.

After a month or so you can make more elaborate purées. Use starchy carbohydrates as a base and combine with vegetables and meat or fish in an approximate ratio of three parts vegetable to one part meat/fish. To add flavour, blend together with some sautéed onion or leek and herbs. Alternatively, use stock made with the water from cooked vegetables or one from a salt-free infant stock cube. Your baby's mealtime can now include a pudding of fruit after their savoury main course. This may consist of one tablespoon/two ice cubes of puréed fruit in a mix of flavours; or you can make sticks of these fruits as finger food if you are using the BLW method.

During the period between seven and nine months, you will be increasing your baby's intake of solid food so that they are having up to three meals per day, with three to four tablespoons of food per meal. Try to offer them foods from all the food groups at each meal.

By nine to ten months the swallowing mechanism has matured and the tongue-thrust reflex (see Box above) is nearly gone. Between nine and twelve months, the finger-pinch mechanism becomes well developed, allowing your baby to pick things up using the thumb and index finger. These features mean that, if you have been using the purée method, your baby can now start to enjoy 'finger food' (see below). Main meals can now be mashed or chopped rather than blended, so that it is coarser and contains soft chunks. At this point, you may want to introduce cutlery, so that your baby can practise feeding themselves. If you have been following the BLW method, they will move on to the same food as you are eating during this stage (but with no added salt and sugar), making meal times much easier in terms of preparation for you.

By the end of the first year, the two weaning methods will have merged, as your spoon-fed baby becomes more adept at feeding themselves. Your baby should be having three meals a day (with pudding) and two snacks; milk becomes secondary to the food and, if you have been using formula, you can now replace it with cow's milk. Your baby's swallowing is much better coordinated, although they have yet to grow molar teeth, so they still use their front teeth to bite and their gums to chew.

Your baby's daily food intake should now be in the following proportions:

- three or four servings of carbohydrates (rice, bread, potato)
- five servings of fruit/vegetables
- two servings of protein (meat, fish, eggs, pulses).

*If your baby starts to grab the spoon you are feeding them with, offer them another spoon to hold so that they feel in control.*

## Top Tips

Keep the atmosphere calm and relaxed: if you are anxious about food rejection and waste, you could communicate this to your baby, leading to battles when they are older.

Try to think of your role as offering nutritiously balanced food in a way that looks appetising. Your baby will then determine how much they want to eat (this will undoubtedly vary from day to day).

When your baby is able to feed themselves finger food, only put a couple of pieces of food on the tray at a time to start with, so that they do not feel overwhelmed.

Beware of making yourself a slave to recipes. While you want to give your baby a variety of interesting flavours, it is all too easy to spend hours in the kitchen knocking up a fantastic meal, only for your baby to reject it entirely!

Try to make eating social: let your baby join in family mealtimes, but if it is just the two of you, chat to them while they are eating.

### Snacks and finger foods
Your baby can be given snacks to eat between meals and these should be things that they can feed themselves: 'finger food' (e.g. strips of toast, soft fruit, cooked sticks of harder fruit or vegetables), sandwiches, pasta, yogurt, dried fruit, homemade biscuits, pieces of cheese, rice cakes, bread sticks. It is always a good idea to have some snack food with you when you are away from home between meals in case your baby becomes hungry. Make sure you give a drink of water at the same time to avoid constipation.

### Milk and water
Breast milk/formula is an important part of your baby's diet throughout the first year. Although full-fat cow's milk can be given from one year, it does

## Constipation and nappy rash

Once you introduce solid food, your baby's poo may change colour and become more solid and smelly. You could also find some undigested food in the nappy (e.g. raisins, fruit skins), particularly if you are following the baby-led weaning method, as your baby may swallow the food without much chewing to start with and the gut is still not mature enough to digest this properly.

It is very common for babies to become constipated when being weaned. Many babies appear to strain when they poo, even if it is the normal consistency (they may have started doing this before you introduced solid foods). This is not constipation and we do not know why they do this (although one theory is that they actually enjoy pooing!). Constipation is defined as hard, pellet-like poos. See also Chapter 2, pp.34–5.

To avoid constipation make sure you are not giving too big a portion of solid food and that your baby is drinking enough liquid by monitoring their breast milk/formula intake and by offering them water in a training cup with their meal. If they still become constipated, cut out the food that you think may be causing it (e.g. bananas, cheese) and try adding prunes, more fruit and vegetables or watered-down prune juice in their diet. Avoid giving more fibre, the gut cannot cope with too much at this stage. Once the constipation has resolved, slowly reintroduce small portions of the foods that may have caused the problem. You will need to continue to monitor your baby's nappy, changing their diet according to the consistency.

Some babies develop nappy rash when they start solid foods. This may be because the pH of the poo changes and it irritates the baby's skin. Change your baby's nappy as soon as you become aware that they have done a poo, so the skin is in contact to the poo for as short a time as possible, and follow the measures outlined in Chapter 2, p.35 for treating nappy rash.

not contain enough iron or other nutrients for under-ones. Once you start weaning, you will find that your baby will want less milk/formula; they may even drop a feed completely. Conversely, if you give them too much milk/formula, they will not want food. So, there is a balance to be made.

Until seven months, feed your baby the same amount of breast milk or formula that you gave them prior to introducing solid foods. At seven to nine months, give a daily intake of 500–800 ml of breast milk/formula spread over about four feeds; at nine to twelve months, reduce this to a daily amount of 450–700 ml in approximately three feeds. By one year, babies can still drink as much as 600 ml per day, although formula can now be substituted with full-fat cow's milk. Bear in mind that this amount includes what you mix with food and that breastfed babies may have more feeds in the day than this, depending on their feeding pattern before weaning.

It is important to introduce a drink of water from an infant cup when you begin weaning onto solid food. This will reduce the chances of constipation (see Box above). It will also get your baby used to the idea of giving themselves a drink, which will help when they become mobile and increasingly thirsty. A cup will enable them to drink greater volumes – by one year, they should be drinking at least two cups of water per day. After six months you do not need to boil water – they can be given tap water to drink (provided the levels of sodium are below 10 mg per litre). Avoid bottled water, as it can contain high levels of sodium.

It is not necessary to give any juice or flavoured drinks unless recommended by your baby's doctor. Getting them used to water at an early age creates healthy habits for when they are older. If your baby is constipated or you would like to introduce juice, it should be watered down to ensure it is mostly water – at least five parts water to one part juice.

### Signs of being full

Whichever method you choose, a really important part of weaning is to let your baby determine how much food they want to eat. Babies have an in-built ability to stop eating when they are full and encouraging them to follow this prevents over-eating and obesity both in childhood and in later life. When your baby has had enough food, they may turn their heads away from the food, push the spoon away if you are feeding them, play with the food or take it into their mouth and spit it out. The purposeful dropping of food on the floor usually happens from nine or ten months and this can become a game to them. Before this age, it is usually another sign that they have had enough.

### Signs of needing more food

Every baby will have a different appetite. If your baby becomes upset when the food is finished or follows you and the empty bowl with their eyes, try offering just a little more. If they are looking

for much larger amounts than this at the beginning, try feeding their milk/formula before the solid food – you want to avoid filling your baby up with so much solid food that they become too full to drink their milk. Too much solid food when your baby is young can also lead to constipation.

### Fussy eating

It is not uncommon for babies to be eating well and then suddenly refuse to eat. Usually this is because they are not feeling very well (e.g. they are getting a cold), are teething or something in their environment has changed (e.g. they are on a family holiday, you have returned to work). The best strategy is to not force your baby to eat: try to follow their lead and do not insist on their eating the amount you think they need – let them 'tell' you when they have had enough, even if they have only had a small meal, by looking for signs of being full. Sometimes, babies will eat lots for a few days and then hardly anything for the next few days, so it may be more helpful for you to consider their food intake over the course of the whole week, rather than focusing on what they have in just one day or even one meal.

Too much food presented at one time can be overwhelming. While there must be a mixture of foods within each meal, show it to your baby in stages, offering them no more than two different foods at a time. Also, putting a smaller portion of these foods into their bowl may help. You can always top it up with another small amount if they finish everything.

If the fussiness continues and they turn their head away when you offer the spoon or push food onto the floor, it could be that they have been having the same type of food for too long and are bored. Try to keep their meals varied.

Whatever their mealtime behaviour, remember no baby has ever starved themselves: in all likelihood, their fussiness and lack of appetite is just a temporary phase. However, if you are concerned that this is carrying on too long, see your health visitor or GP.

## What NOT to feed your baby

The following foods are not recommended for babies under one year:

- sugary puddings, ice cream, shop-bought biscuits, sweets
- adult ready-meals and 'fast foods' – these contain high levels of salt
- tea and coffee – these contain caffeine, which is a diuretic and inhibits iron absorption
- whole nuts, whole fruits containing stones (e.g. plums, cherries) – a choking hazard
- honey – this can (rarely) contain a bacteria that causes food poisoning (botulism) in babies under one; after this, the gut is mature enough to prevent bacteria growing
- cow's, sheep's or goat's milk as a drink – these do not contain the balance of nutrients your baby needs; however, after six months they can be mixed with food
- liver pate – risk of too much vitamin A
- raw or undercooked eggs – risk of salmonella
- raw shellfish – risk of food poisoning
- shark, marlin and swordfish – these contain high levels of mercury
- foods high in saturated fat
- low-fat or low-calorie foods.

## Suggested feeding plan for the first year

| AGE | MILK/FORMULA | MEALS PER DAY | SNACKS |
| --- | --- | --- | --- |
| **6–7 months** | As per pre-weaning pattern | 1–2 (1–2 tbsp of food per meal) | None |
| **7–9 months** | 500–800 ml, 4 times per day (incl. mixed with food); cow's milk can be used in cooking | Up to 3, incl. pudding (3–4 tbsp of food per meal) | None |
| **9–12 months** | 450–700 ml, 3 times per day | 3, incl. pudding | 1 or 2 per day of finger foods |
| **12+ months** | Milk now secondary to food, but still up to 600 ml per day; can be breast milk or cow's milk – formula no longer necessary | 3, incl. pudding | 2 per day of finger foods |

| TYPE OF FOOD | CONSISTENCY |
|---|---|
| **Purées:** sweet potato, butternut squash, pear, apple, baby cereal/rice<br><br>**BLW:** broccoli/cauliflower florets, carrots, sweet potato, parsnips, courgettes, baby corn, pears, apples, bananas, melon, papaya, avocado, cucumber, peppers, fusilli pasta | **Purées:** very smooth and watery/milky<br><br>**BLW:** soft, raw sticks or cooked chunks |
| As above, plus fish, meat, pasteurised dairy products (yogurt, cheese, cottage cheese), low salt/sugar cereals; fruit (mango, pear, papaya, peach, apricot, apple), eggs (well-cooked) from 8 months<br><br>**Purées:** cod, pollock, haddock, hake, lean braised beef, chicken, minced beef/lamb, lentils, carrots, peas, courgette, spinach, cauliflower, broccoli, parsnips<br><br>**BLW:** chicken, meat, fish, polenta sticks, homemade fish cakes, strips of homemade pizza, French toast, pancakes, dips, raisins, peas, rice | **Purées:** thicker and lumpier, combining flavours<br><br>**BLW:** large pieces of slightly harder foods; small pieces of food |
| Meals such as spaghetti Bolognese, fish pie, casseroles with rice, fruit crumbles | **Purées:** mashed not blended (coarser with soft chunks), small pieces of food<br><br>**BLW:** the same food you eat, but with no added sugar or salt |
| As above; can introduce honey | **Purées and BLW:** the same food you eat, but with no added sugar or salt |

# Food allergies

Careful introduction of foods and monitoring ones known to cause problems in your family will help identify if your baby has a particular allergy or intolerance.

### Allergy or intolerance?

Though often confused in common usage, allergies and intolerances are different things. An allergy is an immediate, hypersensitive response of the immune system to a substance (e.g. a type of food, a bee sting, antibiotics). More common is an intolerance, which is much milder and may take time to manifest itself. For example, a baby who has an intolerance will be uncomfortable when they are given the offending food, may be gassy and possibly have diarrhoea. By contrast, a baby with a food allergy may suffer an immediate rash, swelling or difficulty in breathing and will need medical attention straight away.

The symptoms of an allergy or intolerance can be varied and will depend on the area of the body affected. The things to look out for are:

- diarrhoea (watery and sometimes bloody stools)
- vomiting after food has been eaten
- a rash
- wheezing/shortness of breath
- a runny nose (clear, watery mucus)
- sneezing and/or coughing
- red, itchy, watery eyes
- swelling of the face and lips
- anaphylaxis; rare, but needing medical help, ideally at a paediatric A&E.

Sometimes it is difficult to associate your baby's symptoms with a specific allergy/intolerance, as the reactions are shared with a number of illnesses (e.g. the common cold). However, infections such as these tend to produce green or yellow mucus and be accompanied by a raised temperature. If your baby is regularly displaying one or more of the above symptoms and does not have a fever, they could be suffering from an allergy/intolerance.

### Identifying the cause

Isolating the particular food that you suspect is causing your baby's symptoms is often a difficult and painstaking process. The most effective way is to remove one food for a few days to see if the symptoms disappear. If there is no change, you can reintroduce it and move on to another food. If you do notice an improvement in your baby's symptoms, you can check this by giving the suspected food to them once more, carefully monitoring for a return of the same reactions. Bear in mind that intolerance to several foods is not uncommon. If you have tried a number of different foods and are still none the wiser, talk to your GP, who will be able to advise the best course of action. Unfortunately, there are no tests that definitely confirm intolerances.

The common causes of food allergies in children are: cow's milk and dairy products, nuts (especially peanuts), eggs, wheat, fish and shellfish, soy, sesame seeds, berries, citrus and kiwi fruits; common intolerances are to lactose and gluten (a type of protein). There are, of course, environment allergens, such as pet dander (skin flakes in fur), dust mites and pollen, and you will also need to consider these. In babies, one of the most common food allergies is to cow's milk protein. There is often some confusion between a cow's milk protein allergy and cow's milk lactose intolerance.

### Milk allergy

An immediate allergic reaction after drinking milk or eating something with dairy in it affects two to seven per cent of babies. It occurs when your baby's immune system reacts to the protein in milk and may cause diarrhoea (including blood in the stool), vomiting after feeds or simply an eczema-like rash; rarely, it can cause the serious anaphylaxis response. Babies are often miserable and fail to put on weight. Milk allergy is something that goes with time: most children will out grow it between the ages of three to five. However, 50–80 per cent of these children will develop asthma.

If you suspect a milk allergy, you will need to see a specialist, who can perform a skin prick test and/or a blood test (usually a RAST test) to confirm the diagnosis (these are not always very accurate). You will then be advised on the most appropriate treatment (see below).

### Lactose intolerance

Lactose intolerance is when your baby cannot digest the sugar (lactose) in milk and milk products. This is rare in young children. It is likely that your baby does not have the enzyme lactase that is required to break down lactose – it is not a reaction that comes from your baby's immune system – and this can be hereditary (it runs in families) or may occur after birth. Symptoms generally affect the digestive system (e.g. excessive wind, noisy bowel sounds etc) and the response is often proportionate to the amount of milk/dairy products given (i.e. some babies can tolerate a small amount of cheese, but react more severely to a whole pot of yogurt). It can be diagnosed by a lactose challenge test.

Temporary lactose intolerance can occur after a gastroenteritis infection (diarrhoea and vomiting illness), lasting for up to two weeks before it settles and disappears. During this time, you may need to remove dairy from your own diet if you are breastfeeding or give lactose-free formula.

### Treatment for allergies/intolerances

The best way to cure your baby's food allergy or intolerance is to remove the offending substance from their diet. While there are medicines, antihistamines and steroids that can limit the body's response, they only work for as long as they are being taken and may themselves produce side effects if taken long-term. Bear in mind that it can be very difficult, if not impossible, to ensure that your baby's diet is entirely free from the food that causes the reaction. Remember also that it is not a good idea to remove multiple foodstuffs, as this may cause nutritional deficiencies, and repeatedly eating a small number of foods tends to make intolerances worse. Ask your GP for a referral to a specialist infant dietician to ensure that your baby is getting a balanced diet.

### Cutting out dairy

If your baby is not yet weaned and is found to be allergic or intolerant to cow's milk, you will be advised either to change your diet if you are breastfeeding (i.e. cut out your intake of cow's milk – see below) or switch your baby to a soya-based or more specialised formula. Babies can also react to the soya protein, so be aware that this might not fix the problem. The Department of Health and the British Dietetic Association do not recommend soya formula in babies under six months.

Removing milk and dairy products from your diet is a massive undertaking and you will need to read the list of ingredients on all foods that you buy. The obvious things to cut are cow's milk (in tea/coffee, on cereal and so on), ice-cream, cheese, yogurt, butter, margarine and chocolate, but you will be amazed how many foods contain cow's milk or derivatives: cakes, biscuits, crisps, pasta, pizza, soups, sauces …the list goes on.

If your baby is weaned, you will need to remove all cow's milk and products from their diet. Remember that any dietary changes need to be made in consultation with a healthcare professional after a confirmed diagnosis, as milk is an essential part of your baby's nutrition for the first year and beyond. The best way to be sure that your baby's diet is dairy-free is to make all the food yourself, as many ready-made foods contain milk. You will need to find other sources of calcium and vitamin D and possibly give them a vitamin/mineral supplement.

### Desensitisation treatment

Once you have removed the cause of your baby's allergy/intolerance – whether it is milk or another food – you may wish to consider a treatment known as desensitisation. This is when the offending substance is gradually reintroduced to the diet after a period of exclusion, in tiny amounts at first and then in greater quantities as the body learns not to react to it.

# Development

Over the first year, your baby will develop from a tiny, helpless newborn into a mobile and increasingly independent toddler. You will see some fascinating developmental milestones and your baby's personality emerge, enabling you to enjoy playing and doing things together.

# Developmental milestones

All babies develop at different rates. This is due to a combination of genetics, gender and ethnic background. Nevertheless, the order in which they acquire certain skills is mostly the same.

Babies are born with reflexes (see Box in Chapter 1, p.16). These need to disappear in order for development to progress (e.g. they cannot let go if they still have the grasp reflex) and most have gone by six months. A baby's strength develops from the head down over the first eighteen months or more. We can divide a baby's first year of physical development into three-month blocks. The first three months involve developing head control in all planes of movement. This is the first aspect of biomechanical control that needs to occur for normal physical development to follow. The second block, three to six months, shows them advancing their movements in the arms and upper trunk. From six to nine months we see the foundations of the ability to control the lower trunk and pelvis. The final quarter, nine to twelve months, is when your baby becomes more mobile and develops control of the lower parts of the legs, together with an upright stance and overall postural control. All these movements will become more refined as your baby grows.

At the same time as they are acquiring the building blocks of movement – known as 'gross motor skills' – your baby is developing in all sorts of other ways: learning to use their eyes and responding to language and social situations, as well as becoming more precise in their hand, foot and mouth movements, known as 'fine motor skills'. In summary, you can expect your baby to demonstrate certain behaviours, often termed 'developmental milestones', within the following time frame:

## Birth to three months
- moves arms and legs when lying on their back
- develops strength to support their head
- grasps and shakes an object
- focuses and fixes their gaze on a close object and follows it as it moves
- smiles spontaneously and responsively
- coos and vocalises sounds.

## Three to six months
- sits up with the support of cushions
- carries their own weight standing with support
- grasps both hands together
- reaches for objects and looks for objects in their hands
- responds to their name
- smiles responsively and laughs out loud
- has expressive sounds/noises
- may cry if you or your partner leaves the room or a stranger approaches.

## Six to nine months
- rolls over from stomach to back and then from back to front
- sits unaided
- learns to crawl
- picks up small objects with their pincer (thumb and finger) grasp
- learns to feed themselves
- understands 'no'
- waves goodbye
- understands how to play 'peekaboo' and other action games.

## Nine to twelve months
- crawls confidently
- can crawl up the stairs
- cruises around the furniture
- knows the meaning of three words
- may say one word, usually 'mama'/'dada'/'no'.

## When there is cause for concern

It is natural to compare your baby to others of the same age as a way of seeing that all is well. However, it can make parents extremely anxious if their baby is not keeping up with their counterparts. While remembering that there is a range of time in which stages of development take place and that most babies get there in the end, the list below is to help you work out when to take your baby to the GP in order to see whether they feel anything is wrong:

**By two months**
- does not respond to loud noises
- does not notice their hands
- does not fix their vision on an object and follow it when it moves.

**By three months**
- does not pay attention to new faces.

**By four months**
- the eyes are still not moving together and they can appear cross-eyed
- does not reach and grab for toys
- is not babbling or imitating sounds.

**By five months**
- does not have good head control and remains floppy

- seems to have tight, stiff muscles
- appears to be using only one hand
- does not put their hand to their mouth
- does not respond to sounds around them
- does not turn their head to sound.

**By six months**
- cannot sit with support

**By seven months**
- is not able to attract your attention through actions.

**By eight months**
- is not babbling
- does not play 'peekaboo'.

**By twelve months**
- does not crawl
- cannot stand when supported
- does not search for objects that you have hidden while they are watching
- does not say a single word (e.g. 'mama'/'dada'/'no')
- does not wave or shake their head
- does not point at objects.

If, at any time, your baby loses skills that they previously had, you need to see your GP.

Having said all this, every baby is unique and will develop in their own individual way. For example, my first baby never rolled, crawled only very occasionally and did not walk until he was sixteen months. I must add that he is currently a sporty little man with great co-ordination and motor skills! In addition, gender and ethnic differences have an impact on when milestones are reached: for instance, girls tend to walk earlier than boys and Afro-Caribbean babies develop their motor skills more quickly, so are often walking well before the end of the first year. The degree of prematurity will also be a factor (see Feature overleaf). Not only is physical development extremely variable among children, it can be so even between siblings.

It is because of these variations that a wide time frame is given for reaching key milestones. While a 'normal' baby will roll independently by six months, sit by nine months, crawl by twelve months and walk by eighteen months, try not to become too distressed if yours does not do so. Focus on *whether* rather *when* these milestones occur. Ideally, they happen in the order described opposite. Provided your child is able to support their own weight by one year and is walking independently by eighteen months, there is no cause for concern.

## Developmental checks

Your baby will be assessed twice during the first year, at around six weeks and eight months.

### The six-week check

When your baby is between six and eight weeks your GP will check that they are developing well. This will involve a physical examination similar to the one performed in the neonatal assessment shortly after your baby's birth (see Chapter 1, p.14). The six-week check is primarily to monitor for:

- congenital heart disease
- developmental dysplasia of the hip
  (see Feature on swaddling in Chapter 4, p.95)
- cataracts
- undescended testes.

Although these will have already been looked for in the previous examination, they are sometimes not detectable until your baby is a little older. For example, in order to check sight, your GP will see if your baby is able to fix their vision on an object and follow it as it moves around.

In addition to the assessment of their physical features, your baby will be weighed and measured, so make sure you take along your 'red book' (see Chapter 1, p.29). You will also have an opportunity to discuss feeding, ask questions about the immunisation programme (see Chapter 8, p.173) and get further information about aspects of babycare. If you or your GP have any concerns about your baby's health and development, you will be referred to a specialist for further investigation.

### The eight-month check

Later on in the year, you and your baby will be invited for a further check-up. While this typically takes place at around eight months, it can be at any time between six months and one year. The assessment will be carried out by your health visitor or GP and is more of a health review than a formal test. It will cover the following aspects of your baby's development:

- motor skills
- hearing and sight
- language
- feeding and weaning
- teeth and dental care
- sleeping
- immunisations
- playing and social behaviour.

Once again, you should take your baby's 'red book', as their weight and height will be measured. Your baby will be given what is known as the 'distraction hearing test'. You will need to sit your baby on your knee so that they are looking at the health visitor, who will be entertaining them with a visual display (nothing noisy). A second health visitor, who will be behind your baby and therefore hidden from sight, will then use various noises first on one side and then the other. If your baby does not respond on either one side or both, more formal hearing tests will be arranged.

Your health visitor will also chat to you about your physical and mental well-being, as well as your family's general health. If you are having difficulties with teaching your baby to sleep, you think your baby may have food intolerances/allergies or suspect you are suffering from postnatal depression (see Chapter 7, pp.158–9), do raise these issues now if you have not done so before. Your health visitor may suggest you see your GP or be able to refer you for specialist support. They may also ask about your plans for returning to work and give advice about managing this transition and any childcare arrangements.

> Never feel that you or your baby are being 'judged'. Assessments target support where it is needed – and the earlier this is done, the better the outcome.

# The development of premature babies

Babies born before 37 weeks are termed premature. Prematurity can affect the way your baby develops and the earlier your baby was born, the more distinct these differences from other babies will be.

## Weight gain

If your baby has required time in an incubator, their growth and development will have been slow and sporadic, in particular their weight gain. You will notice that on some days they will gain the required weight and on others they may not; they may even lose weight. While this will be monitored carefully, these fluctuations are considered normal for a premature infant and, indeed, doctors look at the general trend of growth rather than the daily ups and downs.

Most babies leave hospital weighing less than comparable infants born at term. This is the case for a few reasons:

- even with advances in modern medicine, babies still develop better in the womb
- the feeds that they are given, either orally or intravenously, are not able to match nature
- many premature babies are extremely ill and so their energy reserves go into repair rather than growth.

Once your baby is on full feeds, they will go through a stage of 'catch-up growth' and you will see the difference in their weight gain.

## Age correction

Premature babies can be given two ages: the first is their actual age from the day that they were born; the second is their 'corrected age' – this describes how many weeks or months old your baby would be if they had been born on their estimated delivery date. So, if your baby was born ten weeks early and is now sixteen weeks old, they have a corrected age of six weeks. It is this corrected age that will be used to assess your baby's development: while a six-week-old baby should have reasonable head control and be able to follow an object as it moves around, a sixteen week old baby would be expected to do a lot more. It is not until the age of two that the corrected age no longer needs to be used in relation to development.

## Acquiring skills

Premature babies can take longer to reach the accepted developmental milestones. This can be because they do not have the physical maturity to perform certain skills and/or because of the time they spent in hospital. For example, if your baby was in an incubator or on a ventilator for a long while, they may lack muscle tone, which could mean that they take longer to learn to sit, use their hands and so on.

Most premature babies (provided they were not born extremely prematurely or have other health problems) catch up with their peers by the age of two. You can help with your baby's progress by staying as relaxed as possible, rather than being tempted to 'push' them. Remember that small babies tire very easily and may find it difficult to cope with lots of stimulation, so always follow their lead. In time, your baby will flourish just like any other.

Try not to worry if your baby's development does not follow the usual pattern. It could just mean that they need a little extra help and in all likelihood there will be nothing seriously wrong. However, never hesitate to contact the appropriate healthcare professional for advice if you are concerned.

# Sight and hearing

Your baby's hearing is developed by the time of birth, but their sight is immature. Over time, both senses will become more and more acute.

## Sight

The eye communicates with the brain via the optic nerve, a bundle of nerve fibres that run from the retina (the area at the back of the eye where the light focuses) to the back of the brain, where the area for sight is located. These connections need to develop over time. Indeed, there is a window of opportunity in which the ability for sight develops. If, for example, a child is born blind and, years later, their lack of sight is able to be corrected, it may be that too much time has lapsed and they can no longer learn the ability to see, even though vision should be possible. This is why every baby has an eye test at birth. Part of the neonatal examination (see Chapter 1, p.14), this very simple test looks for a red reflex from the eye. This shows that light is getting through to the retina, which means that your baby should be able to receive the light and then process its meaning.

## How sight develops

Babies are born with immature sight, which allows them only to differentiate light and dark and nearby shapes and silhouettes (see Chapter 1, p.17). By four weeks, your baby begins to focus on faces and can distinguish your face from others, and their eyes start to move together and objects become less blurred. By eight weeks, they are beginning to differentiate between colours and may prefer bright, strong shades. By three months, they should be able to fix their gaze on an object and follow it around if it moves, as well as focus firmly on a face and recognise familiar people. Their hand-eye coordination is beginning to develop.

By six months, your baby can see you well at a distance of 1–2 m and they are developing some perception of depth. By seven months, colour vision and longer vision matures and they are also more confident in following the movement of objects. By one year, your baby's sight is becoming more adult-like and they can recognise people coming towards them from a distance, as well as focus on small objects close to them. Their vision is now well developed. However, it is not until they are seven to nine years old that they have the capability for 20/20 vision.

## Visual impairment

The neonatal examination may detect a cataract (opacity of the lens within the eye), which restricts the amount of light getting to the retina. This is very rare, affecting about one in every 2,500 babies. Treatment is relatively straightforward and involves removal of the cataract and the insertion of a new lens. As your baby grows, signs to alert you to check with your GP are:

- your baby's eyes remain crossed most of the time
- your baby is not able look in all directions with either one or both eyes
- you have a family history of visual problems
- one or both of your baby's eyes wander outwards
- your baby is not fixing on an object and following it by six weeks.

## Hearing

Hearing develops in the womb and by 35 weeks of pregnancy your baby is able to hear the full range of sounds. Hearing is formally tested in the first few days as part of the neonatal examination and again at the eight-month check. If the test does not show a clear response, has a suboptimal result or someone within your immediate family had hearing loss from birth, your baby will be referred to a specialist for further tests.

One or two babies in every 1,000 are born with hearing loss in one or both ears. There are two main types of hearing loss: conductive and sensorineural.

### Conductive hearing loss

The condition where sound waves are not passed from the ear canal to the inner ear is termed 'conductive hearing loss'. There can be a problem at any of the stages along the route, caused by:

- blockage to the ear canal (e.g. wax, a foreign body, a structural problem)
- absence of or damage to the eardrum (tympanic membrane) or the tiny bones of the middle ear (ossicles)
- fluid within the inner ear after an infection or a blockage to the normal drainage (Eustachian) tube.

Conductive hearing loss is often temporary and can be corrected with medication or minor surgery.

### Sensorineural hearing loss

The type of hearing loss that is associated with damage to the cochlea and the nerves that have attachments to the brain is known as 'sensorineural hearing loss'. Its causes include:

- infection, for example, congenital rubella (during pregnancy), syphilis (during pregnancy), mumps, measles and meningitis
- genetic abnormality – some babies are born deaf or become so because of an inherited characteristic from a parent
- poor function of the hair cells within the cochlear from birth
- medicines – some antibiotics are known to cause damage if the levels in the bloodsteam are too high for a prolonged period of time, as well as some other medications that are more rarely given to babies.

Hearing aids or a cochlea implant can be used in some cases to correct sensorineural hearing loss.

Finding out about hearing loss early is important, as it means that your baby receives the appropriate treatment as soon as possible and you can come to terms with the diagnosis and work out how you can best help. See Useful Resources for details of support organisations.

# Growth

Physical growth is measured throughout your baby's first year and beyond and is a useful indicator of development. Your baby's weight gain is the principal means of assessing that all is well. Head circumference and length can also be used to check general progress.

Your baby's weight, length and head circumference will be measured and documented on the day that they are born. Measurements are plotted on the appropriate chart at the back of your baby's 'red book'. These are compiled from data gathered by the World Health Organisation to create 'centiles' that indicate the range of measurements that is considered to be a healthy pattern of growth. The central curve of the chart is the 50th centile and represents the average (i.e. if 100 babies are measured, 50 will be more than this amount and 50 will be less). Any measurement between the 2nd and the 98th centile is considered 'normal'. Remember that chart centiles are only a rough guide: genetic elements (e.g. how heavy/tall you and your partner are), as well as environmental factors (e.g. diet, health) and prematurity, will affect how your baby develops compared to others.

## Weight

Your baby's initial weight is known as their 'birthweight' and it is very important, as it gives your child a starting point for the rest of their growth. Doctors find it extremely useful to monitor weight: a child who is not putting on weight at the same rate may have an underlying illness and so investigations may need to be carried out.

The average weight for a full-term, newborn girl is 3.5 kg and for a boy is 3.65 kg, but anything in the range of 2.2–4.8 kg and 2.3–5 kg respectively is considered normal – quite a wide spectrum, because babies come in all shapes and sizes. Your baby's birthweight will also depend on the number of completed weeks of pregnancy.

All babies lose weight initially, as there is more going out (wee and poo) than coming in (milk/ formula), but they should be back to their birthweight after fourteen days. If your baby loses more than ten per cent of their birthweight, your midwife or health visitor may suggest that they are seen by a paediatrician. Losing this much weight can make babies sleepy and jaundiced, so they may need to come into hospital for treatment. Thereafter, your baby will usually be weighed at eight, twelve and sixteen weeks and at a year (i.e. around the time of their immunisations). Your baby should steadily gain weight, roughly following these guidelines:

- **five months:** should be about double their birthweight
- **twelve months:** may be triple their birthweight.

There may be some weeks in which your baby does not gain weight and this can sometimes be because they have a cold or other minor illness. This is fine, as what health professionals are monitoring is general weight gain over a period of weeks. While your baby may cross centile lines from time to time, any *sudden* dip in the rate of growth should always be investigated.

## Length and head circumference

Other measurements are taken whenever there is a concern about weight gain. Length can also be used to estimate the potential adult height of your baby (their is a special chart for this). The head circumference allows doctors to monitor the trend of growth. A head that is growing too quickly may indicate there is too much fluid within the brain; conversely, a head that is not growing well may signify a problem with the brain's development.

# Mobility

Learning to sit, crawl and walk are the three major stages of gross motor development in your baby's first year. These stepping stones to mobility are a delight to witness and will give your baby increasing independence and a new perspective on the world.

**What you need**

✓ Rug or playmat
✓ Baby support seat (optional)
✓ Door bouncer (optional)

Although there is a great degree of variation as to exactly when babies learn key gross motor skills, the order of progression is always the same: babies cannot sit independently until they have good control of their head and trunk, and cannot crawl or walk until they have mastered sitting upright.

There are many devices on the market that are supposed to help babies become mobile, not all of them very desirable. Baby support seats are a brilliant way for a baby who has good head control but cannot yet sit to be in a position where they do not have continuous pressure against their head (see Feature on flat head syndrome in Chapter 4, p.103). However, there have been some reports of babies tipping themselves backwards or falling out, so never leave them unsupervised.

I do not recommend the use of baby walkers under any circumstances. Numerous babies have been injured while using them (e.g. by going down stairs) and I am also concerned that they affect the development of the hip joint. When the baby is seated in the harness, the long thigh bone (femur) is angled and, instead of the directional force being directly into the hip joint as it would be when standing, it is now angled. I also find that babies are less likely to crawl, and may even learn to walk later,

as they become more used to the ease with which they can move about in their walkers.

While door bouncers do not have the same hazardous reputation as walkers, a similar directional force is applied to the hip joint. If you want to use a bouncer, buy one with a 'bucket' seat, as these allow your baby to bounce and swing (which they usually love) without weight-bearing.

Remember that any piece of equipment that supports your baby by its very nature also *limits* their movement, so should be used judiciously: only allow limited amounts of time each day and always make sure it is supervised.

## Sitting

Sitting is skill that requires head control and strength in the upper body. Most babies gain this from 'tummy time' (see Feature on p.136), in which they learn to raise their head off the ground and push up on their arms to look around. Babies can learn to sit from about five months, but usually last only for a few moments; they are rarely sitting independently until six to eight months.

I always recommend that, once your baby is able to sit independently, you place them on a carpet, rug or playmat. When sat on slidy laminate or wooden floors, babies tend to 'bottom-shuffle' – propelling themselves with one leg while remaining upright – rather than moving into four-point kneeling and crawling. This is a problem, as it does not allow for continued strengthening of their arms and shoulder girdle (see overleaf).

## Crawling

Crawling is likely to be the first method your baby uses to become mobile. Not all babies crawl – some

'bottom-shuffle' or progress straight from sitting to walking – but there are some benefits to your baby's physical development gained by the action of crawling:

- improves muscle tone around the abdominal and gluteal (bottom) area, which is important for balance, stability and coordination as your baby grows older
- it strengthens the muscles around the shoulder girdle, which helps with the muscle control later required for handwriting
- it helps to develop coordination, in the reciprocal movement required by moving the opposite arm and leg simultaneously to propel forwards
- it gives your child the independence to explore their environment

- it allows babies to develop their perceptive and visual skills by working out how far away an object is, together with a feeling of knowing where they are in the environment; this helps with all aspects of physical strength and development and also with academic tasks at school.

Of course, there will always be exceptions: some children who never crawl will have good balance, handwriting, coordination and core strength, and some children who did crawl will still struggle in these areas. Nevertheless, I would advise you to try to get your baby to crawl before they walk. This can be done through 'tummy time', see overleaf. Even if your child does not eventually crawl, the time spent on their stomach will benefit their normal development. It is very difficult to change a

bottom-shuffler into a crawler, but it can be a good idea to keep putting your baby on their stomach, even if only momentarily, so that they gain strength by using their arms and shoulders to push up.

To start with, your baby will propel themselves around on their front using their arms, often called the 'commando crawl'. This stage may progress to kneeling on all fours, just rocking backwards and forwards. Soon enough, your baby will work out how to get themselves to the crawling position from sitting and will start to use the knees as well as the hands to get around. Sometimes babies even start by crawling backwards!

## Walking

From about nine months onwards, your baby will work out ways to get upright, pulling themselves up using anything within reach, such as a sofa, table leg or even your leg! This is invaluable for gaining strength in their legs and for learning how to balance. Once your baby has got the hang of this, they will start to move around holding onto the furniture, known as 'cruising'. This precursor to walking may carry on for several months until they finally have the skills to balance independently and, ultimately, to take their first steps. There will be a lot of wobbling, tripping and falling over to start with! During this time it is really important that your baby is either barefoot or in soft leather baby shoes, as they need to get a sense of balance and this is much easier if they can feel the floor. Structured shoes are not needed until your baby is walking confidently and has good balance (see Chapter 2, p.38).

# 'Tummy time'

In 1994, the American Academy of Paediatrics (AAP) encouraged parents to place their babies only on their backs to sleep, with a view to reducing the incidence of Sudden Infant Death Syndrome (SIDS), or 'cot death'. This 'Back to Sleep' campaign has proved to be very effective in reducing SIDS by over 40 per cent.

However, it became evident that some babies were being delayed in their initial physical development as a result of sleeping on their back. In addition, the number of babies with flat head syndrome (see Feature in Chapter 4, p.102) increased significantly, as parents were also avoiding placing their babies on their abdomen during the day. The AAP recommendations have since been expanded to include daily, supervised, awake 'tummy time' to address these issues.

## What is 'tummy time'?

'Tummy time' is any activity that avoids your baby lying flat on their back in one position against a firm surface. It is adaptable and changes as your baby grows and gets stronger. For example, a newborn an be held across your forearm, in a sling/baby carrier or over your shoulder. As your baby gets stronger, you can place them on their front on a playmat. 'Tummy time' must always be supervised, as a precaution in reducing the incidence of SIDS.

## Why is 'tummy time' important?

'Tummy time' aids general development, but the most important reason that your baby needs to do it is to encourage them to crawl before they walk (see pp.133–4). The first thing that your baby needs for normal development is head control, more specifically, being able to lift their head up against the pull of gravity. 'Tummy time' promotes this, as your baby learns to lift their head up to look around when in this position. 'Tummy time' also strengthens the muscles that your baby requires for sitting and crawling. The more time that your baby spends playing supervised on their abdomen the better. The recommended amount is 30 minutes per day. This is usually broken up into shorter blocks of time, ranging from just a minute or two when your baby is newborn, and gradually extending this as they get older.

## When to do 'tummy time'

The sooner you begin 'tummy time', the more normal it will be for your baby. It is best to do it when your baby is content and alert – this is often after a bath or a nappy change.

You may prefer to wait for an hour or so after the feed to allow your baby to digest, as this may avoid possetting or throwing up. It is important not to insist on 'tummy time' if your baby is being 'fussy', as forcing the issue can cause your baby to associate the activity with being unhappy.

## Making it fun

'Tummy time' is hard work for babies! Initially, you may need to distract them by making faces, talking, singing and playing with musical or textured toys. Some babies will have very strong opinions about being placed on their stomach. A little bit of squawking is not a problem, but if they become very upset, change position and soothe them before trying again. Placing a mirror or musical box next to your baby may help. Keep working on ways to distract your baby while they are on their tummy, perhaps by introducing new toys or trying massage.

# Playing with your baby

You are your baby's first teacher and friend and they will look to you to help them learn about the world. Stimulating your baby through play is important for their developmental progression and for building the bond between you.

## What you need

✓ Playmat

✓ Mobile

✓ Baby gym

✓ Black-and-white picture cards

✓ Baby mirror

✓ Bubbles

✓ Rattle

✓ Brightly coloured toys

✓ Textured toys

✓ Cloth/board/lift-the-flap books

✓ Musical toys: maracas, tambourine and drum

✓ CDs of nursery rhymes

✓ Building blocks

✓ Stacking cups

✓ Activity board

✓ Mobile car/truck

✓ Push-along trolley/animal

✓ Shape sorter

✓ Cut-out wooden puzzles/jigsaws

✓ Chunky crayons/coloured pencils

✓ Toy telephone

✓ Toy tea set

When children play they learn. In fact, what we may regard as pleasurable relaxation time is actually quite hard work for them! This is because they are still developing physical and mental skills, such as visual perception, picking up and holding objects, spatial awareness and so. Play is a vital part of the learning process, so try to set aside some time each day to focus on playing with your baby.

You will soon learn when your baby is alert and ready for stimulation, although being awake does not necessarily mean that they want to play. Similarly, if they start looking vacant or turning their head away, this is a sign that they have had enough. Most babies are either passive or active in their response – they may, of course, be somewhere in between, too. An active response is when a baby does something as a reaction to what you have just done; a passive baby accepts what you have done and often does not give a response. You also need to consider your baby's personality and tailor the particular activity accordingly (see Box overleaf).

You do not need lots of sophisticated (and expensive) toys – everyday objects in the home, such as a saucepan and a wooden spoon or a sealed plastic bottle containing dried pasta, can be just as fascinating to your baby. They will enjoy the familiarity of certain favourite toys, but try to rotate others so that there is always a fresh selection.

Always follow your baby's lead: never force them to do anything before they are ready. Similarly, limit your role to helping and describing: do not be tempted to take over building the tower or fitting the last piece of the puzzle, but instead gently support and encourage your baby's efforts. Keep talking all the while and make sure you are very vocal when they have achieved something – all children thrive on praise.

### Ideas for newborn to three months

In the early days, all you need to do is to be responsive to your baby and you will find that they will respond to you. Get up close to talk and sing to them, and ensure they get some 'tummy time'. By the time they are a month old, they will enjoy longer periods of 'tummy time', perhaps lying on a playmat that has areas with different textures. Mobiles can be good stimulation for when they are on their back or in a bouncy chair or you could place them under a baby gym, an arch with toys that dangle down that they can see over their head and learn to reach for.

### How your baby's personality influences play

Within a few weeks of their birth you will get the first glimpse of your baby's personality and this will continue to develop throughout the first year and beyond. Is your baby chilled out and relaxed or are they a little more demanding? Do they snuggle in for a cuddle or do they wriggle around? Are they able to remain focused or are they easily distracted?

Psychologists are able to divide babies into different groups according to their temperament. They have identified nine different personality traits, the specific combination of which determines which category your baby falls into: 'easy', 'slow to warm up' and 'challenging'. Not every baby fits neatly into one of these groups: many sit astride a couple. These traits will become more obvious as your child develops, so you should adapt your play to help them achieve what they need to. For example, an inactive and mild child will need plenty of physical activity, motivation and positive reinforcement, whereas an active and busy child may need to be encouraged to focus on the job in hand. It goes without saying that you should never force your child to be other than they are – it is more a case of targeting areas that need a little more support.

Interaction with you needs to be no further than your arm's distance away, which is as far as they can focus at the moment. Black-and-white toys or images on cards are the easiest for them to see at this stage, but over the course of the second and third months you could introduce brightly coloured toys. All babies like looking at themselves in the mirror and you can hold a small, hand-held baby mirror (i.e. one that is not made from glass) up to their face while saying their name. They also love watching bubbles, so you could gently blow through or wave the wand near them and see if they can follow the bubbles as they float around.

By three months, your baby will try to swipe at objects that are dangling down and will be able to grasp objects and shake them. Let them hold a rattle, although it is best to offer one that has a soft exterior to start with, as babies have a tendency to bash themselves in the face! They will also enjoy hand-held toys that have different touch sensations and make noises.

### Ideas for three to six months

While continuing with the activities above, you could now start to read together, using board, lift-the-flap and soft cloth books, which your baby can hold by themselves. They will love the repetition of words and delight in the textures and surprises they find, and you can also spend time describing the pictures, guiding their finger to point at what you are saying. Reading can also be a good part of the bedtime routine (see Chapter 4, pp.93–4).

At 'tummy time', encourage your baby to stretch for toys that are just out of their reach. By the end of this period, they are likely to be sitting up independently, so a selection of toys can be placed at their feet; until then, you can prop them up with cushions so that they can more easily play with the toys attached to the baby gym.

Encourage your baby's physicality by pulling them up by their arms from lying to sitting. By the end of this period, they will be able to support their own weight on their legs with you holding them upright, so put on a CD of nursery rhymes and get them to 'dance' while being supported by you. Sing along with the music and introduce actions, so that they can learn the meanings of the words.

## Ideas for six to nine months

As soon as your baby can sit up reliably, a whole new world of play opens up! As well as creating a racket with a saucepan and spoon or a homemade shaker, they will be able to experiment making sounds with a range of musical toys, such as maracas, a tambourine and a drum. By seven months, they can roll from front to back and vice versa, so you can indulge in some gentle 'rough-and-tumble', perhaps blowing raspberries on their stomach if they enjoy it. Once your baby can crawl, they will want to explore the environment, so allow them to touch all the household objects (while ensuring their safety) to experience texture and temperature, as well as examining different colours and sparkle. Create an 'obstacle course', with cushions and parts of your own body making 'bridges' and 'roads'.

## Top Tips

Play with your baby as often as you can, even if it means abandoning the chores for a while.

Give your baby your full attention while playing (put away that mobile phone!) and make lots of eye contact. Ten minutes of this is more valuable than half an hour with only part of your focus.

Make it fun: while play is a learning experience for your baby, you should avoid setting goals and challenges that could lead to frustration (yours and theirs).

Praise your baby whenever you can: emphasise what they have achieved, not what they are still unable to do.

Always follow your baby's lead: if they are already engrossed in something, leave them to it, and if they are just not in the mood for play today, try again tomorrow.

Your baby's increasing manual dexterity means that they can use their hands to sweep over the floor to pick up an object and transfer it from one hand to another, as well as use their pincer grasp. Ideal toys for this stage are building blocks and stacking cups, so that they can practise making towers and putting objects in and out of each other. Activity boards encourage different hand movements, such as turning, twisting, lifting up and so on. Weather permitting, you can set up some sand and water play outside, or just go around the garden smelling flowers.

A fun game to introduce is 'peekaboo': cover your face with your hands for a few seconds, then bring them quickly away. You can also bring your baby's hands to your or their face (or briefly cover theirs with a muslin cloth), but some babies do not like having their face covered, so only do this if they seem comfortable with it. This simple, fun game starts to get your baby used to the concept that although you may disappear, you always come back. Also try some 'finger games', such as 'Round and round the garden', 'This little piggy' and 'Incey-wincey spider'.

## Ideas for nine to twelve months

Your baby's gross motor skills are improving all the time in this period and you can now introduce a mobile vehicle that they can sit on while you push them along; when they are a little older, they will be able to scoot around the house and garden on it by themselves. You could also invest in toys that allow first supported, then unsupported, walking, such as a wooden trolley filled with bricks or a push-along animal. Ones that make a noise while being pushed around can be enjoyed even before your baby is fully upright and stable.

By the end of the year, your baby should have enough control of an object to be able to let go of it freely, can bang two toys together and successfully put objects in and out of a box or container. You can further refine these skills by giving them a shape sorter, cut-out wooden puzzles and jigsaws. These will also help develop their visual perception. They should also be able to use a pincer grasp to hold a pen, even though they grab it in their whole hand rather than with three fingers, as an older

## Gender and development

Much research has been done on the influence of gender on childhood development and the debate about 'nature and nurture' still rages on. Many parents consider whether they should consciously treat male and female babies differently. There is one very simple answer: a baby has the same needs and wants, whether it is a boy or a girl. They need to feed, sleep and be loved, and that remains constant regardless of gender.

Of course, there are some genuine differences in the development of boys and girls. For example, premature girls do seem to cope better than boys in the early stages. We do not really know that reason for this and, indeed, it makes no difference to the care and treatments babies get. It is also a fact that girls (premature or not) reach their developmental milestones more quickly than boys in the first few years, and this is most noticeable in their language skills; boys are generally better at skills that rely on spatial and mechanical dexterity.

As your baby gets older, however, their gender can influence the way that you treat them. Traditionally, boys like 'rough-and-tumble' and girls prefer more gentle games (although this difference is becoming less noticeable). You can compensate for any differences in your play by not falling into the trap of treating your daughter more carefully while expecting your son to 'toughen up' or of valuing one skill (e.g. sportiness) more highly than another (e.g. linguistic ability).

You will notice in toyshops that there are aisles of 'boys toys', which predominately feature sports and action toys in dark colours, and aisles of 'girls toys', which focus on domestic and nurturing play and are overwhelmingly pink. While it is hard to avoid such stereotypes, you can offer your baby the full range of toys to experience – after all, boys and girls need to acquire the same skills.

Most importantly, you as parents are role models for your child, so from the beginning, you can both get involved in all types of domestic tasks. Fathers can show that they are gentle and loving and mothers can lead by example in being dynamic and strong. That way, your baby will grow up learning that there is no limit to what they can achieve, be they boy or girl.

child would. This means that they can scribble effectively, so you could let them experiment with chunky crayons or coloured pencils.

Reading books can now be a little more sophisticated, with longer stories, more words and interactive noises. Imaginative play can be stimulated by things such as toy telephones and tea sets: show your baby what to do and offer them the chance to do it too. These skills help to reinforce social concepts, such as sharing and taking turns. Good games for this age include 'Hide-and-seek' and 'Find the missing toy'.

### Should I let my baby watch television and DVDs?

Many people have very fixed views on the amount of television or DVDs babies and children should be allowed to watch. Indeed, some professionals think that children under three should not be allowed to watch any television at all, and then, after this time, it should be heavily restricted. I feel that relying on television/DVDs for childcare purposes – that is, putting your baby in front of the screen to amuse them so that you can get on with other things – is not ideal. However, babies and children can receive some educational benefit from good-quality programmes and, later, when they are at school, they can be isolated from conversations with their peers if they do not know about certain characters and programmes. I think the key point is to limit television/DVD time, especially if your child is happy and settled doing something else. Also, be aware that as they get older, the more television they watch, the less physical activity they will do, which can set the pattern for an unhealthy lifestyle later on.

# Teeth

At birth, your baby's gums contain twenty primary teeth (sometimes called 'milk' or 'deciduous' teeth). The first of these typically break through (erupt) at around six months, although some babies already have one or more teeth when they are born, while others have still to gain a tooth by the end of the first year.

## What you need

✓ Teething rings
✓ Teething gel
✓ Infant paracetemol
✓ Baby toothbrush
✓ Infant toothpaste

- irritability and sleeplessness
- diarrhoea
- mild temperature (under 38°C).

Many paediatricians feel that fever and diarrhoea are not specific to teething and it is more likely that your baby has an infection at the same time as cutting their teeth. So, if your baby looks ill, make sure you take them to your GP, as these symptoms may not simply be the result of teething.

Teeth erupt at different times, usually in the order shown in the diagram (see right). By the time that your child is two or three years old they should have all their primary teeth. These will eventually fall out, giving way to permanent adult teeth. However, even though they are temporary, primary teeth serve several important purposes: they reserve space in the mouth for the adult teeth, allow food to be chewed (and therefore optimise the nutrition in food) and aid the development of clear speech.

### Teething

Babies can start teething from as early as three months. The symptoms can be variable and some babies seem to suffer greatly, while others hardly notice it. Signs that your baby is teething are:

- drooling and dribbling more than previously (this can start from ten weeks); can include a rash around the area of skin that is always damp
- red cheeks
- chewing on hands, fingers or other objects
- showing indicators of pain

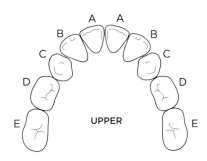

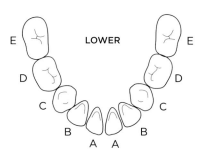

**Order and time of eruption of primary teeth**
**A** Central incisors: 6–10 months (lower); 8–13 months (upper)
**B** Lateral incisors: 8–13 months (upper); 10–16 months (lower)
**C** Canines (cuspids): 16–23 months (upper and lower)
**D** First molars: 13–19 months (upper and lower)
**E** Second molars: 23–31 months (lower); 25–33 months (upper)

Soothing with cool teething rings and infant paracetamol (following the given dosage instructions) are the most effective methods for reducing teething pain. If your baby does not like teething rings, then you can offer them cold food (depending on their age): yogurt, purées from the fridge or a chilled carrot to chew on. You may want to apply a teething gel/cream directly to the gums with your clean fingertip. These products often contain a local anaesthetic (e.g. lidocaine hydrochloride) or an anti-inflamatory (e.g. choline salicylate) to help with the pain and a mild antiseptic (e.g. cetalkonium chloride) to prevent the area from getting infected and therefore helping it to heal quickly and well. Some parents report that homeopathic and traditional herbal remedies work very well for their babies. You should avoid teething products containing benzocaine for babies who are younger than four months old, as there is a small risk of methemoglobinemia (a blood disorder).

You may, on occasion, see a purple spot over the area where the tooth is about to erupt. This is a small blood blister. It will pop when the tooth breaks through the gum but, other than a small amount of bleeding, it should not cause any problems.

## Caring for baby teeth

You should start brushing your baby's teeth with a very soft toothbrush, ideally a special baby toothbrush, and an infant toothpaste as soon as they appear. New primary teeth do not have the strong, protective enamel around them and are therefore very prone to decay and cavities. Moreover, any decay or infection in primary teeth can cause damage to the permanent teeth developing underneath them. It is therefore crucial to establish good oral hygiene from the outset by cleaning your baby's teeth twice a day, once after breakfast and again as part of their bedtime routine. Ninety per cent of all tooth decay in young children occurs in the molar teeth at the back of their mouth. You need to pay particular attention to these teeth, as they have deep fissure and grooves that need cleaning well.

Toothbrushes should always be rinsed well in fresh water after use to ensure that they do not become a breeding ground for bacteria. It is also a good idea to change your baby's toothbrush every three months, or sooner if they are chewing the bristles and they are no longer cleaning the teeth well.

## Should I give my baby extra fluoride?

Research has shown that there is a 20–40 per cent reduction in tooth cavities in babies and children who are given sodium fluoride supplements. Fluoride can be obtained in different ways:

- some water authorities put it in the water supply
- by using infant toothpaste (not all brands)
- as a supplement
- via breast milk (but contains very variable amounts, so not a reliable source)
- by giving powdered infant formula.

However, there is a balance to be maintained here: too much fluoride can lead to fluorosis, a condition which results in white spots on the teeth and less strong enamel. To guard against this, you should be careful that your child is not getting fluoride from multiple sources. For example, if you want to give your baby a sodium fluoride supplement, first check that your water authority does not supplement your water supply and make sure you use toothpaste without fluoride.

### Sugar and tooth decay

Sugar is a well-known cause of tooth decay. Some people feel that babies between six to twelve months should not be given sugary foods, because their teeth are not strong enough to resist decay and erosion. Whatever your decision on this, do not allow your baby to go to sleep with a bottle of milk or juice in their mouth, as the sugar in the liquid will erode their teeth while they are sleeping.

# Learning to speak

Language development is a gradual process that starts from birth. Children acquire language without the need for formal teaching, but parents nevertheless play an important role in helping their baby learn to speak.

Language acquisition is two-fold: it requires the ability both to understand and to communicate. By the time they say their first word, your baby will have already spent many months experimenting with sounds ('babbling') and connecting words with meanings. Their speech develops according to the following pattern. From birth to three months:

- their first sound is crying, a vital method of communication (see Chapter 2, pp.42–6)
- your baby recognises your voice and responds to you with a smile by six weeks
- they babble and coo, making vowel sounds, and turn responsively to noise.

From four to seven months:

- your baby responds to their own name and to the repetition of words
- they are beginning to tell emotions by the difference in tone in your voice and can themselves express displeasure and happiness
- their babbling is more extended as they string sounds together in consonant-vowel pairs (e.g. 'ba', 'goo') and they are learning to understand 'no'.

From eight months to one year:

- they can respond to simple commands
- they are able to sound out some words, such as 'dada', 'mama' and 'oh-oh'
- they start to imitate the sounds that you are saying with more clarity.

If your baby is not doing any of these things, it is worth going to your GP to discuss having a formal hearing test.

## Get talking

How is it that babies can learn the complex system of speech so quickly and easily? Many experts believe that it is genetic (i.e. they are born with the ability to learn), but that there is a critical 'window' until puberty, after which it becomes much more difficult; others say that it is simply exposure and usage that allows fluency in language. However, all agree that interaction with other people is a crucial element in learning to speak – babies will not learn a language if they only hear it spoken on the radio or TV, for example. This is because there are many visual clues in communication that go hand-in-hand with the spoken word. See also section on baby signing opposite.

So, right from the beginning, get close to your baby so that they can see your face, and make sure you smile and nod as you speak to them. You will soon see them moving their mouth as they watch yours. Get into the habit of describing everything while you are doing it – a 'running commentary' – so that your baby hears the rhythm and structure of speech: 'Mummy's changing your nappy now and you're going to have a kick-around while I get the clean one'. Use lots of repetition and ask questions, too (but you will have to give the answer yourself to start with!).

Parents find that they naturally use simpler vocabulary and sentence structure when talking to their babies, as well as exaggerating the intonation and emphasis. This 'baby talk' is absolutely fine, as it really helps your baby to sort out sounds, meanings and word patterns. Some make sure that they only use the 'proper' names for things rather than a pet term or family word, but I do not think it really matters, as children's understanding will soon become sophisticated enough to adjust to this.

## The beginnings of discipline: teaching 'no'

There is very little need to say 'no' to a baby before they are toddling. However, once they are mobile, you will need to set some boundaries in order to keep them safe and secure. While it is important that your baby learns what 'no' means, this can be done in a loving and kind way. So, rather than just saying 'no' all the time to undesirable behaviour, try to explain to them *why* they cannot do something: 'It is not a good idea to get to close to the oven, as you may get burned and that will hurt you – ouch!' Similarly, if they crawl over to an object that you do not want them to have, tell them why they should not touch it and then either remove it from their sight or, better still, distract their attention from the object by introducing something new. You may have to repeat this several times. Using these methods teaches the concept of 'no' in a positive way.

## Baby signing

As I have discussed, communication is not just verbal. A lot of what we 'say' is done through our hand movements, posture and facial expression. Babies are very good at picking up on our gestures. For example, by six months they may start to shake their head if they do not want something. Baby signing is simply an extension of this.

Baby signing was developed by Dr Joseph Garcia, who found that the hearing children of deaf parents were often more content and settled, as they copied their parents' signs in order to express themselves before they had developed their language skills. Children's motor skills develop quicker than their ability to speak, so they are able to sign well before they can verbalise.

The system of baby signing is aimed at children between six and eighteen months. It is very simple to learn and many say that it is intuitive. There are many classes held throughout the UK. See also Useful Resources for website information.

Some people worry that if their baby can sign, they may become lazy with their language development and run into problems with delayed speech. This has been found not to be the case and, indeed, baby signing may even aid speech, as it gives the children a structure of two-way conversation at an early stage.

## Bilingual families

Many children are brought up in homes where more than one language is spoken. While this can (but not always) cause a slight delay in language development, there are lots of advantages to being bilingual from a young age – as anyone who has learned a foreign language as an adult will tell you.

Babies are born with the ability to hear a large number of speech elements, known as 'phonemes', but each language uses only a small number of these. By six months, your baby will have selected the phonemes needed for the particular language they hear. If you and your partner or another family member talk to your baby in different languages, you will naturally increase the number of phonemes they can distinguish, fine differences in sound that will allow your baby, in later years, to speak each language with a native accent. The ability to speak another language fluently ceases by the age of seven or eight.

Parents sometimes worry that their child will mix the languages up and become confused. It is true that children can sometimes use a jumble of words and phrases, but this sorts itself out with time and practice (and you can help by consistently speaking only your language to your baby). Soon enough, your baby will be able to work out that each of you has your own 'code' and which elements belong to which.

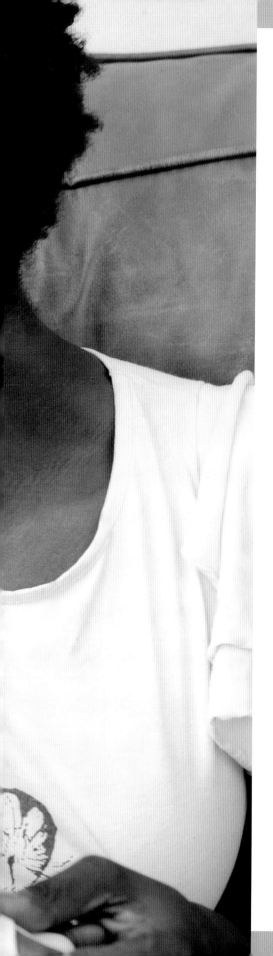

# Looking after yourself

There are so many things to think about when you have a new baby that you often forget about yourself. This is understandable to begin with, but you will soon have to find a balance between meeting your baby's needs and looking after your own physical and emotional well-being, as well as making time for your partner, other children and friends.

# Eating and sleeping well

Life with a newborn can be very demanding, so eating healthily and regularly and getting enough rest should be your priorities.

## Healthy eating

In the immediate postnatal period, you need to replace the vitamins, minerals and that were depleted during your pregnancy. You will obtain these from a healthy, well-balanced diet (see Chapter 5, pp.109–111). However, it can be difficult to make time to eat when looking after a baby. To help you, have some pre-prepared food or ready-meals in the freezer for those first few weeks. You may find it easier to eat little and often, focusing on healthy snacks rather than sugary or fatty foods.

As you settle into a routine with your baby, you will be able to start thinking about preparing fresh, balanced meals and having proper mealtimes. Making yourself sit down to eat is a good way to rest and you will need plenty of that (see below); your evening meal can also be a great time for you and your partner to have one-to-one time together (see p.154).

## Your breastfeeding diet

Breastfeeding does not require a special diet, but what you do eat needs to be healthy and nutritious. Most importantly, you should consume extra fluids to ensure good milk supply (see Box in Chapter 3, p.69). Breastfeeding uses up 300–500 calories per day and some women find this a useful way to lose some of their 'baby weight' (see Box); however, others find that they need to eat a little bit extra and actually put on weight while they are feeding.

Remember that the caffeine that is present in tea, coffee and fizzy drinks will affect your baby and possibly keep them awake. If you have an alcoholic drink, you should be aware that a small amount of alcohol will pass through to your baby, so it is recommended that you leave as long a time as possible between that drink and the next scheduled feed.

## Getting enough sleep

Disturbed sleep is guaranteed during your baby's first year and, most of the time, parents simply live with tiredness as part of their everyday lives. However, sleep deprivation is awful and there will be times when you feel you are being tortured by the demands being made on you! In addition, if you are breastfeeding and are not rested, your milk supply will be affected and your baby will not receive enough; they will therefore need ever more frequent feeds, leading to a vicious circle of further sleep deprivation and reduced milk production.

Sleep deprivation is a common cause of tearfulness and even postnatal depression (see pp.158–9). Mid-morning or afternoon naps do not come naturally to most people, but you will need to perfect the ability to nap whenever your baby does to make up for lost sleep. Lastly, you need to consider whether stress, worry or unhappiness is making you more tired. If so, speak to your health visitor or GP, who will be able to recommend the appropriate course of action.

## Losing your 'baby weight'

You may feel impatient to lose the extra weight you gained in your pregnancy. However, embarking on a serious diet could mean that you lack the energy to deal with the demands of looking after your baby. It is far better to eat sensibly and incorporate some moderate exercise into your routine (see right). That way, the weight will fall off gradually and steadily. Trying to be back to your pre-pregnancy weight by the time your baby is a year old is a realistic and sensible time frame.

# Exercise

The effects of pregnancy and birth on your body should not be underestimated. Being mindful of these as you exercise and go about your daily tasks will aid your recovery and help to protect you from injury.

There are two significant physical factors resulting from pregnancy that you need to be aware of: the separation (diastasis) in your rectus abdominal ('six-pack') muscles that allowed space for your growing baby in pregnancy; and the role of the relaxin hormone.

The gap between your abdominal muscles is completely normal (although it does not appear in all women) and will lessen with time, but it leads to a weakening of the abdominal wall and can place an extra load on the spine. In pregnancy, the relaxin hormone allows the uterus to expand and the ligaments to soften so that you can carry and give birth to a baby. The levels of relaxin take a few months to return to normal, even longer if you are breastfeeding. Soft ligaments can reduce the stability of your joints, particularly around your spine and pelvis, which puts you at greater risk of injuring yourself. Both the diastasis and your soft ligaments mean that you should return to your pre-pregnancy exercise regime gradually and sensibly.

## Protecting your abdomen

You may notice a 'doming' or bulging of the abdominal contents through the separation in your muscles when you perform activities that increase the pressure in your abdomen, such as bringing yourself up from lying to sitting, coughing, sneezing or lifting objects. For the first six weeks, to reduce the effect of diastasis and help with the healing process:

- consciously brace your abdominal and pelvic floor muscles (see the Feature overleaf) when you cough, sneeze or lift an object, by drawing your navel and the area just beneath it towards your spine (commonly known as 'the knack')

- do not lift anything heavier than your baby and avoid twisting and lifting at the same time
- when getting out of bed, roll onto your side and use your elbow and upper hand to push yourself up into the sitting position, moving your legs over the edge of the bed at the same time
- when getting into bed, use your arms to lower yourself down (not your abdominal muscles).

I am a firm believer in women using an abdominal binder/brace or wearing supportive, high-waisted underwear in the postnatal period. A simple elasticated tubular bandage worn doubled over the abdomen works best for the first few weeks. The gentle compression it provides stimulates lymphatic drainage in the abdomen to help reduce residual fluid and is also thought to optimise healing of the diastasis. Support aids can also help you to be more conscious of your posture and to stand up straighter, which will help protect your back (see pp.152–3). You can wear a bandage/binder immediately after a vaginal delivery, but if you have had a Caesarean section, check with your consultant first, as some prefer you to wait a little while. Always check that your midwife or GP is happy with the fabric of your underwear if you had an episiotomy or tear during delivery.

## Safe postnatal exercise

As a general rule (and unless your healthcare professionals have recommended otherwise), I advise that, in the first six weeks after you have given birth, you build up to half an hour's walking at a time and perform only very gentle abdominal exercises. That means no running or high-intensity exercise yet, as tempting as it may be to return to your regular exercise sessions as soon as you have a few minutes to yourself! Sit-ups are the absolute worst exercise you could do in the immediate postnatal period, as they cause your rectus abdominal muscles to shorten, the gap between them to widen and the pressure in your abdomen to increase, all of which will inhibit healing of the diastasis. However, there are some exercises that start the process of abdominal strengthening from the inside.

### Transversus abdominus strengthening

The transversus abdominus are your deepest abdominal muscles and can be felt most easily beside the two parts of your pelvis that stick out at the front (although they run over the entire front of your abdomen). These work together closely with your pelvic floor muscles (see Box opposite) to give stability to your pelvis. To activate them, visualise a point four finger-widths beneath your navel. Breathe in and, as you breathe out, draw your lower abdomen in gently towards your spine. You could also imagine that you were doing up a pair of super-low jeans and needing to pull your stomach in where the button is. With these lowest muscles pulled in, maintain the muscle contraction and take three breaths. Relax the abdomen, wait for a few breaths and then repeat for ten cycles. You can do this exercise while sitting, lying, standing and side-lying, three to six times per day.

### Pelvic tilts

After a few days you can progress to pelvic tilts, which safely engage your rectus (upper) abdominal muscles. Lie on your back with your knees bent and your feet flat on the floor, keeping your elbows on the floor and your hands either beside you or on your lower abdomen. Breathe in and, as you breathe out, gently draw your navel up and under in the direction of your ribs. You will feel your abdominal muscles tighten and your back flatten against the floor. Hold this position and breathe gently for six breaths. Relax your abdomen and repeat ten times, taking care that your ribs do not flare out.

### Resuming normal exercise

To be on the safe side, you could have your abdominal muscles checked by a women's health physiotherapist six weeks after the birth. Depending on how you have healed (it is considered normal to have a shallow, two-finger separation after having had a baby), they will advise you as to whether it is safe for you to return to your normal exercise regime.

If you are given the go-ahead, you should nevertheless proceed slowly. You can begin by swimming (if you are no longer bleeding vaginally) and by attending Pilates and Yoga classes. It is important that classes are either postnatal-specific and or that your regular class teacher is very competent in this area. This is so that they know to avoid very high-intensity abdominal work and any movements that put strain on your loosened ligaments. I recommend that you wait at least three months before running or doing activities such as aerobics, squash or tennis (and, again, only if your diastasis is suitably resolved), as you are still at greater risk of injury.

You should not experience back or pelvic pain, urine leakage or any feeling of vaginal heaviness during exercise. If you do, try slowing down or reducing the intensity of your exercise regime. If these symptoms persist, contact your GP or physiotherapist.

> Returning to your previous exercise regime too quickly after the birth will increase your chances of injury, may worsen diastasis and, ultimately, may delay your recovery.

# Pelvic floor exercises

The pelvic floor is a broad sling of muscles, ligaments and fascia that stretch from your pubic bone in the front of your pelvis to your tailbone at your back. Its function is to evacuate urine and faeces, to support the pelvic organs and to help provide movement control and stability of the pelvis and lumbar spine; it also makes a contribution to sexual arousal.

During the antenatal and postnatal period, the relaxin hormone has a softening effect on all the muscles and ligaments in the body, including those that create the pelvic floor. This, coupled with having to support the weight of a growing baby during pregnancy, can weaken the pelvic floor, meaning that the contents of the pelvis can no longer be adequately supported. As a result, about one-third of women experience urinary incontinence after childbirth. Most commonly, women notice a little leak of urine when they laugh, sneeze or cough. A seriously weakened pelvic floor can cause continence problems for life or a prolapse of the uterus into the vagina. These problems can occur whether you had a vaginal delivery or a Caesarean section.

Studies have shown that women who do pelvic floor exercises while pregnant and after the birth are less likely to suffer with incontinence in the future. These strengthening exercises have also been shown to reduce lower back pain, because of the added stability that they can give to the pelvis. In addition, the pumping action encourages circulation to the area and assists venous and lymphatic drainage, helping remove cell wastes and promoting healing of the perineum. Whether or not you are experiencing any symptoms of incontinence, it is important to do pelvic floor exercises daily for the rest of your life.

## Fast contractions

Draw up the muscles around your vagina and urethra (as if you are stopping your urine flow) and those around your anus (as if you are stopping wind). Draw up for a second, then release for a second. Repeat ten times.

## Slow contractions

Breathe in and as you breathe out, draw up the muscles as described above. Now hold this muscle contraction as you breathe in and out twice. Release and take two breaths at rest. Repeat this cycle ten times.

Make sure that you are not clenching your buttocks or holding your breath. You can practise these exercises in any position and the great thing is that no one will even know you are doing them! Try to do a set each of the fast and slow contractions three to six times per day until six months after you have stopped breastfeeding. Thereafter, do them twice a day every day – it can help you remember to do them if you always associate them with another activity, such as waiting for the kettle to boil, cleaning your teeth or when commuting to or from work.

## Getting help

Women used to be advised to routinely stop their urine flow midstream in order to check their pelvic floor function. However, recent studies have shown that this may confuse neurological signals between the brain and the bladder, so it is no longer recommended. If you are struggling with urinary incontinence, it is essential that you discuss this with your GP. Many women feel too shy to mention it, but early intervention is key in reducing the often debilitating effects.

# Protecting your back

Mothers of babies and toddlers often suffer from lower back pain. The frequent lifting of an ever-growing child can put your spinal discs and joints, as well as their supporting muscles and ligaments, under great strain.

In addition to the physical demands being made on your body, feeling fatigued by the duties of motherhood can contribute to poor posture when doing common tasks and this can lead to injury. While lifting your little one is pretty unavoidable, there are a few things that you can do to reduce the strain on your spine. While the measures described will help you maintain the straight alignment of spine and trunk, if you continue to suffer from back pain, ask your GP to refer you to a physiotherapist to help resolve it.

## Sitting
When sitting in a chair, two-thirds of the length of your thighs should be supported horizontally by the seat and your feet should be on the floor on a stable surface (if your feet cannot reach the floor, place a small footstool beneath them). Your bottom should be as far back as possible, with no gap between the chair back and your buttocks, to ensure that your pelvis is not tilted and that your spine maintains its natural curves. You may want to place a rolled-up towel behind your lower back to support it. See also Chapter 3, p.62 for sitting positions while breastfeeding.

## Lifting your baby
Place your feet shoulder-width apart, keep your back as straight as possible and bend from the hips and the knees. Hold your baby as close to you as can and really feel that you are pushing through your feet, squeezing your buttock muscles so that the power is coming from your legs and not your back. Keep your knees soft rather than locking them into extension and avoid twisting your spine and lifting at the same time. It is especially important to avoid outstretched arms when lifting your baby from their cot – lower the cot side first.

When picking up your baby from the floor, kneel down and place one foot in front of you, so that your knee is at a 90-degree angle. Lift your baby, holding them close to your chest, and stand up by bringing your weight forward into your front leg and pushing off with your back foot.

## Carrying your baby
It is best to carry your baby directly in front of you to maintain the alignment of your spine and trunk. A sling is ideal for this, as it also leaves your hands free (see Chapter 2, p.50). Repetitively carrying your child on one hip, jutting it out to the side, can create an imbalance in the muscle bulk, making one side of your body stronger than the other. This may pull on your pelvis and spine in a lopsided way, which will cause pain in years to come. However, we have all resorted to this at times, so if you are carrying your child this way, remember to alternate the sides on which you carry them.

## Using a pram/pushchair
Try to buy a pram, pushchair or buggy with adjustable handle-height that allows your spine to be neutrally aligned: your back should be straight and your arms at a height that is comfortable and does not cause you to hunch your shoulders. Stand as close as you can when pushing, as having it too far ahead of you may cause your shoulders to rise up. You should feel that the force that you are generating to push the buggy is coming from your whole body and not only from your arms.

## Managing car seats
Getting your baby in and out of their car seat often requires you to twist and lift at the same time – the worst combination for putting yourself at risk of injury. The type of car seat that rotates towards

the open car door can help minimise the risk, but if you have a static car seat, you should place one of your legs inside the car, hold your child close to you and face the car seat as you put your child in.

Carrying the car seat over one arm while your baby is in it is another cause of back pain, as it is very difficult to maintain good body alignment while holding a bulky weight on one side. Instead, put both hands on the handle and, with your elbows bent, carry the car seat directly in front of you, as close to your body as possible.

## Changing nappies

Ensure that the place where you change nappies is at a height that is comfortable for you (usually around waist height) – you should not have to stoop down to reach your baby. Stand face-on so that you are not twisted and place your feet shoulder-width apart, with your weight evenly distributed between both feet and your shoulders relaxed, not hunched.

## At bath time

Bathing your baby can cause you to flex your back and neck forwards, putting the spine out of its natural alignment. To avoid this, if you are using a baby bath, ensure that it is at a level where you can stand upright comfortably – perhaps by having it on a stand or stable flat surface – and that you can stand close enough to it so that you are not lifting your baby in and out of the bath with outstretched arms. When using an adult bath, kneel beside the bath, rather than bend down from standing. Again, hold your baby as close to you as possible when you lift them out.

# You and your partner

'Life will never be the same again', or so they say! The moment your baby is born, your priorities become very different and this will have an effect on your domestic role and your relationship with your partner.

These relationship changes occur more after the birth of your first child than following that of subsequent children. The focus of the day centres around your new baby's needs rather than your own: you are immersed in a world of nappies and interrupted sleep, rather than enjoying the social life you used to have. This will mean less time for everybody else. Despite this, you do still need to make efforts to maintain your relationship.

First and foremost, you and your partner will need to work out the roles each of you will have within your new family and ways to have some quality, adult time together, just the two of you. Just as important is finding the level of intimacy you are both comfortable with. Yes, you will find that life after motherhood has definitely changed, but the experience is so wonderful that, in my opinion, it is all for the better!

### Redefining roles
Even if you and your partner had hoped to split the care of your baby equally, you will inevitably find that, to start with, you tend to carry the majority of the responsibility and decision-making, particularly if you are breastfeeding. This is unsurprising: you are with your baby virtually constantly and are required at every feed (unless you are expressing or mixed feeding). This makes it hard for partners to get involved at first. I think it helps if you both sit down and work out what roles each of you can take and how you are going to share the workload and responsibility. That way both parties know what they can expect from the other. Try to remember that you will be good role models for your baby if you mix and match the household chores, rather than fall into traditional male/female patterns (see also Box in Chapter 6, p.141).

### Making time for each other
Now there is a baby in the equation, your relationship with your partner is bound to alter. It is only too easy to feel too tired or busy to chat about your partner's day and ask about their challenges, triumphs or frustrations at work. You may also underestimate the change that a new baby has on them. For example, if they have returned to work, although many things about their daily life will be the same, they may feel the added weight of responsibility that supporting a family brings.

Maintaining your relationship as a couple is vital, so it is important to make time talk to each other. To help with this, you need to make an extra effort to be alone together. Spontaneous evenings out may be out of the question, but do not dismiss the possibility of leaving your baby in the hands of a competent carer every couple of weeks. You will both be forgiven for phoning home every five minutes to check that all is well, but this separation anxiety gets better with time! Even a small amount of time for just the two of you can make a huge difference to your relationship, especially if your partner senses that they are no longer the most important person in your life. When you are out together, make sure you give your partner your undivided attention and both of you should try not to talk about your baby the whole time (this is harder than you think!).

### Sex
It has to be said that young babies are not very conducive to having a sex life! You are both likely to be tired and opportunities may be few and far between. This is not a problem if you are both reconciled to the situation. However, frustrations can occur when concerns and needs are not openly

discussed, so good communication is essential to avoid the pitfalls. While there are some physical and emotional factors that will impact upon your libido immediately after the birth, you should reassure yourself that there will come a time when you feel like having sex again.

### Healing after the birth

Many women assume that they should wait until their six-week check before having sex (see Chapter 1, p.26). This is not necessarily the case. However, there are some physical considerations to take account of at this time. If you have had stitches to repair a tear or an episiotomy, then it is helpful to allow them to fully heal before you have sex. In addition, having sex while you are still bleeding can increase the risk of infection. Also, your vagina will have been stretched and bruised and, in some places, it will be swollen and tender, so it needs time to heal and regain its pre-delivery shape (in fact, it may not go back to exactly the same shape and size as before). Nevertheless, there are many ways to have physical closeness without penetration – think of it as an opportunity to experiment and explore other ways of physical enjoyment.

### Changes to your body and libido

Many women worry that sex will never be the same again after childbirth and that their partner will look at them differently. This is rarely the case. Indeed, many women say that their sex lives improved and that they enjoy sex more, and even that they are more inventive and experimental than before they had children! This may be because they feel less inhibited about their body and their sexuality.

However, for a while your libido is likely to be reduced due to tiredness and your more or less total commitment to your baby. Your partner needs to know this and both of you need to remember that this is not forever. You will eventually settle into your new role, emerge from the 'fog' of new motherhood and feel stronger both physically and emotionally. In time, your libido will return. Negative thoughts about your body (see overleaf) can have effect on your libido, so make sure you talk these through with a specially trained counsellor if these feelings persist.

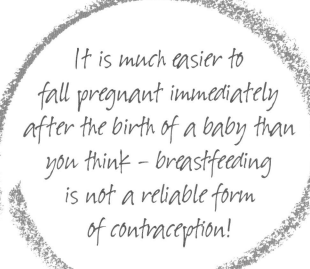

*It is much easier to fall pregnant immediately after the birth of a baby than you think – breastfeeding is not a reliable form of contraception!*

### Taking it slowly

When you do decide to have sex, make sure that you take it slowly. Being anxious and tense may make penetration uncomfortable or, indeed, impossible to achieve. You do not need to rush the moment: make sure you feel ready. You may require some additional lubrication, because penetration may make you sore for the first few times, especially if you have had stitches. In addition, breastfeeding reduces the levels of the oestrogen hormone and consequently your vaginal tissue will be thinner and drier. However, oil-based lubricants can interact with the latex of condoms, making them unreliable – talk to your GP if you need to consider other forms of contraception (see Chapter 1, p.27). Pain during sexual intercourse (dyspareunia) can also be experienced by women who had Caesarean section; in fact, some studies have suggested that it is more common than in women who had a vaginal delivery. Once again, see your GP if these symptoms persist.

# Your emotional welfare

Becoming a mother is a fundamental change in your life and it may take you a little time to adjust to this 'new self'. It is also very easy to forget about your own needs after the birth of your baby. However, to be a good parent you need to be feeling good in yourself and this can be achieved with support from your partner, friends and family.

## Your self-image

It can sometimes be difficult to recognise yourself after having had a baby. These changes are most obvious in your physical shape: your body has been through nine months of gradual change and it will take at least that to return to a semblance of what you looked like before. However, the prevalence of celebrity mothers getting back into their skinny jeans soon after the birth, as well as other social pressures to 'get your body back', can often leave you feeling angry, jealous and defeated. These emotions pop up in odd and discreet ways, for example, when you are getting dressed and cannot find anything to fit or when you are feeding your baby and see some extra 'padding' that was not there before. With so many other adjustments to make, managing your feelings about your body tends not to be a priority. However, just because you are not focusing on these feelings does not mean they are not there. It is just worthwhile remembering that celebrities spend an enormous amount of effort, time and money to get back into shape and usually have plenty of help. Most women's circumstances are very different indeed, so it is wise not to use their lifestyles as any kind of benchmark.

You may also notice how your emotions and responses to the world have now changed. Being the mother of a vulnerable and defenceless baby may make you even more moved by news of conflicts and disasters or cause you to become emotional about things that never would have affected you previously. While this will eventually stabilise, parents report that having a child permanently changes the way they view the world and, in fact, makes them more sensitive and empathetic people. However, before you reach this balance, it may help you to 'disconnect' from the outside world for a short a while: resist the pressure from media and technology to be constantly in touch and focus on enjoying this very special and limited time in your life.

Perhaps the more difficult thing to acknowledge about yourself is that you may be more short-tempered than you used to be, due to tiredness and the number of demands that are being made of you. Snapping at those closest to you and even being impatient with your baby can make you feel upset and guilty, particularly if you do not recognise these responses as typically 'you'. Believe it or not, this is normal. For now, accept that this emotional rollercoaster is part and parcel of the enormous changes that are taking place in your life, try to keep calm and ask that others are tolerant of you while you deal with these foreign feelings. In the medium- to long-term, it will help you to make plans for 'me time', so that you get a chance to recharge your batteries – you cannot care for anyone else if you do not also look after yourself.

## Time for you

While it may make you a candidate for instant sainthood, in reality, if you keep giving of yourself, your energy and personal resources become depleted and you may begin to feel like you have nothing left to give. You therefore need to schedule some 'me time' into your day. This can be hard: on top of looking after your baby and doing all the regular, mundane jobs – food shopping, cooking, cleaning – you may have other children who need some one-to-one time with you, and you and your partner will also need time together. The space at the bottom of the list of this long list of tasks is usually reserved for you.

Nevertheless, it is important to keep your commitment to yourself for some 'me time'. There may well be things you can do while your little one is asleep, such as whizz into a shop changing room to try on some clothes, but in effect you are still in charge of a baby. Remember, it does not count if you have a child with you! Proper 'time off' needs to be time without responsibility for anyone else. It can take the form of a walk, a phone call to a friend, watching some television, going to the gym or however else you normally unwind. You may have to enlist some help so that you can do this. Your partner and your close family will be your first port of call, but it could be that, as time goes on, you need to arrange more formalised childcare.

## Getting out

While, in some ways, having a new baby is about pulling out of the world for a while, research has shown that women who have a strong social network, as well as a supportive partner, cope best with the emotional ups and downs of new

> As soon as you have a little more time, arrange a date with girlfriends and do something completely unrelated to being a mother.

### Parenting websites

Huge changes in your life plus a limited ability to get out and about can make new motherhood an overwhelming and isolating time. Even if you do not normally like that sort of thing, parenting websites can be a ready help at hand. Not only are they a huge source of information, they often have great online discussions, so that you can share your experiences with others going through the same thing. There are lots of different options for sites, and you can browse through a few until you find one that suits you best. See Useful Resources.

motherhood. Try to get out of the house everyday, even if it is only to the local shop to pick up some essentials. This can be especially helpful if you are feeling isolated in your new role, as you will feel part of the bigger community again. You will be surprised at how friendly people can be when you have a new baby in your pram or your sling. A simple hello and a smile from a passing stranger can be very uplifting when you are tired and perhaps feeling low. You could also try some of the many groups and classes for mothers and babies (see Chapter 2, pp.52–5). See also information about postnatal depression overleaf.

### Friendships

With so many changes to your life and so many more demands on your time it can be easy to forget the friendships you had before you became a mother. While you will undoubtedly meet lots of new people – ones that, perhaps, you have far more in common with now – it is wise not to neglect old friends, even if things have to be done more on your terms for a while.

When you do get a chance to catch up, try not to be a 'baby bore' by talking about your baby the entire time and focus on them instead – remember that they will also have important things going on in their lives. It will also do you good to know that you can still kick up your heels once in a while!

# Postnatal depression

It is thought that around one in ten women suffer from postnatal depression, and perhaps as many as four in ten teenage mothers. Despite this, the condition sometimes goes unrecognised, so it is important that you and those around you know the symptoms so that you can get help.

Feeling tearful and emotional for a few days after the birth is totally normal: the majority of women develop the 'baby blues' around the third day (see Chapter 1, p.27). Postnatal depression (PND) is different and more extreme. It can happen at any time up to a year after your baby is born, but most commonly occurs between the second and the eighth week after delivery. The symptoms are similar to those of depression:

- feeling extremely tired all the time
- sleeping problems (either too little or too much)
- anxiety and irritability
- poor concentration and memory loss
- finding that simple things require enormous effort
- loss of appetite
- feeling very low and sad; frequent bouts of crying
- a sense of hopelessness and having little interest in yourself
- feeling numb, as if emotions and experiences are not part of you
- normal behaviours are exaggerated and become obsessive and repetitive
- feeling socially isolated and becoming frightened of leaving the house; panic attacks.

Many mothers with PND feel that they are unable to connect with their new babies and lose interest in them. The reverse is also possible: they constantly worry that something bad will happen to their baby and become over-anxious or even paranoid.

Doctors are not sure what causes PND, but there are certain factors that may contribute: having a difficult, and perhaps traumatic, birth; lacking a strong support network; extreme tiredness and fatigue; strains in your relationship.

You are more likely to suffer from PND if you had a history of depression before you were pregnant and also if you had antenatal depression (depression during your pregnancy). If you had PND following the birth of a previous child, you have a one in four chance of getting it again. Partners can also suffer from depression during this time. Again, the causes are not well understood, but it is thought that the increased pressure and responsibility of parenthood may play a role, as well as a previous history of clinical depression.

Postnatal depression is a clinical condition that requires specialist intervention and is not an attitude of mind that you can simply pull yourself out of. However, it is often very hard to take the

## Post-traumatic stress disorder

It is not clear why women develop post-traumatic stress disorder postnatally, but it can be linked to difficult and frightening experiences during labour and delivery. Symptoms include flashbacks, nightmares, panic attacks, sleep problems and irrational behaviour.

The disorder can occur on its own or alongside postnatal depression. Treatment can be a combination of mood-stabling medications, such as lithium, or an anti-epileptic drug; an antipsychotic (this helps combat the symptoms of psychosis); and a tranquiliser, such as a benzodiazepine, to help you relax. You cannot breastfeed while taking these types of medications, so your baby must be formula-fed.

## Postpartum psychosis

Postpartum (or puerperal) psychosis is serious psychiatric illness that causes new mothers to act strangely. The disorder can develop within hours of the delivery and requires urgent medical care. Symptoms can include high mood (mania), depression, confusion, hallucinations (hearing voices and seeing things that are not really there) and delusions. It is rare (it affects only one or two new mothers in every 1000), but is more common in those with previous mental health problems (e.g. bipolar or schizoaffective disorder).

Treatment involves admission to a specialist unit together with your baby. Most women make a full recovery, but it can take many months. Help is provided by a specialist psychiatric team offering cognitive behavioural therapy, psychological support and medications such as antidepressants and antipsychotics.

first step and admit that something may be wrong, particularly if you feel guilty about having negative feelings. It may be, in fact, that others have noticed uncharacteristic behaviour and confronted you about it. Remember, no one will judge you adversely for the way you feel and admitting that you are struggling is the first step to recovery. So, if you think that you or your partner are experiencing some of the symptoms of postnatal depression, you need to see your midwife, health visitor or GP, who can recommend an appropriate course of action. They can also provide you with reassurance and simple, practical advice.

### Treatment for PND

Counselling, psychotherapy and antidepressant medication are the treatments that are considered most useful in treating PND. Electroconvulsive therapy (ECT) may be recommended if you have severe postnatal depression, but is only used when antidepressants and other treatments have not worked. However, there are also some things you can do to help yourself.

### Social support

Talking through your feelings with people who can relate to your experiences can be really helpful – you will be amazed at what similar stories you may share. Simply chatting to other mothers who feel the same way as you may be all you need to resolve your symptoms of PND. Initially, you may need to be proactive to find a group that you connect with.

### Help at home

Getting some extra help at home, whether it is from your partner, a relative/friend or a paid professional, can free up a little time for you. Perhaps you could indulge in a treat such as a long soak in the bath, time in front of the television or simply some sleep. Even if help is difficult to arrange or happens irregularly, these are things you could fit in to your day while your baby is sleeping.

### Getting out and about

The endorphins you produce during exercise are great for your mental health. Being out of the house and getting your heart rate up is the important thing. If you cannot find any time for exercise, try to change some of your habits. For example, walk to the local shops instead of taking the car, park the car a short distance from the shop rather than outside its door and walk the rest of the way, or put your baby in the buggy or sling for one of their daytime sleeps and go for a walk during this time.

### Healthy eating

A good, varied diet will help you feel stronger. Anaemia on its own can make you feel tired and lethargic, so you may need supplements if this is diagnosed by your GP. You will also feel run down if you are not finding time to eat or because you are dieting to help shift that extra 'baby weight'. Make sure you sit down for at least one proper meal a day and seek help from a nutritionist if necessary.

### Support organisations

There are some support organisations that you can contact for help and advice. You can phone them simply for a chat, and their websites also give tips and solutions to help you through your depression. See Useful Resources for details.

# 8

# Baby health

Most babies will have minor illnesses in their first year. You will want to know how to treat these and also how to spot more serious conditions that may need medical help. Some key first aid techniques are always useful to know.

# When your baby is ill

While their immune systems are maturing, babies are very susceptible to a range of common illnesses. Most of these do not require medical treatment, but you will want to make your baby as comfortable as possible until they recover.

## What you need
✓ Thermometer
✓ Infant paracetamol
✓ Infant ibuprofen
✓ Oral rehydration solution
✓ Saline nasal drops
✓ Nasal aspirator
✓ Syringe

Coughs, colds, ear infections and diarrhoea and vomiting bugs can usually be treated at home (see Chart on p.164), but it is important to keep an eye on your baby to see if their condition worsens or whether there are signs of more serious illness.

### Monitoring your baby's temperature
Normal body temperature is between 36°C and 37.5°C. Anything above this is considered to be a fever. If your baby has a fever, they may sweat and have hot, flushed skin; alternatively, they may feel cold and clammy and look pale.

I am often asked by worried parents how to control a high temperature and at what stage it is appropriate to seek medial help. As a parent myself, I completely understand the concern, as it can be frightening looking after a child who has a fever and is not themselves. Children frequently get fevers, but doctors rarely react until it is above 38°C. For babies under three months, you should get medical advice if their temperature is 38°C or higher; for those aged three to six months, you should do this if it is 39°C or higher. When your baby is six months and older, you can be less concerned and, provided you can get the temperature down at home and they cheer up, they do not necessarily need to see a doctor. See Box for advice on thermometers and temperature readings.

Babies are miserable when their temperature is high, so it makes them feel much better when it is brought back down. A rapidly rising temperature also increases the risk of a febrile convulsion (see p.169). Your baby's temperature should always be brought down in a slow and controlled way. It used to be advised that you put children in a cool bath.

## Thermometers
There are many different types of thermometer on the market. The main thing is to avoid one that contains mercury and/or is made of glass, as these can break easily, leaking the highly poisonous liquid, and the broken shards may cut your baby. Digital thermometers are the best. Ones that go under the tongue or in the bottom are generally not used for under-fives, but other types include ones for the ear canal (tympanic) and under the arm. Follow the instruction manual of the thermometer that you choose – it is worth getting familiar with this before you need to use it – and always make sure that you have a spare battery. If you get an unusually high or low reading, take three readings at least five minutes apart just to confirm (if your technique is incorrect, the readings will be false).

However, this works only momentarily, as their core temperature shoots up again quickly as soon as you remove them from the water. Safe ways of bringing the temperature down are detailed in the Chart on p.164.

## Medication

Paracetemol and ibuprofen are the medicines commonly used to bring a temperature down (antipyretics) and the infant versions are available to buy over-the-counter without the need for a prescription. You can give a baby over two months four full doses of paracetamol within 24 hours, provided they have no liver problems; when they are over three months, they can be given three full doses of ibuprofen over 24 hours, as long as they have no wheezing or kidney abnormalities or blood-clotting problems. When I say full doses, I mean the dose that is recommended on the box of your specific product, as different preparations of liquid paracetamol/ibuprofen vary in strength. Paracetamol and ibuprofen are not licensed for newborns, but special doses can be given in a hospital setting if necessary.

The best way to give these medicines is to try one first and, if this does not bring down the temperature, try the other one. If the temperature still does not come down, start by giving the child a full dose of paracetamol, followed by ibuprofen four hours later and then alternating between the two at four-hourly intervals until the maximum dosage of each has been given over 24 hours. Current advice is against giving both the paracetamol and ibuprofen simultaneously, even though this can be easier. Special syringes can be used for measuring and administering them.

You should see the temperature fall within one to two hours. At this point it is tempting to stop medication. However, the temperature is probably being controlled by the medicines, so if you miss the next dose the temperature may rise again and then you will be back to the beginning. I would therefore advise you to give the paracetamol or ibuprofen for at least 36 hours before you see if the temperature will stay down on its own. If you are unable to get the temperature down at home, you need to seek medical help.

*If your baby suddenly develops a cough and does not have a cold or other illness, check if they have inhaled a small object/ toy and seek medical help to remove it.*

## Dehydration

Children are fine without food during a short illness, but they need plenty of fluids, especially if they have a temperature (because they will lose water through sweating/evaporation). However, they often feel too poorly to drink or may vomit up what they have taken. Babies under six months old can become ill very quickly because of lack of fluids, so you need to monitor this very carefully.

Ideally, you should give your baby cooled boiled water or oral rehydration solution, but if all they will take is milk, diluted fruit juice or squash, it is better to get this liquid inside them than to force them to drink something they do not want or like. Although temporary lactose intolerance can follow a gastroenteritis infection (see p.177), do continue breastfeeding or giving formula if that is what your baby prefers. Signs of dehydration include:

- not having a wet nappy in the last six hours
- vomiting up fluids
- dry lips, mouth and tongue
- sunken eyes with dark circles underneath
- being drowsy and lethargic
- cool hands and feet
- a sunken fontanelle (the soft spot on the top of their head).

A simple test for dehydration is to press on your baby's breastbone with your finger for five seconds, release it, then see how many seconds you have to

## Treating common symptoms

| SYMPTOM | TREATMENT | HOW TO GIVE |
|---|---|---|
| Blocked nose/cough | • humified air | • sit your baby in the bathroom with the door shut while running the bath or shower (N.B. do not give inhalations or add aromatic oils) |
| | • saline nasal drops (available over-the-counter) | • drops of solution as directed in each nostril to soften mucus |
| | • nasal aspiration | • gently sucking out the mucus with a specially designed nasal aspirator |
| | • head elevation while sleeping (to allow mucus to move down the nasal cavity) | • place books under the legs of the cot at the head end (leave the mattress flat on the base) |
| | • increase fluids (dehydration makes secretions thicker) | • breast milk/formula if tolerated; cooled boiled water; oral rehydration solution |
| Fever (high temperature) | • lower core body temperature | • remove excess layers of clothing (stripping down to just the nappy if necessary); place your baby near a fan; give medication (paracetamol or ibuprofen) |
| | • increase fluids to prevent dehydration | • breast milk/formula if tolerated; cooled boiled water; oral rehydration solution |
| Diarrhoea and vomiting | • increase fluids; drink little and often if vomiting (e.g. 5–10 ml every 5–10 mins – use syringe if necessary) | • milk/formula if tolerated • cooled boiled water • oral rehydration solution |
| Sore throat | • pain relief medication | • paracetamol or ibuprofen |
| Earache | • pain relief medication • antibiotics may be needed (but, in most cases, the cause is viral) | • paracetamol or ibuprofen • as prescribed by GP |
| Itching | • prevent scratching • relieve itchiness | • scratch mittens • calamine lotion/cream; antihistamines (available over-the-counter) |
| | • pain relief medication | • paracetamol or ibuprofen |
| Generalised pain | • pain relief medication | • paracetamol or ibuprofen |

## Rashes

Many viral illnesses are accompanied by a rash. These tend to be flat or lightly raised red rashes that disappear when you press the side of a glass on them. The rashes that you need to seek medical advice about are those that do not disappear when you put a glass on top of them. These can be a sign of a serious infection or a problem with the blood's clotting system.

count before the normal pinkness returns to the skin. Count 'one elephant, two elephant, three elephant …'. If you get to three, you should seek medical advice.

If you are advised to go to hospital, your baby will be put on a 'fluid challenge': you will be given a syringe and a cup of water/oral rehydration solution and asked to give them 5–10 ml every five to ten minutes. If they are able to keep this down for a couple of hours, they can go home; if not, they may need to be admitted for fluid support.

### When to see your GP

A baby's condition can change rapidly and you, as their parent, are best placed to notice this. When deciding whether or not your baby needs to see a doctor, ask yourself:

- Are they sleeping more?
- Are they feeding less?
- Are their nappies drier than before?
- Is there a new rash?
- Do they look pale, mottled or blue?
- Do they have a rash that does not blanch under a glass (see Box)?
- Do they have a very high temperature that cannot be brought down?
- Are they irritable?
- Are they inconsolable, with a high-pitched cry?
- Are they lethargic, unresponsive or floppy?
- Does their breathing seem laboured or noisy?
- Is the fontanelle bulging?

Doctors are concerned about these symptoms, because they may indicate more serious illnesses, such as bronchiolitis, meningitis, septicaemia and croup (see entries in the A–Z, pp.174–183). Trust your intuition and **do not be afraid to ask for help.**

### When to go to immediately to hospital or consider calling 999

Regardless of whether or not they have been suffering from an illness, you must go immediately to your nearest hospital or call for an ambulance if your baby does any of the following:

- stops breathing for a short while (apnoea)
- struggles for breath (you may see a sucking in of the ribcage)
- seems disorientated
- becomes unconscious and/or you are unable to wake them
- has a fit for the first time or it lasts for more than three minutes
- has a fever and is either inconsolable or persistently lethargic
- shows signs of severe abdominal pain
- is vomiting continuously and is unable to drink
- has a cut that will not stop bleeding or is too large to secure at home
- cannot use a limb (either following an injury or spontaneously)
- has swallowed a poison or pills.

## Top Tips

**1** Your baby may be quite grizzly and difficult to amuse when they are ill. Be prepared to give lots of cuddles!

**2** Your normal feeding and sleeping pattern is likely to be disrupted and you may have to go with the flow for a while. However, try to get back to your regular routine as soon as your baby seems better – you do not want to still be soothing them to sleep two weeks after a minor cold!

# Infant first aid

It can be really useful to learn some first aid techniques. Many are easy to perform and save unnecessary trips to the GP or hospital. Others are a vital part of treating your baby until specialist help arrives.

## What you need
✓ Sticking plasters
✓ Butterfly strips
✓ Sterile dressing packs
✓ Antiseptic cream
✓ Ice pack

## Cuts and bleeding

If your baby gets a cut (laceration), the priority is to stop the bleeding. Use a clean cloth or, ideally, a sterile dressing pack to press on the wound, but if you cannot find anything, press firmly with your fingers and hand. You may need to do this for ten minutes to ensure the bleeding has stopped. If possible, raise the wound above the level of the heart to help slow the flow. Do not use a tourniquet, because this can stop the circulation and cause further problems. If the blood soaks through this dressing, place another one over the top – do not remove the first one, as this may disrupt a clot that is forming, which will prolong the bleeding.

Once bleeding has stopped, clean the wound with fresh water; you can also apply some antiseptic cream to help prevent infection. If the cut is small (shallow), use a breathable sticking plaster or butterfly stiches (thin adhesive strips) to keep it together. If the wound is big and/or deep and you cannot join the edges, go to hospital, as stitches or glue maybe needed.

If the injury was caused by glass and you are not sure if fragments are still in the wound, you need to get it X-rayed. The glass fragments will show up on the film and can be removed in hospital. Similarly, removal of any other embedded object will also need to be done in hospital.

## Hair tourniquet syndrome

The odd condition known as 'hair tourniquet syndrome' occurs when a piece of hair gets tangled around a finger or toe. As the hair is so fine, it is often difficult to see; often the first sign you will have is that your baby is in pain. On closer inspection, the finger or toe maybe swollen and bluish or pale in colour, but you may need to get a magnifying glass to see the hair wrapped around the digit. When you unwrap the hair, the finger or toe should return to its normal colour, but if you find that you are unable to untangle the hair yourself, seek medical help promptly.

## Where to go for help

Depending on the age and condition of your baby, a number of different sources of help are available to you:

- **Midwife or health visitor:** for minor concerns with your newborn.
- **Pharmacy:** for mild conditions that can be treated without a prescription.
- **GP:** when you need further advice or prescription medication.
- **Hospital accident and emergency unit:** for serious or life-threatening situations.

## Head injuries and falls

Once your baby is mobile, falls and bumps to the head happen quite frequently. Nevertheless, they should always be taken seriously, as every head injury can potentially cause damage. Apply immediate pressure to a superficial bruise, then use a cold compress (a cloth/flannel soaked in cold water) for up to ten minutes. If there is a cut, following the procedures outlined opposite. Concerning signs to look for are:

- excessive crying/being difficult to console
- vomiting more than twice
- being unsteady when crawling/walking; seeming dizzy or disorientated
- not appropriately moving the body or face; weakness or paralysis
- unequal pupil size
- you are unable to rouse them from sleep or they lose consciousness
- abnormal breathing
- obvious serious wound
- blood or clear fluid running out from the nose or ear
- a fit (seizure).

These are indications that you need to take your baby to hospital. Frequently, these injuries occur just before bedtime and your baby wants to go to sleep, but if you are concerned enough about the nature of the fall you should still seek medical help – the staff are very used to monitoring tired and sleeping children with head injuries. If your child has had a significant head injury, but is not confused, is fully conscious, not vomiting and is appropriately moving their body and face, they will be observed for four hours to check that all is well.

If your baby has fallen from a height onto their head, they may have damaged their neck and spine. You should call an ambulance and not move your baby until the paramedics arrive. This is often easier said than done, as mobile babies who are still conscious will want to get up to be comforted. Try to keep them calm and still, ideally in the recovery position (see pp.170–1), until help arrives.

If your baby has fallen from a height and is unconscious, you need to check to see if they are breathing and, if not, move them into a position in which you can perform CPR (see p.171). However, it is vital that you keep their neck as still as you can, so you need to find others to help you, as you must to work together to move your baby's body and head/neck at the same time.

## Burns and scalds

A burn is caused by dry heat, such as an iron or fire; a scald is from something wet, such as steam, hot fat/oil or boiling water. However, the treatment is the same for both. The injured area needs to be put under cold running water immediately – this will reduce the heat of the skin. Only do this for ten minutes at a time, as your baby will get too cold. Allow the area to warm up again and, if necessary, put it under the tap for a second time. If you are not near running water, immerse the wound in any cold liquid you have.

Next, remove any clothing that is near the affected area, but not if it is stuck to the skin. Use cling film to cover the burn or scald to help ease the pain and to protect the area (cling film will not stick to the wound, so it will not be painful to remove it at a later stage). Do not put butter, toothpaste, oil, ointment or anything else onto the skin, as it will have to be cleaned off if further treatment is required. Any blisters caused by a burn or scald will burst naturally, but the raw area underneath will need a protective dressing. While you can treat minor burns and scalds at home, you should go to hospital for:

- burns larger than 3 cm in diameter
- deep burns
- full-thickness burns (the skin looks white and has lost all sensation, so may not be very painful)
- burns to the face, hands, nipples and genitals
- smoke inhalation
- all chemical and electrical burns.

## Insect bites and stings

Bites and stings from insects cause a local allergic response, resulting in itching, redness and swelling. This usually improves within 48 hours. If the area is still hot and inflamed after this time, there may be secondary infection, which will require antibiotic treatment. The immediate management is to wash the area with soap and water and then to apply an ice pack for up to ten minutes. Give paracetamol or ibuprofen for pain relief and elevate the area if possible. You must seek immediate medical help if you notice any of the following:

- wheezing or difficulty breathing
- difficulty swallowing
- vomiting or diarrhoea
- fast heart beat
- dizziness or seeming faint
- confusion/agitation/anxiety.

These can be signs that your baby is having an anaphylactic reaction to the sting or bite. Treatment will vary, depending which of the above signs your baby is exhibiting. For example, they may need a nebuliser of salbutamol or adrenaline to help with their breathing, or antihistamines/steroids to reduce the progression of the reaction.

## Bites
Bites from animals and other children are quite common in babies, and you will know if your baby has been bitten, because the wound edges are often irregular or crushed. Any bite (including human bites) is usually heavily contaminated with bacteria, so if it breaks the skin, your baby will require antibiotics to make sure that the wound does not become infected.

## Splinters
Most splinters can be removed at the time with a steady hand and some tweezers, but do not wash your baby's hand, as the water will make the splinter swell (especially if it is wood), making it harder to remove. If you are unable to remove it, most will work their own way out over time. However, they can cause infection, so if the area appears red, hot and tender 24 hours after the injury, you will need to seek medical help for removal of the splinter and possible antibiotics.

## Objects in the nose or ears
If your baby has something stuck in their nose or ear, leave it where it is (unless you can get it out easily),

as medical help will be required to safely remove it. Be careful not to push it in further in your efforts to get it out; neither must you leave the object there in the hope that it falls out on its own. Objects in the nose cause a serious risk, as they may dislodge into your baby's airway, causing them to choke (see p.170), or your baby may inhale the object into their lungs. If the object is deep in the nose or ear, a small operation may be needed to remove it.

## Ingested foreign bodies
Babies are prone to picking up small objects and putting them in their mouths. You may actually see them swallow an object or your first indication of this is that they suddenly start coughing.

The worst thing to swallow is a battery, as they are corrosive and can cause significant damage if left – small disc-shaped batteries are more dangerous than cylinder-shaped ones, as they do not have the strong protective wrapping of other types and so are more quickly corroded by the stomach acid, causing catastrophic burns. In either case, you need to seek medical help quickly. The team will take an X-ray to see where the battery is and then surgery will be needed to remove it.

Other items that babies swallow often pass through them without any problems. However, coins and larger objects can get lodged in the lower end of the oesophagus (gullet) just before the stomach, because the junction there is tight. An X-ray can be done and then a plan can be made to remove it.

## Swallowing pills or poisons
It is very alarming to discover that your baby may have swallowed pills or poison. The first thing to check is how much has been taken, if at all. For example, in the case of pills, if faced with an empty bottle, it could be that some have rolled under the furniture or that the entire contents is scattered around the floor. If you suspect the worst, take the box/packet or bottle and go straight to hospital – the doctor will need to see the packaging and what remains of the contents. Make a note of the time, so that you can tell them when you think your baby ingested the pills/poisons. In the meantime, keep a close watch on your baby and be prepared to

perform CPR (see p.171). Do not give your baby a salt-and-water solution, or do anything else to make them sick, as this can cause more harm in some instances.

If your baby is in pain or there is any staining, soreness or blistering around their mouth, they have probably swallowed something corrosive. Give them milk or water to sip in order to ease the burning and to dilute the corrosive substance. Get them to hospital quickly.

## Fainting or shock

If your baby looks pale and/or seems unwell after an accident, lie them down. Keep them covered up and warm, but not too hot. The faint feeling will wear off in a minute or two.

## Fits/convulsions

Generalised seizures (fits) are common in children under three. Your baby will become unconscious, their eyes will roll back and they will begin twitching/shaking their arms and legs. Fists and teeth may be clenched and they may begin to foam at the mouth. There may also be some blood within the foam, indicating that they have accidentally bitten their tongue.

Seizures of this nature are usually short, lasting only a few seconds, although they can go on for a few minutes. The most common reason children in this age group have a fit is due to a rapid rise in body temperature (it does not need to be a very high temperature), which can affect their brain. This type of fit is known as a febrile convulsion. Febrile convulsions are not usually connected with epilepsy. However, they can be very frightening to watch, so you will need to remain calm and deal with your baby in the following way:

- look at the time so that you can calculate how long the fit lasts
- loosen anything tight around their neck
- make sure that they are not in a place that could cause them harm from hitting their limbs or head while fitting
- do not put anything in their mouth; if you think they are choking on food or an object, try to remove it.

If your baby is still fitting after three minutes, you need to get medical assistance, preferably by calling for an ambulance. The paramedics will have medication to stop the seizure. For a seizure to do damage, a child needs to be fitting for more than 30 minutes, so you will have plenty of time to seek medical help. I know this all sounds terrifying, but most febrile convulsions are harmless and do not affect your baby's long-term health.

A child who has had their first ever seizure should be taken to hospital to be checked over by a doctor, even if you are sure that it was caused by a rapidly rising temperature. The doctor needs to confirm this and also keep them for observation for 12–24 hours, as it is common for a second seizure to occur within this time period.

## Wheeze

A whistling sound while breathing is termed 'wheeze' and it can have many different causes: infection, allergy or a foreign body lodged in the airway. Asthma is a global term for wheeze that is recurrent. This may be the result of a common cold, allergies (e.g. to cats, dogs, house dust mites) or, perhaps, from exercise, cold air, cigarette smoke or emotional stress. If the wheeze is mild, you can try some simple things at home to help relieve it:

With any cuts, burns/scalds and animal/human bites, always check that your baby's tetanus immunisation is up to date, as infection can occur if the wound comes into contact with soil.

- sit your baby up and lean them forwards slightly
- try to keep them calm and relaxed
- put them in a steamy bathroom (see Chart, p.164).

If the above methods do not help, the wheezing gets worse or your baby is showing signs they are working hard with their breathing, get medical help.

## Choking

Choking is the result of an obstruction to the airway. Knowing how to quickly and effectively clear this and, if necessary, resuscitate your baby (i.e. perform CPR) may save their life.

A choking baby may suddenly be unable to breathe, cry, cough or speak. However, if your baby is still coughing effectively, let them continue, as the blockage is usually and most effectively moved by the coughing mechanism. If this does not fix the situation or your child is unable to cough, you need to try to dislodge the blockage yourself.

Hold your baby face-down along your non-dominant arm with their head lower than their bottom; if they are too big to hold this way, sit them on your knee. Perform five back blows: use the heel of your hand to hit them firmly between the shoulder blades. Then turn them onto their back and perform five chest thrusts: place two fingers in the middle of their chest just below the nipples, and push inwards and upwards up to five times. If the thrusts do not dislodge the object, repeat the back blows followed by the chest thrusts up to twice more. If the obstruction is still there or your baby is not breathing, call for help – this may mean shouting or phoning the emergency services – and progress to CPR (see opposite).

## Secondary drowning

We are all familiar with the concept of drowning, and if your baby has been submerged in water for a length of time, you need to get them to hospital as soon as possible. A less well-known phenomenom is 'secondary drowning'. This occurs when a child was underwater for a very short time, was able to get their breath back and appeared to recover relatively quickly. Later on, anywhere from 1–72 hours, they shows signs of confusion and lethargy. This is the result of a small amount of water getting

into the lungs, which irritates the lung tissue and causes an inflammatory reaction (pulmonary oedema). This inhibits the transfer of blood gases, meaning the oxygen levels in the blood fall and the carbon dioxide levels rise. Your baby will need to have their vital signs (e.g. heart rate, oxygen levels) monitored in hospital, possibly with a chest X-ray and a blood test to assess how the lungs are coping. If necessary, they will be given respiratory support.

## Life-threatening emergencies

The treatment for babies under one who are in a life-threatening condition differs slightly from what you may know about dealing with older children and adults. In addition, you do different things depending on whether your baby is:

- conscious or unconscious
- unconscious and breathing versus unconscious and not breathing.

To find out if your baby is conscious, call their name and tap them on the sole of their foot. If there is no response (i.e. they are unconscious), check whether or not they are breathing by putting your face next to their mouth/nose, at the same time looking along their chest and abdomen for any movement. You may hear the breath and feel it on your cheek, as well as seeing the chest/abdomen rise and fall. Allow ten seconds for this. If your baby is breathing, you should put them in the recovery position until you can get them to hospital. If they are not breathing, start performing CPR.

### The recovery position

An unconscious baby has no muscle control so, when lying on their back, the tongue may block the back of the throat, thereby restricting the flow of air to the lungs. The airway itself also naturally restricts during unconsciousness and, if your baby vomits, they may choke, too. It is important to position babies in a particular way to prevent this happening. Smaller babies need to be held along the length of one arm, with their face looking down to the floor and slightly tilted down. For any baby too big to position like this, lie them on their side on the floor, tilting their chin up slightly. The arm and leg that are on the top (i.e. not the ones touching the floor) need to be placed so that they support your baby and stop them from rolling onto their front: bend the knee and pull the leg forward and bend the arm and place it palm-down on the floor.

## Cardiopulmonary resuscitation (ov)

If your baby is not breathing, you will need to perform cardiopulmonary resuscitation (CPR). Lay them on their back and open the airway by tilting their head back slightly and removing any obstructions (if possible). Place your mouth over your baby's mouth and nose and blow just enough for their chest to rise. Perform five of these 'rescue breaths'. Next, if there are no signs of life, perform 30 chest compressions: for under-ones, place two fingers in the middle of their chest and press down to at least one-third of the chest volume at a rate of about 100 compressions per minute (slightly more than one per second). Follow this with two more breaths. Repeat the cycle of 30 compressions and two breaths twice more. Continue until your baby recovers. If you have not been able to get help already, do so now.

## Life support at a glance

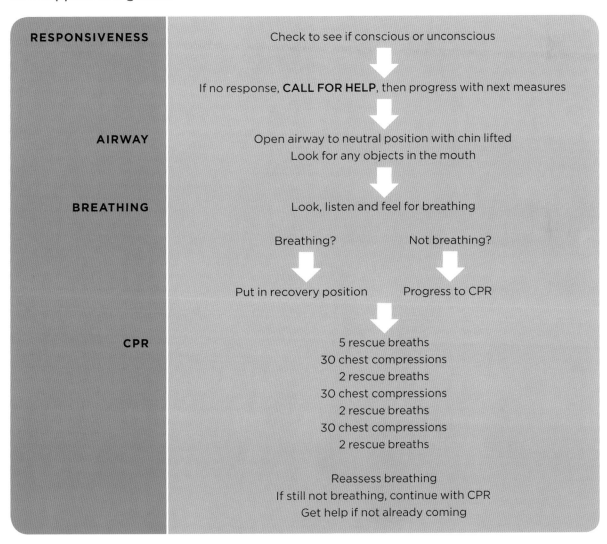

**RESPONSIVENESS**

Check to see if conscious or unconscious

If no response, **CALL FOR HELP**, then progress with next measures

**AIRWAY**

Open airway to neutral position with chin lifted
Look for any objects in the mouth

**BREATHING**

Look, listen and feel for breathing

Breathing?        Not breathing?

Put in recovery position        Progress to CPR

**CPR**

5 rescue breaths
30 chest compressions
2 rescue breaths
30 chest compressions
2 rescue breaths
30 chest compressions
2 rescue breaths

Reassess breathing
If still not breathing, continue with CPR
Get help if not already coming

# Sick babies in hospital

Having an unwell baby who needs medical care in hospital can be a difficult situation for parents, as you have to rely on others for their specialist skills.

If your baby is born with a complication that requires treatment, is found to be jaundiced or to have lost more than ten per cent of their birthweight, they will be admitted to the neonatal unit (NNU). The doctors and nurses there have specialised training, offering three levels of care:

- **intensive care:** your baby requires a ventilator to assist their breathing or they have a condition that requires specialised attention and monitoring; babies are often in incubators and attached to monitors.
- **High dependency care:** your baby will be breathing for themselves, but may need extra support from machines that help them to keep their lungs inflated (e.g. high flow therapy, CPAP); they may also need feeding via a nasogastric tube (NGT) and may be on medications such as antibiotics.
- **Low dependency care:** your baby simply needs to feed and grow; babies born before 34 weeks need to be fed via NGT and others may require a hot cot or incubator to help maintain their body temperature.

If your local hospital cannot offer the appropriate level of care, your baby may be transferred to another one. Babies can also move between different levels of care within the same unit.

In other situations your baby will be admitted to the children's ward. This can be for just a day if they need a simple operation that they can recover from at home, or for a longer time if they need further care. Not every hospital has a paediatric centre (for more specialised nursing), and even if they do, they may not have a PICU (paediatric intensive care unit) or the specialist doctors your baby may need. Again, your baby may have to be moved to a different hospital.

## Life on the ward

Usually, the hospital will be able to provide accommodation for one parent. On the children's ward, this is often a 'put-up bed' next to their cot; in the NNU, you are not given a bed on the ward, but may instead be given accommodation elsewhere.

Wards are busy places and the nurses often look after more than one baby during their shift, usually one nurse to two to four babies in the NNU and perhaps as many as one to eight on the children's ward. They rely heavily on your help with the non-medical jobs, such as changing nappies, feeding and dressing. Not only does this help you bond with your baby (see Box in Chapter 1, p.19), it is also nice for you to feel part of the hospital team and know that you are helping with your baby's recovery.

One of the most difficult parts of your baby's hospital stay is knowing that they are having to go through tests: blood and urine samples, lumbar punctures and so on. Some parents chose to stay while these are carried out; others prefer to leave the room and comfort their baby afterwards. Blood tests are often done with the help of topical anaesthetic, which numbs the skin so the needle cannot be felt. However, these are not licensed for newborns, so very young babies may be offered a sweet solution to suck from a dummy as pain relief.

Always ask the hospital staff if you are unsure about anything – it is their job to keep you up-to-date with your baby's progress. There is often a ward round each morning when the medical team reviews each child. This is a really important time for you to be around, as you can hear the plan for your baby's care that day and discuss things with the doctors. Many parents find it helpful to jot down questions through the day and then refer to the list when the round happens, as it can sometimes be intimidating with so many people in a small room and difficult to remember what you wanted to ask.

# Immunisation

Immunisation schedules are frequently reviewed and modified and you will be given details of the current programme by your health visitor. Parents naturally want to know what benefits immunisation offers and to discuss the issues that surround it.

Some of the diseases targeted by the programme are now very rare. This is thanks to immunisation, as the more of the population that is immunised, the more difficult it is for the disease to spread. In fact, if babies and children continue to be immunised, we may be able to totally eradicate some of these diseases in the way that we have smallpox. The concept of 'herd immunity' occurs when the immunisation of a significant portion of the population (or 'herd') provides a measure of protection for the individuals who have not developed immunity or are unable to be vaccinated. It is therefore the responsibility of us all to maintain the herd immunity effect and have our babies immunised. Immunisations are not compulsory – you do have the right to refuse – but I would encourage you to discuss this fully with your health visitor or GP, so that they have the opportunity to answer your questions and concerns.

A lot of parents worry that their young baby's immune system is too immature to cope. By the end of the first week your baby's skin, throat, nose and intestines are covered by thousands of different bacteria and viruses and the body deals amazingly well with this. Your baby is only being immunised against a relatively small number of infections. The vaccines contain weakened or killed bugs, so they do not cause the actual disease, they just stimulate the immune system.

Side effects are another concern. Common reactions are redness, tenderness and swelling around the site of the injection and irritability; a temperature can also occur two or three days afterwards. In extremely rare cases (one in one million) a baby has an immediate anaphylactic reaction (a rash/itching or difficulty breathing). The health professional who has just given the vaccination will promptly treat this with medication.

There is no reason why a baby with hayfever, asthma, eczema, nut allergy, food intolerances, coeliac disease, cow's milk protein intolerance or other food intolerances should not be given the vaccinations. The only time to be cautious is if your baby has an egg allergy, because egg is used in live vaccines (MMR, flu, yellow fever), or if they have a reduced or suppressed immune system – special medical advice is needed. However, a baby should not be immunised if they:

- have had a confirmed anaphylactic reaction to a previous dose of a vaccine
- have had a confirmed anaphylactic reaction to neomycin, streptomycin or polymyxin B (antibiotics used in the vaccines).

Premature babies need to have their immunisations following exactly the same schedule as a full-term baby. Timings should be calculated according to their actual age, not their corrected age (see Chapter 6, p.129). Postponing the immunisations until your baby is older leaves them at unnecessary risk of infection, particularly as their immune system may not have had the full boost from your immune factors. These transfer across the placenta from you to your baby at 36 weeks of pregnancy and stay in your baby's system for only two to three months.

# A-Z of illnesses and conditions

Listed below are some of the things that can affect a baby in their first year. Many of them are self-limiting (they are temporary conditions that resolve without the need for medical treatment); others can simply be treated at home. Rarely, your baby may need to be admitted to hospital for treatment or an operation. Parents can often tell when their babies are not their usual selves and so you should never hesitate to seek advice from a medical professional if you are in any way concerned.

## Bronchiolitis

A seasonal illness, bronchiolitis occurs predominately during the autumn and winter months. It affects the breathing of babies and infants, commonly between six and eighteen months of age. The softness of their ribs makes any difficulty in breathing very easy to see. Different signs to look for are:

- nasal flaring (the nose widens and the nostrils flare with each breath)
- faster breathing
- noisy breathing (e.g. wheezing, grunting)
- head-bobbing (the head moves forward and back during breaths)
- drawing in of the ribs and breastbone during breathing
- tracheal tug – this is seen as the skin being sucked in at the top of the breastbone
- coughing
- fever
- tiredness and exhaustion
- difficulty feeding or refusing to feed
- vomiting because of the coughing.

Bronchiolitis is caused by a virus and is a self-limiting illness, so antibiotics are not needed. However, the symptoms are very similar to those of pneumonia (which does require antibiotics), so you should see your GP to confirm the diagnosis. Bronchiolitis usually improves after five days, but the cough can last up to fourteen days. The fever and blocked nose/cough can be relieved as outlined in the Chart on p.164. However, some babies find it really difficult to feed if they are struggling with their breathing, so you will need to see your GP for advice and possible admission to hospital for oxygen therapy and feeding support. Bronchiolitis is contagious, so you should avoid contact with other children for three to four days during the worst of the infection.

## Chickenpox

Caused by the virus Varicella-zoster, chickenpox is a mild illness that most children will contract at some point. There is a vaccine, but it is not part of the UK childhood immunisation programme (see Feature on p.173), although your baby can have it privately if you wish. Chickenpox tends to be seasonal, occurring mainly in late winter and spring. The virus is transmitted from person to person via droplets and airborne particles of mucus. The incubation period (the time it takes from contact with the virus to seeing signs of the illness) is 14–21 days and the disease is most contagious one to two days before the rash appears and until the spots crust over.

The symptoms are mild fever, loss of appetite, malaise (feeling poorly and sleepy) and a rash that starts off as flat red spots, which then blister and crust over after three to five days. The scabs will drop off after about a week. The spots can appear anywhere on the body (typically in clusters), even in the scalp and mouth. They can be very itchy, so follow the measures in the Chart on p.164 for relieving this, particularly as spots that are scratched off before they have crusted over will leave a tiny scar; give paracetamol/ibuprofen for the fever.

The rare complications of chicken pox are **pneumonia, septicaemia,** skin infections and **encephalitis** (see **meningitis**) and the effect on the unborn baby if a pregnant woman has chickenpox for the first time while pregnant. Contact your GP straight away if you notice any untypical symptoms, as this may indicate a complication that needs medical treatment.

## Circumcision

An operation to remove the fold of skin (foreskin) that normally covers the glans (head) of the penis is called circumcision. Some cultures and religions require newborn boys to be circumcised and there are also medical reasons for the procedure in boys that are older, such as an unretractable foreskin that is causing recurrent **urinary tract infections**. Other children are circumcised due to parental wishes. Some medical research has shown that there is a reduction in the spread of HIV and other sexually transmitted infections in men who have been circumcised, as well as a slightly lower risk of urine infection.

The procedure can be done at home, at a health clinic or in hospital using a local anaesthetic. The wound will initially be covered with gauze impregnated with petroleum jelly and you will also be given antibiotic ointment to apply later to prevent infection and to avoid the skin sticking to the nappy/clothing; sometimes an oral antibiotic is prescribed as well.

It is recommended that you bath your baby within 24 hours of the procedure. You will need to remove the dressing first – this may have dried to your baby's skin, so moisten the gauze before taking it off. If the wound bleeds a small amount, apply pressure for a minute or two until it stops. If the bleeding is heavy, call your GP or the doctor who performed the procedure for further advice while still applying pressure to the area. Apply the antibiotic ointment regularly (ideally at every nappy change): you can either put some on a clean piece of gauze and place this on the head of the penis or you can put the ointment directly onto the penis and the nappy will act as the gauze. Your baby should be seen again by the doctor within a week of the procedure to check that healing is taking place.

## Colic

Colic is a term used to describe an otherwise healthy baby who cries constantly and inconsolably for an extended period, appears to be uncomfortable and draws up their legs. It is very common and can affect one in five babies. Colic is often worse in the evenings and tends to peak at six weeks, normally settling by twelve weeks.

There is much debate on what causes colic, with no concrete evidence to support the various theories. However, there are several factors that are thought to contribute to the condition:

- an immature digestive system
- maternal diet (if breastfeeding)
- trapped wind
- overtiredness and heightened sensitivity to surroundings.

Before you attribute your baby's symptoms to colic, it is worth checking that they are not suffering from **reflux**, milk allergy (see Chapter 5, pp.122–3) or any other condition that can cause discomfort and even pain.

There is no proven cure for colic. You can try giving gripe water or a preparatory solution containing simeticone or similar with each feed. If these solutions work for your baby, you will see a dramatic improvement within a few feeds, but there is no point in continuing with them if things do not change. If you are breastfeeding, try cutting out spicy foods, alcohol, caffeine and cruciferous vegetables (e.g. broccoli, cabbage) from your diet; if this makes no difference, add them back in. Try to keep your baby as upright as possible during their feeds to reduce the swallowing of air (which will give them wind), but check that they are still latched on properly. If you are feeding from a bottle, again sit them more upright and follow the measures outlined in the Box in Chapter 3, p.83.

Make sure that you wind your baby during feeding, not just at the end (see Chapter 3, p.65). In addition, to release trapped air you can gently massage your baby's tummy and employ the 'colic hold': place your baby face down along your forearm with their cheek by your elbow and your hand firmly between their legs; hold your arm close to your body, using it to brace and steady your baby. See also Chapter 2, pp.42–7 for more about how to deal with crying.

## Common cold

Upper respiratory tract infections such as the common cold are very common in babies and young children, as they have not had a chance to build up their immunity. They are caused by a large number of viruses and babies are expected to get up to eight infections a year – more if they are looked after in a nursery – as they are usually spread easily via hand-to-hand transmission of secretions and droplets of mucus. A cold usually lasts for between three and ten days. Typical symptoms include:

- runny nose
- mild temperature
- sneezing
- blocked nose
- mild fatigue
- loss of appetite.

These can be treated following the guidelines in the Chart on p.164. If you cannot control the temperature at home, the illness has lasted more than seven days or your baby has difficulty breathing, you should see your GP, as antibiotics may be needed. These will not address the cold itself (which is viral), but will treat any secondary infection that your baby has developed (when the body is busy fighting one infection, it is more susceptible to getting another one).

## Conjunctivitis

The condition where the white part of the eyeball goes red is called conjunctivitis. It can be caused by either bacterial or viral infection, an allergy or as a result of an irritant entering the eye accidentally (e.g. shampoo). If something has entered your baby's eye, you need to wash (irrigate) the eye thoroughly. The easiest way to do this is to fill a plastic bottle with fresh cold water from the tap, hold your baby over the bath or sink and pour the water over the eye to rinse it out. Other potential causes of conjunctivitis need to be investigated by your GP as a matter of urgency. Infection can be treated with antibiotic ointment and antihistamines will help relieve symptoms of allergy. See also **sticky eyes** and **periorbital cellulitis**.

### Constipation
The symptoms of constipation are hard, pellet-like poos that are difficult to pass. Be aware, however, constipation is over-diagnosed. For example, it is normal for babies to turn red in the face and cry when they are passing a poo, but this does not necessarily indicate that they are constipated. Similarly, infrequent passing of stools is not a reliable symptom, as it can be normal even for a breastfed baby to poo only once a week – provided the stool is soft, this is not constipation.

Constipation usually occurs because there is too little fibre and water in the diet. Infant formula tends to cause more constipation than breast milk, but breastfed babies can also become constipated. Try to give your baby extra water throughout the day (this must be cooled boiled water that has been made freshly). If you are formula-feeding, add an extra 30 ml of water to the bottle. However, do not give your baby fewer scoops of powder, as they will receive insufficient calories for growth. Beware of significantly increasing the amount of fibre in their diet, as too much of it may inhibit the absorption of iron and other important nutrients.

In babies who are fully weaned, follow the measures outlined in the Box in Chapter 5, p.118.

If these measures have no effect, go to your GP, who may advise either an osmotic laxative or a stool-softener. Constipation can cause **urinary tract infection**, so monitor your baby's wees as well. There are also some rare conditions that can present with constipation (e.g. Hirschsprung's disease), so do ask your doctor for further advice if the constipation does not resolve.

### Cradle cap
The medical condition of seborrhoeic dermatitis is commonly known as 'cradle cap' when it occurs in newborns. The thick layer of greasy, yellow scales covering the top of the scalp is unsightly, but it is harmless and will clear in time. However, if the cradle cap is stubborn, rub in some olive oil and leave it to soften the area. Then use a comb to gently remove it – but even then it may return. Avoid picking at it, as it will only make it sore. If the condition persists, you can use a special shampoo containing an antifungal agent.

### Croup
The childhood condition of croup results from a virus that causes the tissue around the voice box and upper larynx to swell. This restricts the entrance to the lungs, causing breathing problems. It usually affects children between six months and three years. Croup often begins as a cold. Your baby will make an extra noise while breathing in and a barking noise when they cry and cough (some people describe this as a 'seal bark'). Sometimes there is a temperature, which you can treat with paracetemol/ibuprofen. The signs of difficulty in breathing are:

- a fast breathing rate
- noisy breathing
- sucking in the ribs and breastbone
- using neck muscles to help with breathing
- tracheal tug – the skin being sucked in at the top of the breastbone.

If your baby is working hard to breathe, follow the measures to create a steamy environment outlined in the Chart on p.164. If this does not help, seek medical help (at a hospital if necessary) to be given medicine to reduce the swelling.

### Diarrhoea
While most babies have runny poos from time to time (particularly breastfed babies), diarrhoea is a more persistent condition featuring watery, unformed stools, which are often greenish in colour and smell offensive. Diarrhoea can be caused by a virus and may be accompanied by **vomiting** – this is known as **gastroenteritis** (stomach bug). Diarrhoea is self-limiting, but the main issue for babies is dehydration (see pp.163–5), so make sure you treat this promptly.

### Eczema
Around one in five children suffer from eczema, a condition that causes the skin to become itchy, red, dry and cracked. In young babies, eczema is most prominent on the cheeks, forehead and scalp; at six to twelve months, it is often worst on the crawling surfaces (elbows and knees). The exact cause of eczema is not known, but it does tend to run in families and more frequently occurs in people who have allergies such as asthma and hayfever. Most children eventually grow out of it, but the symptoms can be unpleasant, particularly if the skin

becomes infected after scratching, so you should try to make your baby as comfortable as possible.

Try to use only cotton clothing (wool and manmade fibres can irritate the skin) and avoid using bubble bath or soap on your baby's skin. Use a paraffin-based emollient as a soap/bubble bath substitute to keep the skin as supple as possible. Apply a moisturising cream frequently throughout the day if needed. If you feel that this is not enough, try a 50:50 ointment. Itchiness can be worse in the heat and at night – use scratch mittens if possible. Ezcema seems to function in a cyclical pattern, first getting better, then returning as a 'flare up'. Keep going with the treatment even when the skin appears to have calmed down, but see your GP for further advice if there is no long-lasting improvement.

## Gastroenteritis

Commonly called a 'stomach bug', gastroenteritis is actually an infection of the bowel that causes runny, watery stools (**diarrhoea**) and often **vomiting**, too. Vomiting should cease by the third day, but the diarrhoea can last for five to seven days. Your baby may have a fever and also be suffering from crampy, abdominal pains – you can treat these according to the Chart on p.164. Your main concern is to make sure your baby stays well-hydrated (see pp.163–5), as lack of fluids can make them seriously ill.

Gastroenteritis infection is very contagious. You must wash your hands regularly with soap to help prevent the spread of germs, especially before meals and after nappy changes, and do not share towels with other family members. You should also avoid taking your baby swimming for two weeks.

## Glue ear

About twenty per cent of under-twos are affected by glue ear at any one time. It is caused by a malfunctioning Eustachian tube, which fails to drain fluid from the middle ear (the part directly behind the eardrum) into the back of the throat, possibly because it has been affected by an infection (**otitis media**), allergy or smoke irritation (from passive smoking). Glue ear is certainly not caused by water entering the ear canal when swimming or having a bath. Symptoms include hearing loss in one or both ears, which you may notice in your baby when they do not respond to noises or because their language is not developing as it should (see Chapter 6, p.144).

Most causes of glue ear do not need treatment and will clear on their own within two to three months. Babies whose condition does not resolve will require grommets (small tubes that are put across the eardrum to allow the fluid to drain away) – these are put in place during a small operation.

## Head lice

Contrary to popular opinion, infestations of head lice are not the result of having dirty hair or of poor hygiene. It is most likely that your baby will get head lice through contact with older children – they are very contagious, as the bugs can move very quickly and easily from head to head (although they cannot fly, jump or swim). Head lice are the size of a pinhead when first hatched and are therefore difficult to spot, but you may notice your baby scratching their head and some small white eggs (these are the hatched eggs, or 'nits') at the hair roots. Older lice are the size of a sesame seed and grey/brown in colour and can sometimes be seen when you part your baby's hair.

Treatment should begin as soon as you detect lice. You can use a proprietary shampoo, but these sometimes do not kill unhatched eggs, so you may need to repeat a few days later to make sure that all newly hatched bugs have been killed before they can lay. A potentially more effective treatment is to 'wet comb': wet the hair and apply conditioner (this prevents the lice from moving so easily around the head) and carefully comb through the hair with a special fine-toothed comb to remove all the eggs and bugs. Rinse when finished and repeat every three to five days to break the life cycle.

## Hernia

Babies are susceptible to three types of hernia: umbilical hernia, inguinal hernia and diaphragmatic hernia. If the hernia gets stuck and is unable to move freely then it is called an obstructed (or strangulated) hernia. An obstructed hernia is painful, does not push back in, is red/purple/blue and may be associated with vomiting and distress. While extremely rare, it is an emergency situation and you need to seek medical help immediately, as your baby will need an operation to free the loop of bowel to ensure that it regains its blood supply and remains healthy gut tissue.

### Umbilical hernia

Swelling in or around the belly button (umbilicus) is called an 'umbilical hernia' and is more common in African/Afro-Caribbean babies. It is painless and normally resolves on its own by the time your child is two – so there is no need for your baby to undergo surgery unless it becomes obstructed.

### Inguinal hernia

Relatively common in premature babies, an inguinal hernia is a swelling in the groin that grows when your baby is crying and can be pushed back to make the skin flat if your baby is settled. They will normally need surgery – this is a quick procedure under general anaesthetic.

### Diaphragmatic hernia

Occurring in about one in 2,500 babies, diaphragmatic hernias are very rare and are more commonly seen in boys than in girls. The diaphragm is a curved muscle that assists with breathing and separates the chest from the abdomen. A diaphragmatic hernia usually happens at around six to eight weeks of pregnancy, when the diaphragm does not develop fully and a small hole is left through which contents of the abdomen can pass into the chest. This can stop the lungs from developing fully. This condition is usually detected before birth during the ultrasound scan done at around twenty weeks. Your baby will need to be delivered in hospital so that the appropriate medical teams will be present to support your baby.

### Hypospadias

Occurring in one in 300 newborn boys, hypospadias is when the hole through which the urine passes out of the penis is not in the normal place, but is further along the shaft of the penis towards the body. The effect of this is that the stream of urine starts from lower down the penis than it should. Hypospadias is checked for at your baby's routine neonatal examination (see Chapter 1, p.14) and is fully correctible with minor surgery. If the condition is detected, the most important thing

is not to have your baby undergo **circumcision**, as the surgeon will need the foreskin in order to remodel your baby's penis.

### Impetigo

Honey-coloured crusting on any area of damaged skin (e.g. skin around the mouth that is red due to dribbling) is indicative of impetigo. It is most commonly caused by skin bacteria, is highly contagious and will distribute onto other areas of damaged skin. It often disappears on its own, but sometimes requires antibiotics. See your GP if you think that your baby may have impetigo, so that they can advise you whether to use medication or not.

### Intussusception

The rare illness of intussusception occurs when the gut telescopes in on itself and becomes obstructed. Your baby may have episodes of drawing their legs up in discomfort and, while this may appear to be **colic**, your baby will look and become ill, whereas colic resolves by the end of the evening. Other symptoms may include vomiting, not passing stools or passing a redcurrant-jelly-like stool. It is important to seek medical help quickly, so that blood supply is not compromised and the gut tissue remains healthy. Treatment is often with an air enema: air is blown into the gut via the bottom, creating pressure that allows the gut to return to normal. If this is unsuccessful, surgery maybe needed.

### Jaundice

Jaundice is a common condition in newborns. Babies are born with an excess of red blood cells that often cannot be broken down fast enough as part of metabolic processes, particularly if they are dehydrated,

breastfed (breast milk affects the function of the liver) or have an infection. This creates a build-up in the blood of a yellow substance called bilirubin, which causes the skin to turn pale yellow. You can best see this by pressing on the tip of your baby's nose: just before the blood rushes back into the skin you will be able to see if the skin has a yellow tinge. Other symptoms of jaundice are dark yellow urine and pale-coloured stools.

All newborn babies can tolerate mild jaundice – this clears up without treatment in about ten days – but if the jaundice is more severe, they may need medical help to prevent kernicterus, a rare condition that can cause neurological damage. Severe jaundice is when your baby's skin colour is yellow from head to toe and the whites of the eyes have also turned yellow.

A simple non-invasive monitor can be used to detect the degree of jaundice; however, sometimes a blood test is required. The treatment is often a combination of the following:

- **Supported feeding:** giving a bottle of breast milk/formula (so that the amount can be measured); using a nasogastric tube to put the feed directly into your baby's stomach; or administering fluids intravenously.
- **Phototherapy:** ultraviolet light directed at your baby's skin helps to break down bilirubin; it has the same effect as sunlight, but without the harmful rays.
- **Antibiotics**: drugs are given intravenously if infection is thought to be the cause.

Babies improve quickly and are usually able to go home within a few days of treatment.

## Meningitis and encephalitis

Meningitis is the inflammation of the membranes that cover the brain and spinal cord, most commonly caused by one of three different bacteria: Haemophilus influenzae type B, Streptococcus pneumoniae and Neisseria meningitidis. The first two are protected against with the Hib and PCV vaccines respectively; the latter has many strains, but strain C is covered by the Men C vaccination. All three vaccines are given as part of the routine UK childhood immunisation programme (see Feature on p.173) and, at the time of writing, a meningitis B vaccine was soon to be added. These bacteria can also be associated with the very serious condition of **septicaemia** (a large-scale infection in the blood). The condition of meningitis can also be caused by other types of bacteria, such as Listeria and Escherichia coli (E.coli), as well as viruses, parasites and fungi.

Encephalitis is direct irritation and inflammation of the brain tissue. It can be caused by the same bacteria that cause meningitis, but the most common organism is the virus Herpes simplex. It is possible to have both encephalitis and meningitis together and this is called meningoencephilitis.

Meningitis and encephalitis are extremely serious diseases and can kill within hours. Symptoms in babies under one include:

- a tense or bulging fontanelle
- a high temperature, with or without shivering (but often absent in those under three months)
- an irritable, high pitched cry or moaning cry
- sleepiness, difficult to keep awake for a feed
- rapid breathing

- a rash of pin-prick sized red spots that do not blanch when a glass is pressed on them
- cold hands and feet
- seizures
- vomiting and/or diarrhoea.

Children deteriorate very quickly and the quicker antibiotics are given the better. Therefore be proactive if you suspect meningitis – it is a doctor's job to tell you whether it is a medical emergency or simply a common cold. With prompt treatment, most babies who have contracted meningitis/encephalitis survive, but some can be left with life-changing disabilities, such as cerebral palsy, speech problems and loss of hearing/sight.

## Milia

Around half of all newborn babies are affected by milia, small, pearly white or yellowish bumps on the skin. Usually they are present from birth and are seen around the nostrils. Thought to be the result of immature sweat glands, milia are harmless and will disappear in time without leaving a scar, so try to resist squeezing them. See also **rashes**.

## Molluscum contagiosum

A highly contagious viral infection affecting the skin, molluscum contagiosum is easy to diagnose because of its distinctive flesh/pearl-coloured, dome-shaped spots. These have a small dip in the middle of the dome, which gives the spots the appearance of the curled shell of a mollusc – hence the name. Spots can occur anywhere on the body. The infection is harmless and self-limiting, but can take up to a year to clear. If the spots are itchy, follow the guidelines in the Chart on p.164, as scratching them off may leave a small scar.

## Otitis media

Middle ear infection, or otitis media, is most common in babies and infants of six to fifteen months. Earache is often only obvious in a baby if they are pulling at their ear; other symptoms include fever and general irritability. Antibiotics are sometimes given if fluid is seen behind the eardrum or if the infection is not clearing up on its own after three to four days. If your baby is under three months and has a fever, always seek medical advice.

## Periorbital cellulitis

Swelling of the eyelid caused by an infection is medically termed periorbital cellulitis. It is not usually painful, but your baby will not be able to open their eyelid properly or even at all. In children under five, the best way to treat the infection is with intravenous antibiotics in hospital. The reason for this is that there is a direct opening in the skull behind the eyeball that allows the optic nerve to connect to the brain. Infection can spread through this too, potentially causing **meningitis** or an abscess. Prompt and aggressive treatment is therefore vital. See also **conjunctivitis** and **sticky eyes**.

## Pneumonia

Also called a chest infection or lower respiratory tract infection, pneumonia is the medical term for an infection that has affected the lung tissue. (Most infections, such as the **common cold**, stay in the upper airways – mouth or throat – and are referred to as 'upper respiratory tract infections'.) Symptoms of pneumonia include:

- a cough
- increased work of breathing: nostril-flaring, tracheal tug

(sucking in of the skin just above the breast bone), increased breathing rate, drawing in the ribs and breast bone
- a fever
- lethargy
- reduced appetite.

Most infections can be diagnosed by your GP or practice nurse listening to your baby's chest and, if detected, can be treated at home with oral antibiotics. However, your baby may need a chest X-ray to confirm the diagnosis and to be treated in hospital with supplementary oxygen to support their breathing and with intravenous antibiotics (directly into the vein).

### Pyloric stenosis

The rare condition of pyloric stenosis presents itself as projectile vomiting (where vomiting is so forceful that it travels some distance across the room) of all feeds and a very hungry and dehydrated baby who is failing to put on weight and to grow. Pyloric stenosis is usually detected in the first two months and is most common in first-born male babies (with a ratio of 5:1, male to female); it often runs in families.

The treatment is surgery (known as a pyloromyotomy), which is performed under general anaesthesia: a small cut is made in the enlarged muscle that is causing an obstruction to the stomach contents. This can be done by keyhole surgery, which causes minimal scarring. Improvement to feeding is immediate, although your baby will need a little time to recover from the surgery itself.

### Rashes

Three types of rash commonly affect young babies: erythema toxicum, heat rash and nappy rash.

### Erythema toxicum

Around 50 per cent of newborns are affected by erythema toxicum, a nasty-sounding but benign type of skin rash. It appears at around 24–48 hours after birth and presents as flat, red, circular areas with very small white pimples in the centre – hence its common term, 'baby acne'. The rash can appear anywhere on the body (with the exception of the palms of the hand and soles of the feet); it may sometimes be only a couple of spots or it can cover your baby's whole body. It is an inflammatory response and will resolve without treatment, lasting for ten days at most.

### Heat rash

Heat rash, or prickly heat, is particularly common in babies, as their immature sweat glands are more prone to becoming blocked. Crops of tiny red, bumpy spots appear in different parts of the body, usually where the clothes tend to rub, and these patches can be very itchy. Ensure your baby is wearing loose cotton clothing and remove a layer if necessary; simple moisturising cream may help to cool the skin. Heat rashes usually clear up without any further treatment.

### Nappy rash

There are a number of different types of nappy rash. Commonly, a baby will have red skin that does not extend into the creases of their legs and thighs. This is caused by either the urine on the skin or from a reaction to the cleaning materials or nappy. This can be treated as outlined in Chapter 2, p.35. Redness that goes into the creases, with small dots of redness extending from the area of the rash onto healthy skin, could be a sign of an infection of **thrush** (Candida).

### Reflux

Gastro-oesophageal reflux is very common in newborn babies. It describes a situation where milk from the stomach comes back into the mouth because the muscular opening at the top of the stomach is not fully developed and does not close tightly enough. The returning milk is mixed with stomach acid, which can cause irritation and, ultimately, ulceration to the oesophagus. An obvious sign of reflux is vomiting (in greater amounts than posseting, which is normal); however, reflux can also be 'silent', in that the milky mixture travels only a small way back up the oesophagus. The condition is very painful for your baby, causing them to cry at every feed.

You can relieve your baby's symptoms by breaking the feed into stages to allow the milk to pass through the stomach and prevent build-up (pressure in the stomach can make reflux worse). Wind them and keep them upright for at least ten to fifteen minutes after a feed. Raise the head end of their cot (see Chart on p.164); this will allow gravity to help keep the milk in your baby's stomach when they are asleep. Your GP may also prescribe anti-reflux medication. If your baby projectile vomits at every feed, this may indicate **pyloric stenosis**.

### Ringworm

Contrary to its name, ringworm is not an infestation of worms. Rather, it is a fungal infection, tinea, which makes a circular lesion on the skin that often has a clear, unaffected centre and a raised, lumpy border. These patches look scaly and red and are itchy. Your baby may have just one or several at a time. You can treat ringworm yourself with an over-the-counter antifungal cream, applying several times per day until five days after the lesion has gone. Nevertheless, it is worth seeing your GP, as they will take a scraping from the area and confirm the diagnosis and treatment. Ringworm is highly infectious, so employ good hygiene practices (e.g. not sharing towels, frequent washing of bedding) to prevent it spreading to others.

## Scabies

The contagious condition of scabies is caused by mites burrowing into the skin. Your baby may have extremely itchy patches of skin, which are commonly worse at night. It is passed on through skin-to-skin contact and also by sharing clothes, bedding and towels and it can take up to eight weeks for the symptoms to show. Your GP will prescribe an insecticide cream/lotion, which is left on the skin for between eight and 24 hours, depending on the preparation. You will need to treat everyone in the household and wash all bedding and towels. Repeated scratching can tear the skin, creating a risk of infection, so use scratch mits if your baby will tolerate them.

## Septicaemia (blood poisoning)

The body's own white blood cells are normally able to kill invading bacteria. However, occasionally the infection is overpowering or the body's immune system is too weak or underdeveloped to deal with it, allowing bacteria to multiply rapidly. This triggers the condition of septicaemia (sepsis). Once bacteria are in the bloodstream they spread throughout the body, which can be life-threatening and therefore needs immediate treatment with intravenous antibiotics.

The symptoms of septicaemia in babies are similar to those for **meningitis/encephalitis**:

- high temperature
- pale and clammy skin
- rapid, shallow breathing
- floppy and weak response
- unusually sleepy and quiet.

In addition, the skin may develop a pinprick rash (petechiae) or larger purple bruises (purpura) that do not go away when you roll a glass over them. This may signify that the blood is infected by the meningococcal bacterium, which is also a cause of meningitis. You must seek urgent medical help.

There are a few things that help lower your baby's risk of contracting septicaemia. First and foremost, keep up to date with the routine childhood immunisations (see Feature on p.173). Once your baby is weaned, make sure that they have a varied diet that includes plenty of fruit and vegetables. Lastly, seek medical advice if you think that a simple cut, wound or other skin lesion is becoming infected – signs are increasing redness, swelling and heat around the wound, usually about 48 hours after it occurred.

## Sticky eyes

If your baby's eyelashes are heavy with thick, sticky mucus, which may cause the eye to close, it is likely they have what is known as 'sticky eyes'. Babies get sticky eyes for various reasons. In the first days of life this is often because of an infection picked up on their route down the birth canal (in a vaginal delivery). Most often it is both eyes that are affected, but it can only be one. A swab will be taken from your baby's eyes and sent to the laboratory for testing. Your baby will then be treated with eye ointment that needs to be reapplied regularly throughout the day and night. These infections are contagious and, if only one eye is infected, you need to take precautions when washing your baby's face in order to avoid spreading the infection to the other eye (see Chapter 2, p.39–40).

Another cause of a sticky eye is tear duct blockage. This is more commonly seen in the babies under one month and is caused because the tears from the eye are unable to drain away via the nasolacrimal duct due to an obstruction. In order to open this duct, you can perform gentle massage to the area around the entrance by very carefully rubbing in small circular motions just between the corner of the eye and the nasal bridge.

Older babies tend to get sticky eyes because they have a bacterial or viral infection (see **conjunctivitis**). In this instance the white of the eye is often red and itchy. You will need to see your GP as soon as possible for effective topical antibiotics. See also **periorbital cellulitis**.

## Threadworms

Also known as 'pinworms', threadworms are tiny, white worms that survive in the large intestine. Threadworm infection is most common in school-age children rather than babies; nevertheless, if an older sibling has threadworms, they will be easily passed to your baby. Symptoms are primarily an itchy bottom or vagina (especially in early evening and night-time), which may cause difficulty in settling, but you may spot worms on the outside of a stool or around your baby's anus. Eggs are laid around the anus and are transferred to the hands when the area is touched (they are very sticky), so washing your hands, particularly after changing your baby's nappy and going to the toilet yourself is important to prevent spreading and reinfection.

It is wise to treat the whole family for threadworm infection with a single dose of either mebendazole or piperazine (available over-the-counter), but see your GP for advice as to the best product for your baby; sometimes a second dose two weeks later is needed to kill any newly hatched worms. Remember to wash all bedding and towels.

### Thrush

The condition commonly known as 'thrush' is caused by a yeast/fungus called Candida albicans. It can occur around the bottom and/or in the mouth. Oral thrush is more common in premature babies, as their immune system are not mature and they did not receive the full amount your antibodies via the placenta (see Feature on p.173). Another cause is alteration of the body's normal flora by antibiotics.

The sign of oral thrush is a white coating on the tongue that is not milk residue (it will still be present some time after the feed). Perianal thrush presents as a rash around the bottom that is patchy and often in the creases (unlike classic nappy rash), with tiny red dots around the edge of the rash. Thrush is passed readily between mother and baby and can cause problems with breastfeeding (see Chapter 3, pp.74–5 for how to treat yourself).

The treatment for small babies is a prescription of liquid antifungal to be taken orally and a topical antifungal cream (available over-the-counter) for the bottom rash. Use the cream even if there is no sign of a rash – there is a risk that thrush will travel through the gut from the mouth to the bottom and cause infection. Treatment usually continues for two weeks, and sometimes longer (check the prescription or the packaging for the correct dose). When your

baby is symptom-free, continue to give the medication for another five days to ensure all the infection has been cleared, otherwise it will simply return when the treatment stops. If there is no significant improvement after two weeks, seek further medical advice, as you may need a different medication.

Fungi like warm, moist environments, so (for perianal thrush) time without the nappy, frequent changing of the nappy and making sure that the skin is dry before you put the new nappy on will all help too. See also Chapter 2, p.35.

### Tonsillitis

The tonsils are two small glands on either side of the back of the throat. They are one part of the body's immune system and work to kill infections. If they become infected, they enlarge and look red. Symptoms include a sore throat and difficulty swallowing, a high temperature and coughing – you can treat these as outlined in the Chart on p.164. Although the cause is generally viral, bacteria can cause tonsillitis, so your GP should do a throat swab to confirm which it is and prescribe antibiotics if appropriate.

As the immune system gets stronger, the tonsils become less important and usually shrink. Sometimes, however, there are circumstances in which doctors consider removing them:

- recurrent severe attacks of tonsillitis – as a rough guide, at least three episodes per year for three consecutive years; or four per year for two consecutive years; or five episodes in one year.
- peritonsillar abscess (quinsy)
- inability to swallow easily due to enlarged tonsils
- enlarged tonsils that lead to

obstructive sleep apnoea (snoring while asleep, noisy breathing at night, episodes of not breathing during sleep)
- recurrent ear infections (**otitis media**) associated with tonsillitis
- hearing impairment due to blocked Eustachian tubes (connecting the inner ear to the throat).

If an operation to remove the tonsils (a tonsillectomy) is considered beneficial, this will be done under general anaesthetic using one of a number of different procedures. Swallowing will be painful for a little while afterwards but, if your baby is weaned, continue to give solids, although you should avoid acidic fruit/fruit juices, as they will sting.

### Umbilical granuloma

After the umbilical stump drops off (see Box in Chapter 2, p. 35), some babies are left with a small overgrowth of skin from within their belly button, which forms a red nodule. This is termed an umbilical granuloma and is easily treated with a prescription of silver nitrate, which cauterises it and causes the tissue to dry up. Alternatively, you can treat it yourself using salt or alcohol wipes. For the salt treatment, you can use a sprinkle of ordinary table or cooking salt and cover the area with gauze. However, there is not a standard form of treatment using these methods; some say you need to repeat the salt treatment twice a day for up to ten days for ten to 30 minutes each time. If the granuloma is still present or you notice any sign of infection (e.g. offensive smell, discharge), seek medical attention as soon as possible.

### Undescended testes

During the development of the male fetus in the womb, the testes start inside the abdomen before descending to occupy the scrotal sac. If they remain in the abdomen after birth, there is a risk of infertility and testicular cancer in later life, so they need to be located and brought down to their proper place. There are various ways in which this problem occurs:

- One of your baby's testes is down in the scrotal sac, but the second is felt higher up along your baby's upper thigh crease (inguinal region). In this case, the affected testis will probably descend on its own.
- One testis might not be felt on examination and therefore an ultrasound scan is needed to find it. Depending on its position, an assessment will be made as to the appropriate course of action.
- Neither of your baby's testes is in the scrotal sac. An ultrasound scan will be performed to find out where the testes are and, depending on what this shows, your baby may need blood tests before a decision on treatment can be made.

If by the end of the first year the testis or testes are not in the scrotal sac, your baby will need a corrective operation.

## Urinary tract infection

Although urine infections are common, doctors take them more seriously in children, especially if your baby has more than one within their first year. Symptoms include:

- pain when passing urine
- cloudy-looking urine (best identified if your GP does a 'clean catch' sample)
- possible dark or smelly urine
- vomiting

- fever
- irritability
- lethargy/sleepiness
- abdominal pain (indicated by tension in the area and drawing up the legs and crying when the abdomen is touched).

If your baby is under three months, they may need to be admitted to hospital for intravenous antibiotics. An ultrasound scan may also be performed to check that the kidney and bladder and the tubes that connect them are all in the normal position and look healthy.

Constipation is a common cause of urine infections (see entry on p.176 for how to treat). If your baby is suffering from recurrent infections, further tests will be needed to investigate why this is.

## Vomiting

A symptom of a variety of illnesses, vomiting can also be quite normal for babies, especially if they are in the habit of swallowing air when they feed (see also reflux). If your baby is being weaned, vomiting after a meal can sometimes indicate a food allergy or intolerance (see Chapter 5, p.122), so you will need to monitor this carefully to discover whether the vomiting was an isolated incident or whether it occurs every time your baby is given a particular food to eat. When vomiting is accompanied by diarrhoea, it is usually a sign of gastroenteritis (stomach bug).

Occasionally, vomiting can be a symptom of a very serious illness or condition (e.g. intussusception, meningitis, obstructed hernia), an anaphylactic reaction to a sting/bite (see pp.167–8) or a head injury (see p.167). This is particularly so when the vomiting is more persistent and your baby seems generally unwell.

In these instances, it is important to seek medical help as soon as possible, especially if your baby has been vomiting continuously and is unable to hold down fluids.

Projectile vomiting (vomiting that travels some distance across a room) in newborns can be a symptom of pyloric stenosis.

## Whooping cough (pertussis)

The infectious disease of whooping cough is less prevalent than it used to be, thanks to the routine childhood immunisation programme (see Feature on p.173). Nevertheless, it has not yet been eradicated and the most vulnerable group are babies under one. This is why you were offered a pertussis vaccination during your third trimester of pregnancy, so that your antibodies could cross the placenta and protect your baby until they have been fully immunised against it.

Whooping cough is spread from person to person via droplets of mucus. It tends to be seasonal, being most prevalent in late winter and early spring. Symptoms are sustained bursts of coughing, with a characteristic 'whoop' at the end as the person catches their breath. This can lead to vomiting, poor feeding and exhaustion. Your baby may also have a mild temperature.

Your baby can be given antibiotics – this is principally to shorten the length of the disease and help prevent it spreading to others. Otherwise, you can treat the symptoms as outlined in the Chart on p.164. Very young babies may need to be admitted to hospital for treatment in case of serious complications. The cough can last for up to three months – it is also known as 'the hundred day cough' – although your baby will cease to be infectious after about three weeks.

# Useful Resources

## 1 The early days

**Newborn checks**
www.babycheck.org.uk

## 2 Caring for your baby

**Equipment**
www.babylist.co.uk

**Equipment for hire**
www.thebabyloft.co.uk
www.minilodgers.co.uk
Baby Equipment Hirers Association: www.beha.co.uk

**Cloth nappies**
www.goreal.org.uk
www.realnappiesforlondon.org.uk

**Clothing (footwear)**
The Society of Chiropodists and Podiatrists:
www.scpod.org

**Crying**
www.cry-sis.org.uk

## 3 Feeding

**Breastfeeding support**
www.nationalbreastfeedinghelpline.org.uk
www.breastfeedingnetwork.org.uk
National Childbirth Trust: www.nct.org.uk
www.laleche.org.uk
www.breastfeedinginc.ca
Lactation consultants of Great Britain:
www.lcgb.org
International Lactation Consultant Association:
www.ilca.org
www.thetruthaboutbreastfeeding.com
Association of Breastfeeding Mothers: www.abm.me.uk

**Equipment**
Breastfeeding pillow: www.mybrestfriend.com
Breastfeeding bra: www.simplewishes.com
Nipple cream: www.lansinoh.co.uk

**Expressing**
Breast pump:
Medela Symphony Double Electric Breast Pump
www.medelabreastfeedingus.com
www.expressyourselfmums.co.uk

## 4 Sleep

www.lullabytrust.org.uk (SIDS)
www.thechildrenssleepcharity.org.uk
The National Children's Bureau: ncb.org.uk
www.millpondsleepclinic.com

## 5 Weaning

**Weaning**
www.annabelkarmel.com
Baby-led weaning: www.rapleyweaning.com

## 6 Development

**Baby signing**
www.babysigners.co.uk
www.babysignlanguage.com

**Hearing loss**
The National Deaf Children's Society: www.ndcs.org.uk

**Teeth**
www.dentalhealth.org

## 7 Looking after yourself

**Postnatal depression**
www.beatingtheblues.co.uk
Association for Postnatal Illness: www.apni.org

**Parenting**
www.mumsnet.com
www.Mybaba.com
www.childcare.co.uk
www.netmums.com
www.parentdish.co.uk
www.parenting.com

## 8 Baby health

**First aid training:** www.redcross.org.uk

# Index

# Acknowledgments

I have an enormous list of fabulous people who have had important input for this book. It was vital for me that true experts were giving the advice – I think their years of experience and dedication in their area has been invaluable and has added a sense of honesty to the book. Thank you so much Beth Graham (Lactation Counsellor and Midwife), Lulu Becker (Women and Children Health Physiotherapist), Dr Alexandra Seddon (General Practitioner), Holli Rubin (Psychotherapist with a special interest in women's health and pregnancy), Dr Mark Anthony (Neonatal Consultant and Founder of Babycheck.org.uk) and Anita Woolridge (Founder of Babylist.co.uk). I have also relied heavily on the sound medical advice and reassurance of my friend and colleague Dr Charlie Briar, who has helped me to keep to the facts and stay focused on the evidence.

Thanks to Quadrille, especially Anne Furniss, who has been a continued support and reassurance throughout, thank you. Behind the scenes Victoria Marshallsay and Pauline Savage have been tirelessly editing and re-editing to keep me to the all important word counts – not an easy job, as I had so much to write about! Thanks to Jim Smith who designed the book and brought it all to life on the page. Thanks to Tiffany Mumford for her wonderful photos. She is a true artist. Also, a huge thank you to all the wonderful families who have allowed us to photograph their babies: you have added a truly beautiful and colourful dimension to the book.

The biggest thank you has to go to my long-suffering but happy and smiling family, in particular, my fabulous children Olly and Emily for allowing me to practice my parenting skills on them and who totally complete my world.

**Editorial Director** Anne Furniss
**Creative Director** Helen Lewis
**Project Editors** Victoria Marshallsay and Pauline Savage
**Design** Jim Smith
**Photography** Tiffany Mumford
**Production Director** Vincent Smith
**Production Controllers** Sasha Hawkes and Tom Moore

First published in 2015 by
Quadrille Publishing
Pentagon House
52–54 Southwark Street
London SE1 1UN
www.quadrille.co.uk

British Library Cataloguing-in-Publication Data.
A catalogue record of this book is available from the British Library.

ISBN 978 184949 473 1

Printed in China